Messy Bitch Magic

Ani Ferlise

The contents of this book explore many difficult and sensitive topics, so it may be triggering at some points. I want to be clear that this is a book of nuance, healing, and complexities. The thoughts, beliefs, approaches, and perspectives in this book mirror where I was at the time they happened, and may not reflect anything presently. I'm going to show you a really intimate look at what a "healing process" could look like (not pretty) and some of the reasons I needed the healing (definitely triggering). I changed a bunch of stuff so I don't tell anyone else's story (or get sued). This story is mine, from my perspective. Okay, I think I covered it. Thank you for indulging this part. And the whole thing, honestly.

Big love, Ani

Cover design by Tate Eknaian of Toadstone Illustration
Interior layout by Chriswilliamsdesign.co.uk
www.the-numinous.com

This book is for every other person who
craves to know what it means to be alive.

And to A.D. - until we dance again.

Contents

Messy Bitch: A Definition

Messy Bitch [meh-see biCH] (Noun)

1. A nuanced, complex individual, regardless of gender, who has experienced all the different facets life has to offer.

2. A person whose life has been chaotic, awkward, hilarious, embarrassing, deep, filled with big moments (painful, beautiful, and everything in between) and even bigger magic.

3. Someone who has rejected, either consciously or subconsciously, the conditioning of being perfect and palatable.

4. A real, raw, honest, authentic modern-day mystic who shows up to life again and again, letting it crack them open, transform them, and finds the beauty in it all ... eventually.

5. The revered, holy, intricate hunnies who can actually make sweet love to life itself, not *despite* their mess, but because of it.

Introduction

I am a Messy Bitch.

Like, truly, a Messy Bitch.

Like possibly one of the messiest bitches. And I wear that title proudly.

I've thrown up that fluorescent purple "liquor" (which, honestly, what even is that stuff?) in the club. And I've had the most spiritual, profound, real conversations about betrayal, loss, heartache, and what love really is in the bathroom there, too.

I've gone to spiritual circles with people I wished wore more deodorant, and who hugged me for way longer than necessary. And those gatherings have likewise brought nuggets of wisdom, connection, and insight (deodorant *is* a great invention!).

I've had my left tit pop out at a rooftop nightclub after tucking a rogue hair extension away in my purse. I'm the gal that always has one tit out. Metaphorically and literally.

I've turned up to an ecstatic dance event in platform boots and a leather dress, fashionably late, only to walk into a full-on cacao circle with someone playing a sound bowl and everybody chanting. I couldn't sit cross-legged because my boots were too high and my dress was too tight. I'm still haunted by the echo of my heels walking to find a spot amidst the chants.

I've been shamed for wearing lipstick in spiritual circles, for not wanting to eye-gaze with a complete stranger, and for having a passionate love affair with Italian food (that's not vegan, organic, or gluten free).

Oh, and did I mention that my emotions have a tendency to hit me like a tsunami? I feel them so strongly it knocks me on my ass sometimes. I can also unconsciously leak them onto other people. But every wave of fear, pain, sadness, and rage, has been equaled by the same amount of bliss, aliveness, and ecstasy. If you ask me, ALL of it is what makes life worth living.

You're about to find out how my overall messiness, my general just-cannot-hold-it-all-togetherness, has brought me to my knees too many times to count. Like, my-life-is-a-shambles-who-the-fuck-do-I-call-now. Like everything fell apart, especially me. And it's in these low places that I have found the most magic, connection, and beauty. You're also about to find out: when you've been down to the underworld enough times, you learn that no matter what, you will rise again.

THE MESSY BITCHES ARE THE ones who don't have it all figured out yet, who love to get glammed-up, who have felt the kind of pain that knocks the wind out of you, who belly laugh the hardest, who come alive when their favorite song plays, and who don't care who sees them dance wildly to it (except when they do).

We're the ones who dwell in the past while dreaming of the future, who feel constantly too much or not enough, and who probably grew up way too fast or blossomed way too late - whatever those even mean. We're the ones who know how to make love to life (and have gotten fucked by it, too). Who find God on the dancefloor and have wide open hearts that really FEEL. We're the ones who know how to love, even when love has ripped us apart from the inside out. We're the ones who came for it all—the agony, the ecstasy, and the sauce-dripping-off-your-chin unlimited dim-sum carts in the wee hours of the morning after meeting yet another person we're convinced is "the one."

And I am in DEEP reverence of us, of you. Because while we may never feel welcome in sanitized spiritual spaces, all flowing robes and the coiling smoke of culturally appropriated sage. And while we may doubt our free-spirited, imperfect-but-not-in-a-cute-way beings, I believe it's our magic that is needed the most. Because our magic is raw, real, unfiltered, and unadulterated. Like Cher's endless farewell tours, every time we mess up, fall down, say goodbye, and think we're done, we come back out in a sheer Bob

Mackie black and sparkle bodysuit and motorcycle jacket, ready for more.

I want spirituality to be for us Messy Bitches, too.

I want spirituality for the ones who immediately look up their new partner's ex and compare themselves to them.

I want spirituality for the ones who find solace in a song that plays at 4am, when the only people left on the dancefloor are the ones who can't bear to go home alone.

I want spirituality for the ones whose emotions are so MUCH that sometimes it's easier to shove them away by scrolling on your phone or partying it all away. I want it for the ones who have made the BIG mistakes—and lived to tell the tale.

I want it for the ones who don't fit in.

I want spiritually for the ones who have felt beyond broken and fucked up, mascara down their face.

I want spirituality for the ones who bite their nails or pick at their pimples with way longer-than-practical acrylics. For the ones who are insecure. Who work a regular 9-to-5 or cannot find a job. For the ones who wonder how the fuck they're going to survive this thing called life.

I want all the Messy Bitches to know that spirituality is for YOU, too. That your journey is one of the most sacred, even with your mascara-stained pillowcases.

THIS MESSAGE AND THIS BOOK was born from the messiest times of my own life. 2020, the year that led me here, was a time of loss for many. I ended up grieving almost everything: a relationship I thought was my forever, a home, a city, a job. I lost my faith, my sense of self, and even my mind for a while. And I was one of the privileged ones. I tried to fix that mess, I tried to heal up, grow up, pray it away, surrender it to smithereens!

But there I was. Again. And again. On my bedroom floor in a satin robe, writhing in pain, unable even to cry, just doing that weird gasping/writhing/out-of-breath thing like a suicidal goldfish that's leapt out of its tank. Have you ever felt abandoned? Too disgusting to be wanted by anyone? Like a loser, failure, nothing, and a fraud, all at once? But then you catch a glimpse of yourself in the mirror, and get a twinge of hope 'cause you kinda look pretty when you cry?

I have. Because, behind the tears, your power is beginning to surface. The dawn is breaking on your very aliveness. It is often in these moments that we experience an absolutely raw, real, and true homecoming of the self. And it's also when the Messy Bitch comes into their power.

The path of the Messy Bitch is an initiation into some of the deepest portals of magic. It means feeling everything deeply and not expecting to cruise through life on autopilot. It means accepting ourselves unconditionally, even when it's scary. It will bring you to a place where there's no longer anything to hide. To a place where you will know your power. Because let me tell you, no matter how "spiritual" or conscious you try to become, your inner Messy Bitch has always been the wisest sage of all.

In this book, I'm going to share my messiest Messy Bitch moments with you, and how they brought me closer to God and myself than anything else. In a world that is constantly trying to shame us into perfection, being a Messy Bitch is about embracing the fuckups and choosing to love life, even as it goes up in flames. It's about getting to know every part of you intimately and deeply, especially the parts that seem like they're deliberately trying to fuck you up and make you seem like the worst person on the planet. It's about redefining spirituality on your own messy terms, and seeing it in everything. The Taco Bell take-out because you're too lazy to cook; the belly laughs to relatable TikToks when you thought you were the only one with rampant main character syndrome; the times you wanted so desperately to say what you really felt, and you didn't say anything at all. Being a Messy Bitch is not limited to a certain style or stereotype, it's about you being you. Yes, YOU, the magical, spiritual, divinely messy being that you innately are. So are you ready?

1
The Beginning

I'm about to go into my senior year of high school and I've never been kissed. I need to do something about this ASAP. So I do what any girl desperate for love and attention would do: I sign up to be a janitor/kitchen staff at a Christian sleepaway summer camp!

Other seventeen-year-old girls have been partying, boys, traveling, whatever. Me? I'm just *beginning*. I've also just made what feels like my first real friend. Her name is Joni. The friend before Joni was Melissa. "No guy will ever dance with you unless you lose, like thirty pounds," she'd casually taunt me in the cafeteria. The friend before Melissa was Emily. Emily only invited me places because her dad wouldn't let her hang out with boys—unless I was there. Yes, I was *that* friend. The one deemed funny before I even opened my mouth.

But with Joni, it's different. I met her at this very camp last summer, and we happen to live exactly an hour and four minutes away from each other with no traffic. We talk on the phone every single day when I'm home from school and die laughing about made-up scenarios or fantasize about what kissing will feel like. Once a month, our parents drive us to see each other. In those sacred hangouts, we watch '80s movies, trade CDs of '70s compilation albums to burn on our iTunes, and eat our body weight in peanut M&Ms.

We are the good girls: Drew Barrymore in *Never Been Kissed* adjacent. We bond over hating our bodies and our mutual lack of romantic experience. And this summer we are determined to live our best young, wild, and free lives. Christian Camp Counselor style.

And now it is a June afternoon in Connecticut, and I'm surrounded by trees, probably about to scrub poop off of toilet stalls. Not the toilet—the actual stall. Kids are fucking gross.

"Anus, is this for real? We are literally going to be living together. For a whole entire summer. I ... cannot," Joni gleams, as we make our way to the spot where we're having our very first team meeting. Did I mention she calls me Anus?

"I'm ... dying. We get to actually redefine ourselves now, too." We link arms, and I look up at the sky. "Like, I know they put us in the misfit cabin when we were campers, but I for one am going to use this summer to break out of that. To start really living, you know?"

"The drama," Joni laughs. "Anus, you're stunning, your face is like, made from clay. And you're the coolest, funniest, person I've ever met, for the record." I look at Joni's massive brown eyes as she turns her head toward me, making sure I catch her gaze so she can drive the point home. That's the thing about Joni: she knows what it's like to not feel good about yourself. In my case, I think I am a fundamentally gross human on like, every level. Body, mind, and soul. But Joni, she has this thing called "Body Dysmorphic Disorder," where for some reason she thinks she's the ugliest person that has ever lived. She can't show her body in public.

I sneak a peek at her sweatpants and long sleeves and think about how hot she must be right now. I don't understand it. Joni is beautiful. But we haven't ever been able to take a picture together because she erupts into a panic at the sight of one. I look back up at her eyes and smile.

"And don't you forget it," I bellow, giving my best trashy game show host. Joni roars with her iconic laugh. It doesn't take much to get her going. We finally get to the gathering place, arm in arm and smiling ear to ear.

I will be working with Joni, five other girls, and four guys on this team. We are the "Staff In Training" (a.k.a. "too young to actually look after kids, and just young enough to want to clean poop for no money just to socialize away from home"). Everyone on my team is sixteen or seventeen, and the actual counselors range from age eighteen to forty. It's kinda like going to college: no one knows who you are or where you come from. No one knows if you're the "weird kid" at school or if, like me, you've never been kissed. Enter the overwhelming cringe of a bunch of young people exaggerating their life stories while trying on their new nonchalant personas, and feeling "cool" for the first time in their life.

My best "cool girl" impression looks like: unbothered, kind of an asshole, a little flirtatious. Remember, this is a Christian summer camp, so there really isn't a whole lot of "coolness" to compete with.

We get separated into two different groups: one will do the kitchen work, and the other clean-up. Our boss is a bulky twenty-four year-old man with kind eyes and a bellowing voice. His name is JD (which for some reason my strange brain always makes stand for "Jesus Died" or "Justin Dustin" instead of James Daniel, his actual name). I hold my breath as he begins to divide us. It's obvious the cool kids are going on the kitchen staff, while the nerds are on clean-up duty.

"Lacey? Clean-up," JD coos somberly. Lacey wears khaki shorts (by choice) and only talks about her traveling choir shows. I saw that one coming.

"Alex—Kitchen!" JD cheers. Alex is a short man who puffs out his chest and makes fun of the girls he's slept with.

"George S? Clean-up." Once again, it's as if JD is giving a eulogy, as poor George sheepishly makes his way over to the clean-up misfits.

"Julia? Kitchen!" No one is shocked. Julia wears lipgloss as thick as chicken grease, and looks like she dates her teachers.

"Joni?" The sound of her name makes us both hold our breath, and her long nails dig into my arm. It feels like we are waiting to hear the winner of *American Idol*.

"... Clean-up." I look over at Joni expecting her to drop to her knees, but she just lets out a little sigh and shrugs.

"Ani ... " My heart pounds and my stomach feels like a lava lamp, which I know means if I don't calm down I've got about five minutes of playing time before I'll need to bolt to the bathroom.

"KITCHEN!" He cheers.

Time stops for a moment and my vision blurs as "Dirty" by Christina Aguilera starts blaring inside my head. My cells are turning into confetti and my heart is violently twerking. Reel it in, Ani. Play it cool.

The song suddenly stops like a record warping when I realize I'm not going to be with Joni. This was supposed to be our summer, and now that we're separated, are we even going to see each other? I look over at her and we make eye contact. She forces the smallest smile and gives a little wave.

I flare my nostrils and suck my lips in to try and make her laugh.

Neither of us do.

AND SO BEGINS MY SUMMER of "cool" at Christian Camp. I take on this persona pretty effortlessly over the coming days—laughing at Alex's Will Ferrell impressions, pretending to relate to Julia's party girl stories—all the while keeping my never-been-kissed life-truth locked away in my ever tightening chest. I am officially living a lie. Joni and I barely see each other or talk, and at night time our usual hours-long conversations are replaced with us sitting with everyone, forcing laughter at bad jokes. But hey—we have to branch out, right? It can't be just us forever.

One night, we are all huddling by the pond after a long day of prepping food and cleaning. The kids are all tucked away in their cabins, and the night is ours. Even the older counselors come and join us. Suddenly, Joni grabs my arm. I look at her eyes go wide and she nods to my other side, where JD sits down next to me. Joni and I talk about how much we have a crush on JD like, every night. But it's a fake crush, like having one on Ashton Kutcher in *That 70s Show*.

"I dare you to hang your thong on the flag pole!" George chortles to Julia, who bravely accepts and makes her way there, slips off her baby pink thong (that mysteriously has no weird stains on the crotch) Girl Scout style without taking off her shorts, and clips it to the flagpole. She sits boastfully back in the circle as everyone looks at each other, giddy with disbelief. The hormones are palpable.

"Alex," Julia purrs, "Truth or dare?"

Alex puffs his chest out and smirks. "Truth." He nods his chin at Julia in his best "gimme-what-you-got" way.

"Where's the craziest place you've ever hooked up?" she asks with big, probing eyes.

"Oh, hands down, in the McDonald's drive-thru, waiting in line. She was sucking me off as I was waiting for my McChicken." Alex bursts into hysterics and everyone follows suit. A twinge of tightness in my stomach and I hear Joni force a giggle, so I follow suit.

Suddenly, Alex darts his eyes to me. "Ani—truth or dare?" I fucking knew it.

I can't do dare. I cannot. What if he dares me to do something humiliating like the thong thing and I have to show my floral print hole-y granny panties? What if he dares me to kiss someone and they all laugh? What if he dares me to flash him and everyone sees that my torso is so bloated it looks like Kermit the Frog's face?

"Truth," I chirp with false confidence.

"How many guys have you fucked?" he pries, with a cocky grin and signature puffed-out chest.

Of fucking course, Alex, you fucking dick. I look over at Joni, who's wide-eyed, knowing that this is my biggest secret.

Lying at Christian camp is definitely a sin, right? Also, I have an Italian father who has drilled into me that my word is the only thing that truly matters, so I have to tell the truth. I am a failure. My time being "cool" is up. I take a sharp breath in and hold it.

"... None," I mumble, eyes to the floor. As I stare into the dirt, I hear a clutter of chuckles skitter like rats down a dark street at night.

"Well, how far have you gone?"

I pause, waiting for someone to interject because he can't double truth me. Can he? I'm met with a heavy silence.

Here goes. "Um, well, I've actually never kissed anyone." Everyone gasps in horror. "I'm really picky! I don't know ... I need to be corrupted." I keep my eyes fixed on the ground. I *refuse* to watch everyone stop liking me. Maybe if I don't look, it won't happen. "Oh, this is fucking epic! Little Virgin Ani! New goal this summer—Ani gets corrupted!" Alex jeers. Every boy in the circle hoots in agreement.

"Ani! What?! I can't believe you didn't tell me. Bitch—we have so much to discuss!" Julia pulls her thick black hair to one side and sits her body up straighter, as she calls from across the circle. I feel JD's arm snake around me and squeeze my shoulder. I look up and he's staring at me. "Hey, there's nothing wrong with that. I think it's beautiful. Someone who looks like you and has so much going for them—*saving* themselves? That is rare and special. Don't let anyone tell you otherwise."

I feel glittery inside. I never in my life thought I would not only be accepted, but deemed special for my inexperience. Perhaps this whole not-having-been-kissed thing is my edge. A rush of adrenaline-fueled glory sparkles in my brain. I wonder if this is what doing ecstasy feels like.

BEFORE LONG, EVERYONE AROUND CAMP catches wind of my "innocence." The gossip is hot and spreads like wildfire.

"Ani! Have you been corrupted yet?" hormone-laden boys ask me every day.

"Okay, how are we gonna corrupt Ani tonight?" they ask each other, in front of me, every night.

I like the attention but I also feel a little like a sock puppet.

One night, I'm sitting on a swinging bench under the stars listening to the crickets and the frogs hum their hymns as I pray to God that someday, someone will actually want me. Not just want to "corrupt" me.

I hear footsteps on the gravel. Before I have a chance to panic, I see JD hoofing to the bench next to me. "Mind if I join you?" he asks softly. That's the thing with JD—everything from his footsteps, to his voice, to his round eyes is so ... soft.

"Yeah, sure thing!" I scooch over to make room for him.

"I won't bite! Come sit close to me." He smiles, and pats the empty stretch of bench right next to him.

My spine straightens. A rush of nerves floods through me. I move closer to him. We stare at our feet as we lightly move the swing back and forth.

"You know, it's been really great to get to know you this summer. It's really rare that you meet someone like you. You have this way—I don't even know how to describe it. You are such an old soul, but you're also so ... *pure*." He speaks tenderly, with gentle earnestness. "It's really beautiful. I just want you to never, even for a second, doubt yourself. Whoever gets to be with you would be so lucky." It's like his voice is *wrapping* around every word like a hug.

A lump forms in my throat. I don't speak. I don't want to start crying. This is everything I've always wanted to hear and it's coming from an actual man—not a boy. The feelings of relief and validation are so intense, it's like they're emerging out of my pores like steam.

"JD, I want to be wanted so fucking bad that sometimes it hurts. I don't get it, I really don't. I don't *think* I'm that ugly or intolerable ..." I'm not just talking. I'm *sobbing*. Hot, wet, tears stream down my face. JD folds his big arms around me, hugging me close and tight.

"You are beautiful, Ani. Truly." My body stiffens and my heart widens. He continues. "Just because stupid high school guys can't see it doesn't mean it's not true. You are so beyond them."

I continue to sob, not sure if they're tears of happiness or pain or both. JD continues to hold and soothe me. I finally pick my head up from his now soaked shoulder and wipe my eyes.

"I don't usually sob and complain, it's just been a lot. I'm sorry. I can be a bit dramatic sometimes," I giggle, wiping a tear from my eye. "Thank you for being so good to me. I know this isn't exactly in your job description and I'm sorry if I crossed any lines."

"I'm always here for you, Ani. I mean that. Always." He gives me one more squeeze on my knee and takes off, leaving me dumbfounded on the swing.

I run to my cabin so quickly that dirt from the path flies up my calves and I eat shit on a tree root, but barely react; and when I burst through the cabin door, I limp right over to Joni's bunk.

"Joni!" I hiss. "Get up! I have to tell you something!"

"Whassamattah?" she says, imitating her Nana's thick Massachusetts accent.

" I think I'm in love with JD."

"Like, actually? He's like, graduating from college, isn't he? What happened?" And with that, I tell her every minute detail of our talk.

AS THE WEEKS GO BY, JD and I begin to connect on the swing on a nightly basis. He listens to all my stories about heartache, loneliness, and rejection. I listen to his stories about how he wants to have kids one day and sing them lullabies.

JD is my dream guy, and soon I've decided I won't settle for anything less than an ambitious, family oriented, Prince Charming. I daydream about how my future husband will be just like him. How he's probably out there somewhere dreaming of me, too, and how we're going to meet when we're in our twenties and have a *real* relationship, not just a stupid, *immature* high school hookup.

And then I blink and it's mid-August. I am feeling all the feels, as we only have two days of camp left. This has been the most incredible summer of my life, and even though I wasn't corrupted, I'm walking away fully knowing that it's this—my innocence—that makes me special. It's not a flaw. I now understand that a man like JD is going to love me one day not despite my lack of experience, but *because* of it.

After the campers go to bed, all of the staff gather to reminisce and tell each other how much we love each other. JD stares at me from across the circle. He nods his head to the trail. Is he asking me to follow him? He is!

I get up and start to walk down the trail. Moments later he is sneaking away to meet me there.

"Hi! Where are we going?" I ask excitedly.

"Just follow me, I have a surprise for you." He smiles and puts his arm around me as we follow the trail to a dark, empty field.

"JD! What are we doing? Tell me right now, I hate surprises!" He gives me a sly gaze, like he has a trick up his sleeve. Then he grabs me by the hand, leading me even deeper into the field. I can't even hear the roaring laughter of the group anymore.

We finally get to a run-down bench that is tucked in the trees on the edge of the field. Now we're in total darkness. I feel a ping in the pit of my stomach.

"Okay, now tell me, what's the surprise?" I pry, trying to slow down my heart rate.

"Sit down," he demands, calmly and sternly. His soft smile has been replaced with a piercing gaze that makes my stomach feel like it's about to explode. I try to shush my rattled insides: *This is JD!* I tell myself. *You love him and he loves you and he is the best. Stop being dramatic. Just sit. Calm down.*

He is staring at me. For some reason, my stomach churns.

He sits down next to me holding my gaze, still not speaking. I'm not going to be the one to break the silence, mostly because my throat feels like it's closing up. What I want to say is: *What is happening right now?*

The flashlight he's holding makes his face look old. Big, hard bags form under his usually soft eyes.

"So, you want to be corrupted, right?"

"I mean, I want to wait to have something special with someone that loves me," I say quietly, trying to coax that comforting, soft side of him back out.

"And you really haven't done anything?"

"No, the furthest I've gone is cuddling, you know that."

"Everyone knows that you want to be corrupted, though. You even said it. You want to." His glare is stern and unmoving. "So what do you want to do to be corrupted?"

Nothing is happening. Relax.

"I mean, if I am going to be corrupted, I'd want it to be with someone I love. There's a reason why I haven't done it yet, and it's because I want to be with one person and have all my firsts with them," I blurt, dry-mouthed.

"Or we can do it here," he responds dryly. "I know you want me to corrupt you."

He's still staring at me. I rub my palms on my shorts over and over again.

"There's a guy back home I think I'm into, and I think I want it to be him," I lie.

"Flash me," he dares flatly. Everything about him is eerily calm and unmoving, which makes me even more nervous.

I lift up my shirt for the quickest microsecond and flash him my bra.

"That was so middle school. Longer than that," he deadpans.

"I don't want to do anything dumb like that, I've already done it before. I lied before," I say. Now I'm lying about lying but honestly, I just want to get the fuck out of there.

"Kiss my neck." I see his eyes devour me in my peripherals, while I look intently at everything else in the field besides him.

Any chance of me holding back the panic I am feeling crumbles. My vision blurs.

"I can't, I don't know how and I'm going to embarrass myself." I fake smile, to hide the cracking in my voice.

"It's totally normal to feel scared when you're doing this for the first time, Ani."

"I really don't want to, I seriously know I want to wait for the right person." I want to get up and end this scene, right now. I want to be in my bunk with Joni. I want to be anywhere but here. But my body feels so heavy and shaky, and I am so dizzy, that I can't physically move.

I start to pick a mosquito bite scab on the side of my thigh.

He is still staring at me, not responding.

"I can't, like I can't do it. My mouth is physically dry."

"If your mouth is dry, then let's get you a drink."

I try to stand but I can't. My legs have also stopped working.

He pulls me up from the bench by my arm and we take very slow intentional steps to a water fountain in the corner of the field. He waits as I try to take a sip, but my hands aren't working properly. I let the littlest bit of liquid brush my lips and stop. The sip of water feels like an ocean in my belly. I am seasick and about to barf. He starts to walk and I fall behind him.

I could go. Right now. Just leave.

He suddenly whips his head around and laughs. "Wow. Jesus, Ani, you're making me feel like I'm a bad guy or something. I feel like the biggest dick right now."

"Why?" I ask, keeping my distance.

"Because you're walking so far behind me and you're clearly uncomfortable."

I look at the trail and consider bolting down it again, but my locked knees stop me.

I laugh because I don't know what to say. He grabs my arm again and leads me back to the bench and we sit.

"Kiss my neck," he demands quietly again.

I close my eyes and kiss/peck his neck for a second with my lips closed. He smells like cold sweat, Axe cologne, and clothes that were left in the laundry for too long with extra fabric softener. I boomerang quickly back to my place on the bench.

"What was that?" he snaps. "This is how you do it," he breathes as he pulls my hair back from my shoulders and neck, and moves his lips and tongue over my neck. A bolt of lightning electrocutes my insides. It *does* feel kind of good. I start shaking even harder and he puts his hand over my bouncing leg to steady it. This is officially the furthest I've gone with a guy.

"Now, do that to me." And with that, the lightning is gone and replaced with a desolate, vast, radiation wasteland. I can't look at him.

"Okay," I lean in and immediately jerk back again, "...Okay...um, okay." I bob my head toward him then away, like a pigeon trying to suss out food on the sidewalk.

"Say 'okay' one more time." He is caustic, sarcastic.

I can't breathe. The taste in my mouth is metallic and my saliva is so thick I can barely swallow.

"You have three more tries or I'm leaving," he threatens.

"Okay, oh fuck, sorry. I ... I just—" *I'm fucking pathetic.*

I close my eyes. I lean in. I kiss his neck exactly the way he kissed mine. Now I've gone even further.

"Now suck my earlobe."

"What? How?"

"Right here, go," he points to his ear, then shoves my head toward it.

I choke back tears as he forces his ear into my mouth. I pull away.

"Umm ... how was that? I'm sorry." Why am I apologizing?

"Really good, actually. I have a boner right now. Wanna see it?"

"That's enough corruption for one night." I get up, but he suddenly grabs my left hand with a force I would never have expected from soft, sweet JD.

"Wanna touch it?" he moans with a whisper. He whips out his dick. Reflexively, I swing my head the other direction, as he wraps my hand around it. He places his hand on top of mine, guiding it up and down. Up and down. Tears sting my eyes but my body is so tightly clenched that none of them fall. He lets out a slight moan.

"Ani," he sighs. "I'm not going to kiss you because I don't want to be your first kiss. But you're doing so good. This feels so good. Holy shit. You're a natural," he whispers.. His hand is clutching mine, moving even quicker over his groin.

I stare at the illuminated patch of grass lit up by the fallen flashlight.

This is happening.

I can see myself from the outside looking in, giving some version of a hand job to a man who doesn't even want to kiss me.

"Do you want to kiss it?" He asks.

"No."

He doesn't respond. He just frantically glides my hand up and down, up and down.

"I haven't had my dick touched in like, nine months. You're amazing. But let's not tell anyone about this, okay?"

He wipes his hands on the grass beneath us.

"Let's keep this between us because it will cause some drama if the higher ups find out, and I also want a chance with Laurie. I don't want me doing you this favor to get in the way of that. What happens on the bench, stays on the bench. I'll go back to the group first. You wait five minutes and come after," he instructs, with as much feeling as when he was teaching me how to properly sweep the kitchen floor.

I stare forward. My words have evaporated with my emotions.

"See, Ani? It's not that bad. Ani, trust me, you're going to make a lucky guy so happy one day," he says, taking off down the long, pitch-black trail.

New York, 2011

By the time I get to college a year later, there have been a few innocent kisses, but I am still pure. As in virginal. I even bought myself a purity ring at Kohl's, to remind myself that I am waiting for my one and only. But my insides feel tarnished.

When I arrive at my dorm room (that actually looks more like a jail cell at minimum security) I unpack my baby blue leather journal. It's filled with letters that I'm going to give my future love on our wedding day. Updates on my life, love poems, funny anecdotes. Whenever I feel hopeless—whenever I feel like I am the most disgusting human I've ever met—I look down at my ring and write him a letter.

Two parties featuring jungle-juice fueled makeout sessions on sticky frat house floors later, and I realize I have been getting it all wrong. I don't need to wait for someone to come and save me from my own self-hatred and love me like in some Hallmark movie. I've been depriving myself of all this fun—for what?

I throw the ring away and bury the letters far under my bed.

One Saturday night, I find myself talking earnestly to some bro about the refugee crisis in Syria. He interrupts me mid-sentence, pushes me against the wall and mauls my entire lower face, down to my chin, with his beer-scented tongue, moaning about how hot it is that I know so much about current affairs. I push him off, slip under his arm and walk back to my dorm.

Although I took off my gold purity ring, I still want to save myself for something special. I have to have just *one* special first. So I keep a metaphorical ring on my finger as I drink myself into enough false bravado to want to hook up with someone. I never take it further than "heavy petting"—as they'd say in the 1950s. But I also trade my cardigans for leather; my curly hair for sleek, straight, black locks; always rock a perfect cat eye and bright red lips; and develop a reputation of being a badass tease.

But even with all the fun I'm having, thick, globby tears form when my head hits the pillow alone every night. I guess I want what every human wants but won't ever dare say out loud—I want to be wanted. So I go out again, every night in fact, and I drink and smoke some weed and find somebody to hit on me to keep the loneliness at bay.

And now here I am.

Age 18, and sensually defaced.

Seductively hurt.

Rolling a blunt on the big, stained, tan couch of a frat house party.

"Holy shit, I am going to marry you," I hear a deep voice say from behind me. I turn around to see a bulky frat bro.

"Yeah, take a number and get in line, honey," I clap back, as I look back down at my perfectly rolled masterpiece with pride.

"No, really, what's your name?" He comes closer.

"Ani." I still don't look at him.

"I'm Michael." Like lightning, he grabs the blunt out of my hand and locks eyes with me.

"Ani. I'm going to marry you. Mark my words. You're my wife." He holds my gaze. My stomach flips slightly. But before the flip turns into a kick I shut the feeling right the fuck down.

"Show me the ring and then we'll talk." I wink and grab the blunt back out of his hands and traipse outside, looking over my shoulder to check out his face. He looks like the Looney Toons in love: Big cartoon eyes with beating hearts popping out of them.

FOR MONTHS, MICHAEL CHASES ME. He leaves me flowers. He writes me notes. He asks all my friends to tell me that he *actually* loves me. I refuse to give him the time of day. But he never stops trying, which I find kind of ... endearing.

"I'm a virgin and am not going to have sex until I'm married. You have no shot," I snap at him while Pitbull glares over the frat house speakers during another party.

This makes him even more persistent. He waits for me at parties—even when I hook up with other people—to walk me home and make sure I'm safe. He tells me "how much better" he's going to treat me if I will only give him a chance. I don't really get why I'm not into him. What he's saying is everything I ever wanted, but I feel a massive retraction every time he's around, like my top lip wants to curl up and my nose wants to crinkle. I feel nothing but disgust. *I'm such a dick.*

And then one night in some random guy's room, while he tries to finger bang me as the song "Sandstorm" blares in the background, I snap back into reality in a hot blaring second. I see the horrifying mass-produced poster on the wall of two generically hot girls making out in a bed; a *Fear and Loathing in Las Vegas* poster taped next to it; empty well liquor bottles on display in the window; dirty socks on the floor. *What the fuck am I doing?*

I run out of the house as panic rises in my chest. I can't exhale and I'm shaking, my perfectly curated "bad girl" image breaking apart right there on the side of the Turnpike. I power walk in my Jeffrey Campbell Litas down the street, hiding my face in my hands as I bolt back to my dorm.

What the fuck is happening? How did I end up here? Nothing has changed from high school. I'm pathetic and disgusting. I am a fucking mess.

"Ani?" Michael calls out from down the street. Fucking Christ. I power walk faster. So does he.

"Ani, what's wrong, are you okay? What's wrong, baby?" I've waited my whole life for a guy to call me baby, but this is not how I imagined it to be. He grabs my shoulders and puts me in front of him, trying to meet my eyes with his, and I can't look at him.

"Nothing, I just ... nothing." Despite my best efforts I can't help but break down, and I start having a full-on anxiety attack, inhaling sharply like a fish out of water.

"Tell me, I'm right here." He speaks softly and brings me closer to him. I still don't answer.

"I'll show you my scars if you show me yours," he whispers. This is getting real embarrassing, real quick, very angsty teenage movie. But I would be a liar if I said that his words didn't spark some sort of desire in me.

"Okay," I sob, and follow him back to his dorm.

We spend the rest of the night in his dorm sharing our woes, our struggles. I tell him about my boss at camp and how gross I felt. I tell him how I feel so unlovable. That no one has ever really wanted me and how I get so anxious sometimes I want to rip my skin off.

He tells me that he had to beat up his stepdad nightly to stop him from choking his mother. He tells me about how much trouble he got in at school. That he never talks to his dad now because he left when he was ten.

"Ani, I knew you were special. You are so fucking perfect. I know this sounds insane, but I love you, Ani. Actually. This isn't just a game to me. I really love you."

I see tears welling up in his eyes. Panic rises from the inside of my gut again, and my hands start to shake almost immediately.

"I gotta go, thank you Michael. Have a good night." I bolt out of the room and head toward the elevator before he can respond. But then:

What are you doing? He is a good man! He has been through so much, and he actually gives a shit about you! So what if you're not that physically attracted to him. Are you really that shallow? This could be love. This could be love!

And so I pivot and walk back to his dorm and bang on the door. He answers without saying anything, and I run into his arms. He feels kind of good, even though my body is still shaking. I look up at him and meet his eyes with mine, and then he kisses me.

He starts kissing me harder.

And now he's pushing me on his bed.

"Hey, hey, hey. Slow, okay? Relax," I whisper nervously.

He pushes his whole body on top of me and kisses me even harder.

"Michael, relax, slow down!" I shout as he rips down my pants and jerks me towards him. I try to find his gaze but his eyes are darting frantically around my body. He jerks me even harder towards him.

His mouth is on me and he plunges his fingers inside. It hurts so bad that I say it even louder, "Michael slow the fuck down!"

He aggressively pulls his pants down. "Ani I need to put my dick inside of you right the fuck now, please baby."

"No!" I yell, rage bubbling up inside of me.

"Just the tip, okay? Just the tip—please—baby I've wanted this for so fucking long, you're so perfect and beautiful, you are my wife. Please, baby. I won't go in. I love you so much. I am in love with you."

He thrusts himself on top of me. I feel his dick on my vulva. My whole body tightens.

"Michael, NO. I really don't want to do that," I cry hysterically, as I feel him plunge into me and start to frantically thrust in and out. I turn my head to the side as I try to catch my breath. Exasperated tears are pouring from my eyes.

He puts his hand over my face to cover it up as he continues to thrust.

"I really don't want this," I say between sobs. I feel him slow down as he gasps, holds his breath, and shakes, then collapses on top of me.

"Baby, I love you. You're fucking incredible. That was amazing. Did you want me to stop?"

"I want to kill myself," I whisper vacantly.

"I've been there, too, baby. That's why we are meant for each other. We'll get through it together. I got you. I'm always here for you, Ani. I mean that. Always."

There is no more emotion in my body. I feel my heart harden and my eyes glaze over. He falls right to sleep, and I stare at the wall until it's morning, listening to the voice in my head:

I mean, I knew what would happen if I went to his room. I liked his attention all these months, and I guess I have been leading him on. What did I expect when I knocked on his door and let him kiss me? I knew exactly what I was doing. I'm like, actually sick in the head. This could be love, Ani. Real love. Get over yourself. This is what adults do, and this might just mean he actually is the one.

I DATE MICHAEL FOR ALMOST two years. We live in his frat house. The frat house becomes my prison.

Have you ever heard of the frog in boiling water metaphor? It goes something like: if you put a frog in boiling water, it jumps right out. However, if you put it in warm water and slowly turn up the temperature, it will boil alive.

Michael is nice to me after we have sex. For a week at least.

Then, he kisses another girl because he says he didn't know we were "official." And he is so sorry, he even buys me flowers, writes me poems, and cries his eyes out when he realizes he's hurt me.

The water starts to heat up after that. He starts to critique my clothes, saying I always look "goofy." He tells me I'm gaining too much weight to wear my favorite skimpy clothes. But he does that to make sure no one else makes fun of me. He has my back. He's honest.

I eventually stop hanging out with my friends. I even stop talking to Joni and leave all of her calls and messages unanswered. She tries to get in touch every day, but I can't face her. I have nothing to say. This is my life now.

I smile at a stranger passing by us on the street when we meet eyes—a sweet looking guy I've seen on campus before.

"What the fuck was that?" he barks.

"I'm being friendly ... what do you mean?"

"So this is how you get back at me? You flirt with guys right in front of my fucking face?" He grabs my arm and leads me to an alleyway, and pushes me against the wall.

"I don't even know him! What, do you want me to never look at someone again? I was literally just being nice, you used to like that about me, remember?"

"Fuck this, and fuck you. You know what you're doing." He storms away. I run after him.

Because *he's gone through so much in his life, and he loves me so much, he can't help but shut down when he feels this. He had it so much rougher than I did.*

If I dare to go out with my friends, he calls me all night and screams bloody murder at me when I get home. When I try to address his temper, he breaks down and tells me how badly he needs me and how much he loves me.

He never outright hits me, but he will hold me down as I try with all my might to squirm away, screaming at him to let me go. He watches me struggle, devoid of any facial expression. Afterwards, he tries to kiss me or be gentle with me, and always says it's because he doesn't "know his strength." He does the same thing to his little sister, he says, and she never reacts so strongly, so he is confused when I do.

If I don't want to have sex with him, he presses his head against mine as hard as he can, and tells me that I'm going to be the reason that he kills himself. He writes me a poem saying the reason he gets so passionate and physical with me is because he can't take how much he loves me, and it scares him. And he will do anything to keep me safe, to protect me, to honor me. He will try harder, do better, he says, and learn to control his temper.

One particularly brutal night of "fun" involves him tickling me as hard as he can in my underarms, digging in so deeply and with so much gusto that I'm sobbing and screaming. He insists he is just tickling me, and doesn't get why I'm so dramatic. He won't let me leave the room that night, blocking the door with his body as he watches the TV. I give up trying, crawl into the bed, and fall asleep. When I wake up early the next morning, I frantically pack my bag while he is still sleeping in an attempt to make it to my dorm room. But I know it's going to be fruitless. He always wakes up, and drives to my dorm, arriving faster than I can run. He waits for me at my door, pissed off and ready to show me just how pissed.

Sometimes I get frantic calls from his mother, crying and begging me to make sure her son isn't dead after receiving yet another suicide text because I have left him to go to class.

"Yeah, Ani, you are disgusting in a lot of ways. But I love you, I see you beyond that." He says it to me every day.

"I never think about you when we're having sex. I don't know—your body just doesn't do it for me in that way—but I love you beyond that." He says it to me every night.

When he drinks, it only gets worse. One time, he sees a man I've kissed once at a bar. He corners me, his body towering over mine.

"Why the fuck did you choose that fucking douchebag over me for so long, huh? What the fuck is wrong with you? Make me a list of every fucking guy you've hooked up with right-the- fuck-now so I know who my slam-pig girlfriend teased. I bet you actually did fuck them too, and you weren't a virgin when we met."

Suddenly a bouncer appears and stands between us, arms folded.

"If you push her again, I'm going to fucking kill you," the bouncer says, his voice eerily calm.

"Don't worry sir, he's my boyfriend," I interject, and stand between him and Michael.

Michael storms out of the bar and I chase after him, panic rattling my bones. I'd rather him be screaming at me than vibrating with silent rage. The silent rage is scarier.

He rips the banister off of the stairs and starts breaking all of the gifts I got for him. Picture frames, trinkets. Then he grabs a Yankees glass filled with water by his bed, and throws it against the wall.

"I'm leaving. I can't keep doing this," I gasp between sobs, trying to avoid the glass as I walk to the door. I can't help him when he's like this. I can't do this.

He picks up a broken shard of the glass.

"If you walk out that door I will kill myself," he threatens, deadpan and monotone, razor sharp glass pressed against the soft crook of his arm, over his vein.

"I need to go. I can't keep doing this, Michael." I place my hand on the door knob and turn, and hear him inhale sharply behind me.

I whip around and he is looking in my eyes, expressionless, shard of glass in hand, slowly gliding over his forearm, blood bubbling over.

"MICHAEL, NO!" I scream and fall to my knees in front of him. His frat brothers rush in, think that I caused this, and tell me to get out. They refuse to call 911 because they don't want him to get kicked out of the frat. I'm banging on the front door of the frat house like a psychopath trying to figure out what's going on, and get him to the hospital. We finally go, just he and I, and he tells the doctors he got into a car accident. I smile at the nurse and thank him, to which Michael gets blinded by rage.

"Really, Ani? While I'm in the hospital? You're going to flirt with someone in front of me you sick fuck? After what I just went through?"

I apologize. He writes me a letter later that explains that sometimes he can't take how jealous he gets because of how much he loves me. It is all out of love.

And now it is March, Saint Patrick's Day.

I'm dressed in green and happy as a clam to be hanging around his frat brothers, or at least trying to be. We're at a bar, and Michael leans in to kiss me, but instead bites my lip as hard as he can.

"Ow, why the fuck would you do that?" I hiss.

He says nothing, but grabs my hand and leads me out of the bar and to his frat house in silence.

As soon as I enter his room, I sit down on the floor by his futon.

"Why are you being so weird, are you okay?" I ask.

He is still silent, but approaches me quickly, grabs my hair on the side of my head, and bashes my head on the wooden frame of his futon.

"Michael, what the fuck? Why?" I am in shock as blood pours out of my nose. He is expressionless, emotionless.

That night, I will endure hours upon hours of physical and sexual abuse. At certain moments, I am not even sure if I will survive.

My face is covered with bite marks and my hair is matted with blood. I finally manage to trick him into stopping by saying we should shower off the blood.

***

I told you I was a Messy Bitch.

I definitely did not intend for these to be the first things you knew about me. In fact, I did everything I could do to *not* write this part. I really didn't want to. This probably isn't what you expected to find in this book. Guess what, I didn't see it coming either.

But it turns out that this was the beginning of my spiritual path. And whether I like it or not, abuse, rape, self-hatred, anxiety, self-sabotage, gaslighting the fuck out of myself, and days of dissociation—all of it, and more, are a part of my story. And this book has to begin here.

When people think of a spiritual path, they think manifestation, magick, self-help, growth! Well, let's get one thing straight: I did not manifest being abused by my boss at Christian camp. No, being raped was not my "soul's blueprint." I do not think it was written the stars, or God, or "karma," and I do not believe that any part of me "chose" this path.

We live in a world where this shit happens, and it happened to me. Just like it happens to way too many others.

I wasn't somebody who was born clutching crystals and stating affirmations. I wasn't someone who just always loved spending time in nature, and feeling the warm presence of an all-powerful force in the breeze. I did not start down my spiritual path because I was so moved by the beauty of the world.

The first time I dropped to my knees wasn't in prayer; it was out of defeat and disbelief, because I couldn't fathom how a God that was supposed to love all of humanity, unconditionally, could also create a world where this kind of soul-sucking pain is possible. The first time I truly talked to the Divine, it wasn't out of gratitude; it was screaming in anger about how it could create a world where hearts go cold and bodies and souls are violated.

The bittersweet truth is that my story is not unique in its specifics or its essence. Not many a spiritual quest begins when everything is shiny and sparkly and sweet. Most people who start meditating get on the cushion because they're so stressed and anxious they can't live this way for another second. Most people who are on their knees praying to God are there because they are begging for a breath of hope. Most people who collect crystals and pray to the Moon are doing so to feel some sort of version of okay, or to try to manifest something that will make them finally feel like they belong in this world.

I'm not here to make out like you can't be spiritual until you've experienced pain. The traumas I have shown you shut me down and caused me untold suffering and confusion for years. My healing is still unfolding. And I'm also not here to try to make you feel bad for me, or more importantly, like me. Because as you'll see, I'm not going to be all that likable.

I didn't make my mess, but have had to clean up. It sucks. But it's *because* of this shit that I started on my journey. Like most everything else in nature, my story begins in the darkness. The underground. The underworld. But these painful experiences planted me, like a seed, in dark, fertile soil. Eventually, my roots cracked through and deepened down, and I began to grow.

And if that isn't big fucking magic, I don't know what is.

The miracles are in the moments that come after the blow; the glitter that settles into the hole that pain has made inside of you. *That's* the homecoming. The magic is in the times you laugh, even when you thought you may never be able to again. The times you open your heart to love again, the times you say yes to hanging out with a friend, even though you aren't sure you were going to make it through the day. The magic is choosing to come home to yourself again and again, no matter what kind of hurt, pain, person, conditioning, or voice inside of you tells you otherwise.

So no, trauma isn't the juju here. This isn't about romanticizing pain. This isn't about even making meaning from it. And this definitely isn't about fucking claiming that "everything happens for a reason."

This is about seeing that life can be a really shitty teacher.

But as cruel a teacher as life can be, you can be an even more amazing student. You, Messy Bitch, will take whatever shitty lessons life throws at you and run with them. You don't even make lemonade from lemons; you take the black matter that comes from a Dark Night of the Soul and turn it into the damn fucking cosmos. And every time you say yes to this power, and remember who you really are, is when you come home.

Maybe the pain didn't have to happen. Maybe it is completely unfair, and fucked up, and undeserved.

But here you are, making magic; sometimes despite it, sometimes because of it.

The #spiritual space looks so serene on the surface as you're scrolling through the gram. Like everyone has their shit together, and were born peaceful, loving, decent people. And maybe that's true for some.

But, if you have been burned,
If you have felt like the biggest fuck up,
If you have felt the depths of shame and self-hatred,
If you have cried hot angry tears,
Or felt nothing at all,
If you've numbed out,
Trusted too much,
Don't trust ANYone,
If you've leaked your trauma onto others,
If you've hid yourself from the world,
And you desperately want to believe that there's magic out there, somewhere (but you secretly doubt it),
And you have known deep loss and darkness,
And felt the most earth shattering loneliness and profound brokenness ...

You are not broken.

You are magic.

The pain isn't the ending.

It's the just the fucking beginning.

2
Party Bitch

Clack clack clack CLACK clack clack CLACK.

I'm in my Toyota RAV4, listening to my newly purchased, battery-powered daisy string lights hit the windows as the car shakes down the highway. There are bright pillows and bohemian-inspired blankets adorning the back seats along with a giant cooler filled with deli sandwiches and wine. I adjust my new, dark green circle glasses so they rest on the perfect spot on the bridge of my nose—the aim is to look less like a 1940s professor with pants up to their nipples, and more Janis Joplin.

Call it avoidance of my recently destroyed life, or call it the pathway to enlightenment. I don't really give a fuck what you call it, because I'm on my way to my very first music festival!

Naturally, the story of me and the frat guy spread like wildfire. You know how it goes; some people's life-altering, severely traumatizing, barely survivable experiences are other people's hot gossip.

After hours of feverishly Googling "What do I wear to a music festival?" and purchasing a plug that connects to the cigarette lighter so I can straighten my hair in the car, I'm finally driving down the tree-lined highway with Michelle. Michelle lived in my building my freshman year of college and is a spaced-out hippie chick who never not looks like she just stepped out of a PacSun ad.

Clack clack clack CLACK clack clack CLACK.

After what feels like decades in the car, we CLACK our way into the festival. We pull right up to a giant tent teeming with twenty or so of Michelle's best friends. I'm awestruck taking in the setup. I'm clearly with the seasoned pros, the real deals, the true blue free spirits; they have invested in a literal circus tent because of how often they frequent these events. I scan the rows of sleeping pads and mats. I guess we'll all be sleeping in the tent. Gas bubbles begin throwing their own rave inside of my stomach. I clench my butt-cheeks in anticipation.

A slew of brightly colored tapestries hang from the sides of the giant tent, both for privacy and decoration. Sublime's "Santeria" is blasting through fancy portable speakers someone brought, while long haired girls are hula hooping to the beat. Two other girls are sitting on a tapestry on the ground, one braiding beads in the other's hair while she looks in a hand mirror, meticulously applying face gems to her forehead. Everyone is passing around a bag of wine and playing a game I quickly discover is called "slapping the bag" (which basically just involves slapping and chugging wine from the plastic bag that is tucked inside of the boxed wine).

I have a feeling, or maybe a hope, that this weekend is what will finally connect me to something bigger than myself.

I make my way around the tent feeling impressed with myself. These are clearly the most experienced people at the music festival. They even have a velvet rope lining the big communal tent, making it feel extra VIP. In front of one of the tripped-out tapestries, a dude with long, dark, flowing locks and a Ganesha muscle tee is posing in a *V for Vendetta* mask, and one of the braid girls is taking his picture with a fisheye lens as he crouches down with his hands in prayer position. I instantly feel not cool enough; I'm not wearing baggy pants, I don't have a fisheye lens, and I definitely don't have a *V for Vendetta* mask.

"Everyone! This is Ani! Ani, this is everyone!" announces Michelle, casually-yet-loud-enough to hear over the blaring speakers.

"Whatsaaaaahhhpppppp," a bearded man croons, very à la that Budweiser commercial from the early 2000s.

"Hi everyone! Thanks for having me!" I chirp like the nerdiest good girl of all time. This is a crowd that's literally slapping a bag of wine. I have clearly lost all my social skills after the year from hell. I take a deep breath and search the crowd for something—anything—to connect with them over. Some common ground ...

I see the wine bag coming my way. It's time. The bearded man, who I find out is named Kyle (of-fucking-course), hovers it over my mouth.

SLAP.

I begin to chug frantically, like my life depends on it, while trying desperately not to barf. I keep chugging. Vomit crawls up my throat. I keep chugging. I swallow the liquid down along with my dignity. I keep chugging. The tingles flush through my whole body and I feel myself coming alive. I hear a few "Oh my Gods" and it only empowers me to keep chugging. And chugging. And chugging. I keep chugging despite the fact I'm fully aware that I'm using my coping mechanism of dissociation to fit in with a group of festival freaks, until Kyle lets out a full "HOLY SHIT!" in disbelief. I slap the near-empty bag again to tap out—and bitches—I am BACK.

"Hell yeah, Ani!!! She is SO one of us!" bearded Kyle gushes. I feel a surge of electricity course through my veins. I'm unsure if I'm buzzing from the half bottle of wine I just downed or if it's just the sweet little hit of good ole validation. Who cares? I feel *good*.

We keep passing the bag along, and seemingly out of nowhere, the sunset turns to nightfall, the portable lamps in the tent switch on, and the hula hoops light up with neon-colored LEDs. The music festival officially starts the next morning, and my anxious nerves are finally turning to excited nerves thanks to the wine warmly coursing through me. I look around our communal tent and see a few guys strumming their guitars and writing music together, and a little subgroup talking about the concept of "oneness and consciousness." Everyone's laughing and smoking pot and reminiscing over the hundreds of other festivals and concerts they've attended.

This could be my life now, a traveling festival Queen who knows all about music and has discovered the magic of being alive.

At the witching hour of 3am, I crawl into the back of my car, which I have converted into a full bed by putting all the seats down, and settle in for the night. I'm too lazy to set up on the floor with everyone else, and also still conscious of farting in my sleep. I lie there half-asleep, half-electrified by the possibilities, before I finally doze off.

WHEN I WAKE UP IT'S SUNRISE, and I realize no one else has gone to bed yet. I drown my disappointment in myself for being a weenie who needs sleep with a massive cup of instant coffee. Everyone else is sitting around in a circle on a pink tapestry in the center of the tent, in the same clothes as yesterday, passing around cocaine.

My teeth clench down and aren't budging when I see it, as if they are trying to tell me: "stop being such a fucking pussy, bitch." The irony is that I used to tell people I did coke all the time just to sound cool—but I've never actually even been this close to it. Until now.

What if we get arrested? What if someone overdoses? I worry lamely.

sniiiiiiiiiffffffff

It feels like my teeth are totally wired together and my lips are sewn shut and I pull the blanket in my trunk over my head so no one sees me up and tries to invite me over. My whole body is tense, looking at everyone carelessly passing around something that could get us in huge trouble or be laced with something.

sniffffffffffffff *cough*

But I do wonder what it's like? I mean what if it's not *careless*? What if it's care*free* and I'm a big fat uptight baby? A fierce, electric determination takes over my body.

I fling off my blanket dramatically, crawl out of my trunk, and plop down in the circle.

sniiiiiiiiiffffffff

The conversations about "consciousness" are still being had around me, and everyone is getting deeper—in cocaine and conversation. Passionately talking about everything from Nietzsche, to Buddhist concepts of suffering and oneness, to the glory of Beatnik poetry, and how life is meant to be lived "on the road." I sit and quietly observe the scene, too scared to chime in but frantically trying to retain every ounce of information so I can Google it later and have more to contribute next time.

sniiiiiiiiiffffffff

"Ayyyyy, Ani! She rises!" Kyle briefly coos with a plate of cocaine settled into his lap, before immediately jumping back into his rant.

"But yeah man, the only way any of this life makes sense is if we hit the road. No corporate job is stealing my soul." His face contorts after snorting a fat line and he passes the plate to the skinny, bearded, tatted-up dude next to him.

sniiiiiiiiiffffffff

"Humanity needs a whole reset, man. Everyone needs a bit of ganja and a new perspective. I saw a man wearing his sunglasses while ordering a sandwich at the deli, and I was so angry. You're missing eye contact, man, real human connection, man. Social media is destroying us." Another coked-out dude whose name I'll never remember adds this while strumming his guitar, his linen pants stained with dirt.

sniiiiiiiiiffffffff

"Yeah man, consciousness is being destroyed by the constant influx of validation streaming from the dopamine hits of social media. I want to just start a commune, live off the land," muses the guy who was wearing the *V for Vendetta* mask when I first pulled up (the one posing for a picture for his socials with the fisheye lens).

Ok, Ani, you can be spiritual and cool here, add something worthwhile! You got 'em with the wine, now give 'em the old razzle-dazzle with your deep thoughts.

"Yeah!" I start ... then stop. "... yeah. I agree."

Nice. Brilliant. Articulate. Way to fucking go.

My jaw starts to clench again.

I realize I have absolutely nothing to contribute here, mostly because I happen to think that most Beatnik writers tend to be very privileged members of society with not very much to complain about, so I don't waste my time reading too much about them. Also, because I'm not sure I know what the fuck "consciousness" even is?

It dawns on me that I don't actually agree with anything they're saying. I love taking selfies. I love social media. And I don't think working a 9-5 is demoralizing to the point at which your "soul gets sucked out of your skull." It's the reality for most people who need jobs to survive and take care of their families, and there are really cosmic connections that can happen there, too.

But what the hell do I know?

I've only played around with spiritual concepts, reading quotes from

Eckhart Tolle and Louise Hay but not their actual books. I've also tried to meditate but I'm too ADHD. When I meditate, flashes of *The Muppets Take Manhattan* randomly pop in my brain, while Seal's "Kiss from a Rose" plays loudly in the background, while I can't stop thinking about that time I said Boob Dylan instead of Bob Dylan in 8th grade, while thinking of how the shark from *Jaws* isn't named Jaws but Bruce, while also thinking about why humans need to suffer, while thinking about how beautiful it is that Martha Stewart and Snoop Dog are friends.

I look around at the harem pants adorned with Om signs and the perfectly placed face gems. I eavesdrop on the big words everyone keeps casually dropping into conversation, like "cosmosogny" (?) or "transcendentalism." Words I keep trying to secretly type into my phone, but I butcher the spelling so bad, not even autocorrect seems to understand.

My chest suddenly feels like it's on fire, tears like pinpricks behind my eyes. I try my best to casually pretend to be stoned and lay on the floor while they go on about their philosophies.

NO. Enough crying.

I belong here. I need to belong here. Because belonging means hope after watching my life go up in flames. Belonging means that there could be a reality where I'm not so fucking alone and sad, and would mean access to another life that's way better than I could've ever imagined. Belonging here means God is real and consciousness is up-leveling and cocaine is okay, and that I could have a carefree, blissful time just having fun, instead of falling down another shame spiral.

Belonging means surviving.

I put my hands over my lower belly, and breathe the spliff-coated air. I decide to do what the festival kids would do: silently recite some affirmations and hope to God I believe them!

I am going to belong here. I am loved. I am lovable. I am safe. I am beautiful. I have value. I belong.

No one actually wants you here. And you look like an idiot with your Forever 21 outfit, btw.

I press my eyes closed so tight they twitch to cut off the thought. Deep breath.

I belong. I am ...

... SO fucking ugly, and dumb.

I rocket up into a tall-spine, cross-legged position and look around the circle to release myself from the shackles of my mind.

The cocaine plate magically appears in front of me.

I pass it to Kyle. "Really? Don't want a little kickstart?" he so kindly offers.

"I've never done it before," I giggle.

Everyone in the circle's mouth drops open and smiles wide. And suddenly the innocent halo I sported at camp is back, hanging over my head, feeling like a noose.

"Do you ... want some?" Kyle pries, his smile turning into a smirk. Fuck that halo. I'll curb stomp that shit into the ground! I nod. Yes, I'd like some cocaine thankyouverymuch.

"We got a first timer!" Kyle calls out triumphantly. "Okay, listen, just take this card, line it up ..." I fumble with the card for a second, knocking a little coke on my lap. I hear a gasp rumble through the crowd.

"... No, no. Here—I'll do it for you." He cuts it up into three nice, neat lines. "And then you just snort it up with this bill, okay? Just really inhale it all the way down. Careful though, it burns a bit, but that's cause it's the good stuff ya know?"

I bend over and place the bill in front of the line, and try to stop my hand shaking.

DO IT.

I snort the first line.

"YEAHHHHHH!" Kyle cheers. He's nothing if not supportive. "Do another one, catch up with us!"

I do another one. I swallow the burn and wipe my nose.

I can *feel* my pupils dilate. A huge, rabid grin stretches over my face.

I do the third one, inhaling sharply. I swell in the pride of overcoming fear. Of overcoming like, everything honestly. Of having friends who want to include me.

I pass the plate and the deep conversations start again, but suddenly, I really want to talk. Like really, really want to talk. I have stuff to say!

"You know you guys, I think that connection is the most precious thing a human can experience, like, ever, and I am really glad to be connecting with you all. Like, super glad. Thank you for welcoming me in. I think God is connection," I ramble to everyone. They nod their heads and smile.

"We're glad you're here," says *V for Vendetta* guy, putting his hand on my back.

"Really glad." Hawaiian shirt guy adds.

After a few more rounds of plate passing, we all stand to head towards our first set of the day—some crunchy band I wouldn't be able to dance to if I wasn't crawling out of my skin with energy right now.

As we get our stuff, I feel an arm slink around me from the side.

"Welcome, Chica." It's Hawaiian shirt guy. I'm too happy to even cringe.

"Here, save this for later, then come find me." He hands me a little capsule with yellow-y rock candy looking stuff in it.

"What is it?" I ask, too coked out to be coy.

"Molly. Not too much, just a taste. We can have some fun if you're down." He runs his hand down my back and I whip my head towards him. Suddenly the only thing I can hear is "Hot Stuff" by Donna Summer blaring in my head and all I see is him.

"I'm so fucking down," I smile. He spins me towards him, pulls me close, and gently guides my chin towards him and we look at each other for a second.

"Take it during Nectar. I'm about to blow your mind," he whispers in my ear, and scampers off with the boys while I wait for the girls to catch up in solidarity or safety.

NOT TO STATE THE OBVIOUS but I haven't done *any* drugs before. I mean, I smoke weed, but that's a plant. Plus it makes you tired and boring. But this? This is my jam. I put the pill in a microscopic jean short pocket (more like denim underwear), nice and close.

By the time we make our way to Nectar's set (which I quickly find out is some DJ dude named Bassnectar) I am fully loaded, on a lovely little cocktail of cocaine, wine, and the Molly capsule I just swallowed and am eagerly awaiting to kick in.

This Nectar dude is apparently the main event and everyone is losing their minds. Like everyone in our group has his symbol tatted onto their flesh, which I had thought was a tribal peach or some *Star Wars* symbol. I've never heard his music because if I'm being honest, EDM music is like—Abercrombie & Fitch music? One song that feels like it's going to have a build up, only to just repeat, over and over. It reminds me of those times you can't get off with your vibrator, so you end up laying there for an hour only to feel like you're *almost* gonna cum but never do.

But apparently this guy is different. Michelle says that I'm thinking of house, and that this is dubstep. Never heard of that either—but, it's a day of openness and firsts, right?

And Hawaiian shirt guy has suddenly become wildly attractive. In fact, I REALLY want to make out with him (his name is Ty, I later find out from Michelle). And I don't care if it's to Abercrombie Blue Ball music.

I peer into the crowd, eagerly trying to spot him, my eyes so gapingly open I'm surprised I can't get a wide-angle view of the whole scene. My jaw keeps doing this weird inverted clenchy thing but the sudden influx of feel-good chemicals makes it so I don't really give a shit that I'm probably cracking my teeth.

The sky is hot pink. No really, it's like electric pink. *Wow.* Holy fuck. The sky is beautiful. I suddenly understand why people lose their minds over nature. I mean this, this looks like God took a highlighter and went to town!

I look around me to see if anyone else is in as much awe as I'm in. Everyone is so antsy in anticipation for their Nectar God that they look like they have a jittery filter effect on them. I love my happy, vibrating friends. Or maybe *I'm* the one vibrating. Either way, I love them so much and it's way too much to look at. The sky is insane, holy shit! I wish Ty would find me already so he can see this too!

BEEWOOWOWW

My head snaps towards the stage, along with the entire crowd. A primordial sound that just bellows from the speakers and abruptly stops. We're meerkats who've popped out of their holes, waiting excitedly to hear the sound again. This is ***insane.**** I feel so much excitement bursting through my heart that I almost can't contain it. And I don't even know what it's for! What is happening? My cheeks hurt from grinning.

BEWWOOOWWWWWW!

OH GOD, IT HAPPENED AGAIN! The SOUND!

BEWOOOWWWWWWWW!

BEWOOOWWWWWWWW!

BEWOOOWWWWWWWW!

Back-to-back primordial noises? And then more silence? It feels like the crowd is about to burst (along with my heart).

The air is so tense I feel like a fish in a too-hot water tank, gulping and bug-eyed.

"COME WIT IT, NOW"

And suddenly, I've reached ascension as I am greeted by the beginning of one of my all time favorite songs, "Bulls on Parade" by Rage Against the Machine. But this is a remix—and not a perpetual pre-cum remix, but an orgasmic, primal remix.

You know when the Hulk, like, totally transforms, his body starts to twitch, his eyes go wide, and suddenly he's an entirely different, indestructible beast?

Well, same.

I smile a devilish smile. And I start losing. My. Damn. Mind. And everyone around me is as electrified as I am.

The only time I've heard this song blasted before was in my car. I didn't even think this was a thing! People dancing to Rage Against the Machine? Like this? I'm used to throwing my ass in a circle at clubs, but this is not sexy.

This is feral.

I throw myself around and the only thing I can think of is how amazing this moment is. This is heaven on earth. Look at the sky! It's proof!

And suddenly, I feel someone twirl me around.

It's Ty.

We start aggressively making out. But I want to still dance! I thrash around again, then go aggressively make out, then thrash, then aggressively make out. This is the least sexy I've ever been in my life probably—I mean I can *feel* my jaw moving like Popeye's—but I've never cared less. And never felt better.

Ty and I dance and maul each other throughout the set, and the second it's over, we dart towards the tent, stopping every few feet to makeout again. We can't even make it all the way there. We melt down to the grass on the hill by the tent, and continue to furiously makeout.

Ty is on top of me, his Hawaiian shirt still unbuttoned, and I feel the buttons tickle my side whenever he shifts his position. The cold, damp grass feels nice on my back.

Heaven.

He makes his way to the button on my jean shorts.

"May I?" he asks. He actually waits for me to answer.

My body tightens and the ground is suddenly cold. I start to shiver. I want to say yes, but I cannot even bear the thought of sex. I don't even really know how to do it. I like *this* so much, why did he have to ruin it?

"Hey," he moves his hands over my arms and shoulders, noticing that I'm shaking like a leaf.

"No pressure, Ani. This is perfectly enough for me. Let's just stick with this and if you change your mind, let me know, is that okay?"

I nod my head and pull him back on top of me, trying to recreate the situation we were in where I was lost in his scent and warmth and lips.

It works. Even more passionate this time.

"Can I join?" I hear a British accent ask a few moments later. I am too enthralled to pay attention, but feel Ty lift himself off of me.

"You'll have to ask her." Ty says, very respectfully. What a good one.

Unable to speak, I just reach my hands out, welcoming her on top of me.

She puts Ty to shame. Holy shit. My body explodes with goosebumps and I want more.

I pull away and smile at the mysterious girl with the British accent.

"Thanks, that was amazing," she whispers, trotting off.

Ty rejoins me back on the wet, damp grass by the tent and we continue to kiss. I feel disappointed for a second, but quickly forget as we get more passionate.

I didn't think I could kiss like this. I didn't think I could dance like this. I didn't think I could be with someone as nice as Ty. This is the best day of my whole life.

I also have to pee.

WOW.

I *really* have to pee.

I politely excuse myself and weave through the sea of LED lights and glow sticks and giant signs on poles with phrases like "Bass made me do it" towards the port-a-potties.

Suddenly, things are not so magical. Everything is kind of overwhelming without Ty by my side, and there are like 900 port-a-potties and I can't tell if there's a line or not? I can't see through the dark mass of people. I run up to a stall, pretty sure I cut a huge line but what are you gonna do? I scramble in and latch the door.

Never in my life did I think a stench like this could exist. Oh my GOD.

I pee and sanitize my hands, then rush out and gasp for a fresh breath. The crisp evening air feels like it's cleansing my whole soul after that.

Then I feel sharp nails dig into the side of my arm. Someone is grabbing me with everything they got, like I am the last turkey on Thanksgiving.

I whip my head around and see a young girl desperately clinging to my arm, her eyes as big as saucers, her skin ghostly pale. She can't be older than eighteen. She doesn't utter a single word but the second our eyes meet, I instinctively know that she is not okay. The mix of the cool air, her tightening grip, and the gravity of her terrified presence pulls me down from Heaven and back to Earth.

"Hi, my love, are you doing alright?" I gently breathe as I soften my eyes to ease hers.

"I'm ... scared. I'm so scared. I took too much acid I think." Tears stream down her face. I may not know a single thing about being on acid, but I certainly know a fellow Messy Bitch in distress when I see one. We might not be in the stall of a Long Island nightclub crying over her broken heart, but a girl in the grips of fear, confusion, overwhelm, and needing to get the fuck out of Dodge is something I know to show up to immediately.

And (of course) as soon as the words "I took too much acid" fly out of her trembling mouth, a man emerges from the swarm of bassheads, carrying a giant cutout of Bob Saget's head that is larger than both of us. He starts dramatically fanning the two of us with it, swinging the head right into our bewildered faces, then all the way back up, and back down again. This would be trippy for anyone, let alone a girl in the throes of a bad trip. I look over to see her about to lose her fucking mind, her eyes pleading for mercy, but unable to break away from Bob Saget's aggressive head bobbing.

"Hey, I'm with you, I'm not going anywhere. Where are your friends?" I soothe.

"They ditched me and said I was annoying them because I was crying." She cries harder.

I take in the crowd and orient to what's around me, something I didn't do in my hazy tunnel vision trip here. I see a man wearing a shirt that says "peace, love, unity, respect" actually step over someone who is passed out on the ground, without even glancing back.

I try assessing the situation as best as possible, but the sounds coming from all the different stages seem to be swirling around us and smothering us, just like the huge cloud of cigarette smoke coming from the passersby. Surges of LED light-up gloves and pacifiers, loaded men chanting "Eat, sleep, rave, repeat," and fluffy boots cocoon us, making it hard to breathe. Luckily, I'm a seasoned pro at being over-stimmed and anxious, and if I zoom out, this is actually what it's like for me most of the time.

We both need to get out of here, ASAP.

"We're going to get you somewhere safe, okay? Does that feel okay?" I ask this cheerfully as I calculate how best to disarm her, attempting to channel my best East-Coast older Italian mom vibe. She nods gratefully and follows me, as I elbow through the crowd, practically singing the words "Excuse me! Comin' through! Pardon us!" back to the big tent. Someone there will know what to do and where to find help.

"What's your name?" I chirp. I link arms with her and guide her away from the swarms of neon tank tops. "Lauren," she hums hollowly, still fixated on the chaos, refusing to look me in the eyes. I think back to the moments I've been this terrified and overwhelmed and feel into what I have needed in times when I've lost my grip on reality. Comfort. Presence. Distraction. Getting the fuck away from anyone wearing a shirt with aggressive party statements on it.

I keep leading her back to my decked-out camp.

"You're okay, we're in this together, okay? I got wicked overwhelmed out there too, don't worry, you'll be feeling as good as new in no time," I say as soon as we are far enough away from the swarm. Her large sobs are replaced by short sniffs and a small smile.

"Thank you. I really appreciate you, you don't have to stick around with me if you don't want, I don't want to ruin your time," she says between sniffs. I see the circus tent from a distance.

"Nonsense tawk" I say in my Long Island mother voice, "we're officially too sensitive for big crowds right now. We're in this together, and I need to decompress after being in the traumatizing port-a-potty." I giggle.

"Oh my GOD, I'm pretty sure that was why I started crying!" she says and starts to giggle too.

We stumble into the giant ass tent. Nobody's here and the lights are all out. It suddenly looks dark, empty, and chaotic, littered with the remnants of substance use. Big yikes.

I clear a space on a tapestry among the drug paraphernalia and bring over some pillows from my car, turning on a portable lantern. I grab my phone and start playing Joni Mitchell's "California." Then I start to ask her questions about her life. She tells me how amazing her mom is. How close she is with her brother. All the ways she's devoted to sustainability. For the first time, there's a tiny beam of light in her eyes.

"This world is so beautiful, we get to see it every day. We get to see a sunset every day." Now her excitement feels almost electric. I can see the fear inside of her dissipating into the air, as she falls deeper and deeper and deeper into her passion.

I spend the rest of the night asking her more questions, getting to know her, and listening to her tell stories about her life. I introduce her to the music of Jim Croce and the like. I braid her hair. And as she is telling me a story about a backpacking mishap, my mind begins to trail off.

Of course I am here, dutifully braiding the hair of a girl I just met to the comforting sounds of 1970s soft rock, while listening to her wax poetic about the wonders of composting and her dad's quirky sense of humor.

Even if I can turn off my own shit for a night, I can't turn off the crippling, overwhelming empathy I feel when I see messiness in someone else. I can't step over someone when they are passed out. I can't pretend that someone is okay when they aren't. Because I know that feeling so well. Lauren drifts off to "Operator" by Jim Croce and I drape a blanket over her and tuck her in. Scenes from my life of similar Hedonistic Healing moments flash in my mind.

I AM LEAVING THE BATHROOM at a frat party when I'm flagged down by a bro who I've never spoken to before, but have seen at almost every party this semester wearing his frat letter jacket and bedazzled True Religion jeans.

"Hey, uh. You're Ani, right? You're into like, the spiritual stuff? Like the moon and the aftalife?" he nervously mumbles, unable to hold my gaze but trying his hardest. His eyes dart from the ground to mine for a split second, only to drop back down—making the briefest pit stop at my over-the-top cleavage—before respectfully training his gaze on his very clean, very white fancy sneakers again.

Hearing this dude say "aftalife" in a thick, New York accent, while trying not to stare at my tits is enough to melt my heart.

"Yeah, you could say that. Why do you ask?" I probe slyly through a smirk, unable to hide my growing amusement. He wets his lips and looks around the room.

"Well, can we talk for a quick sec? Like, alone?" he pleads. His forehead gleams with either sweat or hair gel. Ordinarily, walking off alone with a frat bro would be a huge FUCK NO. But I don't know; something— something strange—washes over me.

The next thing I know I'm sitting next to this nameless dude on a damp, ripped up, duct-taped couch in the yard next door to the party. He exhales.

"So, uh, I'm going through a really hard time right now. My aunt died. It was awful and sudden, but I can, like, *feel* her. I have dreams about her every night. She even came to me before the night she died in a dream and told me that it was about to happen," he chokes. His eyes are glistening.

"When my mom called me in the morning, I knew what she was going to say. And I don't know what this means ..." Now he is sobbing, thick, fat, saltwater tears streaming down his face, like a true Messy Bro Bitch.

And in this moment, we are cracked open wide.

"And Ani, I swear, I don't know anything about those like, chakras or nothin' like that, but I swear to GOD, I can, I'm pretty sure, like, talk to dead people in my dreams," he tells me this proudly now.

We talk all night, and I'm truly in awe of this man's wisdom. He shares with me his take on what the Bible meant when it said to not "conjuh up the dead" and how he thinks his dreams are different, and how he has felt so alone in this, growing up so Catholic, but how he thinks God gave him this gift to be in service. And I sit and listen to him, asking him questions, and as it turns out, he just needed to be heard and seen. And I was happy to hear and see him.

I find magic with this man. This boy. This salt-of-the-earth Italian frat bro from Long Island, sluggin' back jungle juice with eyebrows more groomed than mine, with jeans more bedazzled than mine—teaching me how to reach people on the other side in my dreams.

I AM A FRESHMAN IN COLLEGE at a hip Brooklyn apartment. Somewhere in Williamsburg. There is a girl named Magnum.

She is short. Forty-something. A vixen covered in tattoos. She rocks Amy Winehouse eyeliner and bright red lipstick. Her thick black ponytail of extensions wraps perfectly around her curves.

Magnum is the definition of fucking cool. My mouth hangs open as she tells me tales of hanging out with Lady Gaga before she got famous and "sold out."

There is cigarette ash everywhere. Tattered up couches. I'm transfixed by Magnum. She tells us wild stories about her cool New York life, only pausing to do bumps of cocaine from the most ornate coke vial I've ever seen. Her nails are red and sharp and navigate the tiny bumps of coke like she's performing surgery.

Then something suddenly shifts. It's like the bright, intoxicating light that burned so brightly inside of her has been snuffed out. She goes from alt-party-girl scene queen to empty shell, mid-sentence. She walks out of the room.

Everyone else is too fucked up to notice.

Even though we've only just met and I'm wildly intimidated by her and think she might actually be the coolest girl in the world—something—something strange—washes over me. I walk out after her.

I float like a ghost through the halls of this strange Brooklyn apartment looking for her. I peer into every room. She is nowhere. Even the melodramatic scent of her spicy vanilla perfume has vanished. Gone.

I make my way to the fire escape and crawl onto the rooftop, where I find her sitting on the ledge, staring down into the void. My chest tightens. I walk over to her.

Her breath is heavy and rapid, the street lights reflecting off her black shiny corset like a strobe light flashing across her curvy body.

"I can't do this anymore," she whispers, not breaking her gaze from the street below. "I really can't."

"Wanna tell me about it?" I ask.

She slowly looks up from the street and plops her body onto the floor of the rooftop. Big, black mascara tears cascade down her face, down her body, landing in her tattooed hands.

She tells me about her pain. Her broken heart. The constant second-guessing of herself, her fucked up family, her addictions. "I don't know what it feels like to just breathe," she says. "I don't think I ever have."

Her pain is palpable. I can see it. I can feel it. I get it.

I look down at my wrist. It's adorned with a massive cuff shaped like a phoenix. I quietly slide it off and hold it in my hands.

"Magnum, do you know what the phoenix is?" I ask, nervously. She shakes her head no.

"The phoenix rises from the ashes. It gets dragged through the fire to the point where it burns into nothingness. It disintegrates. And then, when it's time, it rises in its full power, made of flame and magic. It kinda sounds like you. You are the fucking phoenix. And you are the fucking flame. You are fucking magic. And you will rise from this moment in all your flaming glory, more powerful than ever." I smile and slide the cuff onto her mascara-tear-stained wrist. "And in the meantime, we can eat White Castle together and hang out."

And that is exactly what we do.

We leave the party and eat burgers, talk about movies, and hope to God that *this* is enough to make the mess tolerable.

I don't see her again after that night.

Until, six years later, I get a Facebook message request from a woman named Amanda. It's just a picture of a wrist with tattoos perfectly surrounding a phoenix cuff, and one, brief message that says: "Hey. I rose from the ashes motherfucker. Thank you for that night. I am sober, sexy, and so fucking happy."

AND THEN THERE ARE THE COUNTLESS intoxicated girls in tight dresses that I always just so happen to stumble upon in the club bathroom, thick glitter tears streaming down their faces, as they finally get to release the pain they've been carrying that they are too proud to show while they're trying to prove what sexy, got-it-all-together bitches they are.

"I gave him EVERYTHING and he tossed me aside like I was NOTHING!" I hear from the bathroom line of the hottest NYC rooftop bar.

I enter to see a perfectly adorned woman in a tight dress with pumps that could kill, in hysterical tears.

I catch her eyes in the mirror, and pry gently, "Are you okay?"

"NO!" she sobs, collapsing into my arms, her tears now running down my cleavage.

She tells me the story of her pain, her heartache, how she opens her heart again and again, only to get used and tossed aside. And so I hold her and let her cry.

And then everyone else in the bathroom gathers around and holds this woman, helping her clean up her make-up after her huge purge and vent session, telling her their WTF moments, and sharing stories of when life knocked them on their ass and how it all got better.

And we all find divinity there.

AND THEN I FLASH ON ME, freshman year, rocking my leather jacket, fingerless gloves, streaks of dark green and black in my hair, walking into a party and beelining it straight to the jungle juice. My grandfather had just died, and the last words he ever said to me were "I wish you were more like your cousin," after looking me up and down in disapproval. I was consumed by rage, but underneath that was so much raw hurt. So, I drink. A lot. Not consciously trying to numb out, but determined to "just have a good time for tonight."

And the next thing I know, I'm punching an innocent rain gutter. And that's when Jesse, a red-headed library hipster chick, sees me and approaches. She is wearing dark blue ballet flats, opaque orange tights, a pencil skirt, and a cardigan. To a party. I never would have thought this chick would be the type to struggle. She seems more like the kind of person who calls movies "the cinema" and loves tea.

But it turns out Jesse is a fellow Messy Bitch, and that she has the Hedonistic Healer magic, too.

"Hey," she coos as she grabs my hand. "I just saw a TV by a dumpster, wanna go smash it?"

I catch her eyes beaming very sacred "I get it and I got you" energy directly at me.

"Fuck yes," I confirm, and follow this perfect stranger to a dark alley down the street.

We make our way to the dumpster and smash the TV with rocks while huffing, grunting, and laughing. Years later, in my spiritual practice, I will find out this is a great "somatic release" technique. I am wearing massive chunky black combat boots, and I kick in the screen for my final purge.

Jesse, getting carried away in the moment in true Messy Bitch fashion—and completely forgetting she is wearing ballet flats—also kicks the now completely shattered screen, cutting the top of her foot so badly we spend the rest of the night in the hospital together, getting her stitched up.

It was the start of one of the most sacred friendships I have ever had.

I AM PULLED BACK INTO REALITY by my iTunes shuffling and immediately playing the intro to "Paperback Writer" by The Beatles, which is truly one of the most jarring intros of all time. Lauren is still sound asleep, and I close my eyes and Thank God for every part of today.

I do feel reborn, in a way ... I got to let loose for the first time in my life. I felt safe with a man when I never thought it would happen again. I made a new friend.

I experienced the realness of humanity, where people let down their guard and reach out to one another. Maybe parties have always been portals for our raw, real shit and our raw, real glory to come out and play with us.

My eyes shoot open. *You also did drugs. What if someone filmed you and posted it online? You're going to destroy your family's life. Now you're probably gonna get addicted because there's no way you will ever be that free without cocaine and molly.* I start to shake, unsure if it's from the cold or nerves.

But I suddenly stop quaking, my body and inner demons too tired from the excitement of today for our usual song and dance.

You know what? So what if sometimes people need drugs to let go? I've been told to move a certain way, look a certain way, act a certain way my whole life—no wonder I need a little something to help me not go there. I literally hate my body more than anything, and today, I moved in front of other people without even a second thought. Just because it felt good.

3
Sexy Bitch

September, 2013

I am not inspiring, or strong, or brave, like people told me all the time after the whole horrible marathon-abuse fiasco. I am just a gal trying to piece together her new identity with hair extensions and some nail glue.

And I'm back, getting ready for school again in Good Ol' Long Island—yes, it's the same one, and yes I'm a kinky masochistic bitch for going back—but what can I say, I got somethin' to prove and nothing is gonna stop me.

I live in a small, old-lady looking house behind a makeshift frat house and a McDonald's. There are six hormonal, normal, non-traumatized girls living there. Most of them are party girls. I live in a little basement room with a small window and a carpeted floor that I am making into a little oasis.

Mood lighting LED strips, a tapestry to cover my bed, a giant Jimi Hendrix decal that says "music is my religion," and a huge light-up Buddha next to my dresser/altar where I'll store my crystals. I have all the pieces splayed out in front of me to put my dresser together, and that godforsaken little IKEA-man pamphlet that I am desperately trying to make sense of but am not fully able to focus on.

Here's the thing—I'm trying to settle in. I want to show people I'm a better person than who I was. I'm not that girl. I'm not a mess. I'm not untrustworthy nor do I have bad judgment. I'm not like, scary or unhinged, which is what I could imagine people think of me.

I don't blame anyone for not reaching out or checking in on me during my absence.

I mean, I had been gone for two semesters. What the hell is there to say anyway? *Hey, sorry you almost got destroyed in a frat house, how ya feeling?*

I was a pretty horrible person when I was with Michael. Honestly, I was a pretty horrible person before him too, but this was my worst. If he got in my face, I would get right back in his. If I was a true victim, I would have been flinching and trembling with fear, not telling him what a sack of shit he was and trying to headbutt him when he would hold me down. I stepped over him and ran out the door after he would bash his head in the mirror and lay there bloodied and crying. I kept my mouth shut when he and his frat bros would mock other girls' selfies and call them sluts, and would recoil under a blanket. I would join him in making fun of people too sometimes, because it felt good to bond over something instead of fighting. I would even do shitty things that had nothing to do with him, that's how I really know I was fucked: like spend all day on Tumblr and steal other people's posts to put on Twitter. They were all mean and nasty jokes, too.

Is it even abuse if I was a fucking shitty person too?

My chest is so tight that it feels like my muscles are playing cat's cradle with my veins.

He was kicked out of his frat house, but the school is allowing Michael to come back because they need the money or don't care or whatever—even though the school had to go on lockdown after they couldn't find him the night he attacked me.

You're a fucking monster. You got exactly what you wanted, you wanted him to do this to you so you can be the victim. He didn't rape you, you knew what would happen. And you told people he did?! You were like, barely raped, he was your partner. The things you're willing to do for attention are sick. You're fucking sick.

My hands begin to shake.

Fuck.

It's happening. I see spots of black. My heart is pounding so hard I can't hear anything else.

Fuck.

Not again.

I sit on the edge of my IKEA bed and try to distract myself with Instagram, but I can't focus on any of the pictures or read any posts, and my hands are shaking so hard that I can't scroll fast enough to find something that will catch my attention.

No. No. NO.

A little squeak of desperation escapes my throat. It's all over. My whole body starts convulsing and I can feel every pore on my dampened, clammy body.

He was your partner. He didn't rape you. You KNEW what would happen.

I gasp for air and move to the ground to try and feel some kind of stability, kneeling over and pressing my head to the floor. My whole body hurts from shaking, I roll over into a fetal position and try to hold myself but that hurts worse and I need to cover my eyes. I keel over on my knees again and take a shaky, shallow breath, only to feel a pain so sharp in my chest that a forced gasp and guttural croak escape my mouth.

I close my eyes tighter and begin to pray.

Please God, not again. Please hold me. God, I'm scared. I'm yours, please, God, hold me, protect me. I'm so sorry. I'm trying to be better. Please show me how to be a good person. I just want to be good. I want to be good. Pl—

You're so fucking gross. If only people knew who you really are. But don't you worry, he'll expose you. That's what he's planning. That's what he's doing when he's away from you. He's going to leak your nudes, he's going to tell people all the fucked up things you said about them. And these are just the things you remember ... It's just a matter of time ...

My whole torso flies up from the ground and I begin to retch and dry heave, my body shaking so hard I can barely stabilize myself, but manage to go into all fours as I continue retching.

I open my eyes to be greeted with a pool of yellow bile on my brand new room's carpet, centimeters away from my face. After I puke, my body is usually so tired that I just lay down and pass out. I'm not sure how long I was gone for, and I look out my tiny window to gauge the time. Sunset. That was probably an hour.

I get up like I'm moving through molasses, lifting my torso first, then my head—all dramatic, like in the movies when the underdog picks themself up after getting beat down by the villain. I slowly stand up and look at the tons of random screws, planks of wood, and puke all over my room. I have arrived, and I have risen.

I then clean it all up, make my way to the bathroom, shower and brush my teeth, and call my mom to ask for help getting a much-needed therapist to help me with these panic attacks I've been having twice a day.

Just kidding!!

I half-heartedly hop over everything, accidentally stepping on a plank and cracking it. Then I walk over to my emergency Pop-Tart stash that I keep on my mini fridge and break off a bite to mask my puke breath.

BEFORE I CAME BACK TO SCHOOL, I had only seen Michael once since the attack. The morning after it went down, my poor father had to come get me from school. I packed an overnight bag of my things from my dorm, and left everything else behind.

So, naturally, a month-and-a-half later, I had to go back and clear it out so the new batch of hopeful students could come and live their dreams. I brought my friend Sage with me. She is my height, but no one dares mess with her. She's been my protectress since high school, and if I ever needed one, it was that day.

When we pulled up to the school, I immediately felt humiliation. Not fear. I didn't want to see a soul. Having friend-telepathy, she realized that immediately.

"I'll go get the bags, you stay here and run them up," she said, and hopped out of the U-Haul we drove up.

I was sitting in the front passenger seat, scrolling away on my phone as per usual, when all of a sudden, the hair on my neck stood up. This is how I know we're animals—it's like in nature documentaries when you see a gazelle randomly whip their necks around and check behind them, only to be greeted by a lion silently stalking them.

I looked up. And there he was. Rushing toward me. I tightened my grip on my phone so hard that I heard something start to break, and locked the door as quickly as a gazelle bolts away.

Suddenly, his face was in the window.

"Ani, I'm sorry. I'm sorry, please, PLEASE talk to me, I'm sorry"

"Go Away, Michael."

"Please, baby, please talk to me, I'm sorry I was fucked up, please, I love you, don't do this."

"GO AWAY. Get the FUCK away from me. Get OUT!" I screamed like a banshee and hit the window so hard with my phone it almost shattered.

And as if by telepathy again, Sage appeared out of nowhere, jumped into the front seat, started the engine, and drove away while dialing public safety.

And that was that.

Now, I have a restraining order against him, and it's been two weeks since I've been back at school, prepping for the semester to begin and settling in. But there he always is, staying the designated number of feet away from me wherever I go, smoking a cigarette, staring at me. Sometimes he even sends his only friend to try and scare me. He'll say things like, "you ruined my friend's life, now I'm going to ruin yours." Or just make the tacky hand-slitting throat move to signal that I'm dead meat or whatever.

I don't know if anything legal is going on. I never once had to go to court, I just had some random public defender make sure he legally couldn't come near me or something. But I don't even really understand what a public defender is, what he's being charged with, if I'm the one doing it, or if I'm going to get in trouble too somehow because I didn't report that he sold weed, and I would subtweet responses to his insane rants about me.

Was that breaking the restraining order? How did I even get that, anyway? How else is he going to attack me? He's probably going to leak my nudes, and I'm going to ruin my whole family's life. Or he's going to say I'm the abusive one. Am I the abusive one? Not having him next to me felt even more terrifying than when he was in my face screaming. At least I knew what was coming then. I would refresh the Tumblr he made to get cryptic messages across to me without breaking the restraining order like I was waiting for updates about a nuclear war erupting.

I look in the mirror hanging on my closed door that makes me look like a wavy, funhouse character, and clean up my smudged mascara a little bit so it looks like an intentional smoky look. Then I make my way to Cara's boxy, windowless, highly illegal basement room next to mine.

"It's time ... I am ready to be a slut. Like one that goes all the way, like a sex slut," I declare with pride and fierce determination to my three house-mates, T, Cara, and Alexa.

"Dude, you gotta fuck Tony C," T says in their magical monotone voice. T is the kind of person who wears a black t-shirt that's like 900 dol-lars and always smells like clean laundry and spicy perfume and has a shaved head with loads of black ink tattoos. Ordinarily, I would be intim-idated by someone like T, but I sealed my fate the first time we met when I was trying to show them a picture of my room—and swiped one too far to reveal the largest dump I've ever taken to date. It actually wasn't and still isn't funny for me, but it did create a bond based on pure vulnerability and authenticity.

"YESSSSS TONY C!" squeals Cara as she jolts up from her bed. She's dressed in her signature long black side pony and cropped sweater/skin-ny-jean combo.

"Do it," Alexa vocal fries, her huge brown eyes focusing on sealing her blunt with sharp precision.

"Who the fuck is Tony C and why do we have to include the C?" I inquire.

"It rolls off the tongue, TONY C! And also he has like, a 12-inch dick I heard. Like it's huge. And he's TOTALLY DTF," Cara shrieks as she falls back on her bed and rolls around dramatically.

"Yeah, he definitely would be down. I can introduce you. And I did hear about his dick, that's like the sole reason to fuck him," T instructs.

"Ew," Alexa joins.

"Okay well like ... how do I even, like, do it though? Like how do I get from point A to point B? And is he hot? Like how do I know he's down? What do I need?" I'm spiraling.

"Ani. Relax. We got you. Go shave and get ready and leave the rest to us," T soothes, and I look down at my armpit hair. It is long enough to braid after exactly one week without shaving it. On it.

I spend the next hour meticulously shaving every single hair from my bikini and beyond (I'm half-Armenian—let me live). Then I glide to-wards my room looking like a raw chicken breast and see a box of mag-num condoms, a water bottle by my made-up bed, and the IKEA wooden planks stacked neatly in the corner. My friends have prepared my room and thank GOD the puke spot is too subtle to notice in the dark.

Next, I slather body oil all over me, squeeze into my black skinny jeans and black long sleeve crop, apply the perfect liquid line, and adorn myself with a rose quartz wrap to enhance the romance vibes (and to give me something to anxiously fiddle with, if we're being honest).

I feel like there's an army of fire ants under the first layer of my skin and I want to scratch it all off. Burning hot panicky magma churns like a broken and bubbled-over lava lamp in my gut. I'm reminded of how much time I wasted in the darkness, while everyone was else was off being wild and free and young—and the wind is knocked out of me.

Here's my deepest darkest secret: I have faked every orgasm I've ever had. Every single time I had sex with Michael, every random hookup that ended with someone jamming their fingers in or around me. The pleasure I expressed? Put on. Not real. A performance.

Why? I got fucking nervous and it was taking way too long. I'm also sure I fucking desensitized myself by using a vibrator twenty times a day. But mainly, I just couldn't *not* get lost in my thoughts. Not to mention I was always trying to frantically gauge where the other person was. I didn't want to fucking make anyone feel bad, so I faked it. Every time.

Tonight though, I'm going to bust it open and try my best to hoe out and cum in the name of freedom, Goddamnit! Amen.

T, CARA, ALEXA, AND I head to the bar McCladdens—the not-so-iconic bar up the road from our college that lets us drink as long as we are nineteen. I guess the owner pays off the cops or whatever but that's none of my business. The owner's name is Elliot. He drives an extra-large white Escalade, is in his late thirties, and is channeling enough cortisol to make my anxiety-ridden ass look like I'm a monk. Elliot also owns all the houses around here that the college students rent. Everyone hates him because he's, well, the worst. Questionable morals and whatnot. But for some reason, this man has my back SO hard. Ever since he found out what happened to me with Michael, he constantly checks in with me, and he's honestly the only one.

It took Michael exactly two days to figure out where I lived, and he started leaving shit on my car. First, an old headband I left at his house. Then, some weed and a note. (I will never forget *that* panic attack.) I didn't want to call the police, but I didn't know what else to do. When he saw the cop car outside, Elliot BURST through the front door to make sure I was okay. He installed security cameras for me that night, even though other people couldn't even get him to get their toilets to work.

He is my very flawed, very stressed, very questionable, but very rock-solid guardian angel. *And* he lets me and all my friends skip the line!

I walk into the bar like a rockstar, and Cara smacks my arm and points dead ahead. There he is—Tony C. Blue micro-mohawk and all. Tongue ring. I walk up to him with gusto so I don't lose my nerve.

Wait, is he wearing ... khaki shorts? And a black tee? And ... are those knee socks?

"Rugby socks," T corrects, reading my mind.

"Oh ... okay. Bold. I like that. Okay!" I chirp.

I begin my approach to him, letting false confidence fuel every contrived strut until I'm tapping him on the shoulder.

"I'm Ani. My housemates say you are *the* person to meet!" I add coyly.

He looks me up and down. "Hey, you're hot. Yes."

"So, shall we like ... fuck?" The words fall out of my mouth awkwardly. I suddenly realize that I've completely forgotten how to be a functioning member of society.

"Straight to the point, I like that! Hell yes. Let's get outta here. My place or yours?" He leans closer to me, lifts my chin to meet his, where we hover for a moment.

Here it is. The fireworks part. I remember this part pre-Michael.

Wait for it ... Wait for it ...

I give him my signature soul-sucking gaze, which is more than just looking someone in the eyes. I throw my whole soul into it until it radiates out of my eyeballs and then I suck them in. It works every. Damn. Time.

He starts to maul my mouth with his, kissing me with such ferocity and passion I lose my balance.

But there's no fireworks sounding off in my gut. No butterflies doing the Macarena in my stomach lining. I'm grossed the fuck out. Swapping spit with someone you don't want to is fucking vile.

He pulls away and I almost visibly wince seeing a spit string from his mouth. I'm going to need a drink for this.

"Let's grab one and go," I say, waving down the overly stressed bartender to get my whiskey neat. I gulp it down easier than that kiss.

We get back to my LED-lit room, and I suddenly want to cover up my giant Jimi Hendrix wall decal by my bed to spare the soul of Jimi the disgust of what he's about to see. We flop onto my bed.

"So, you're sure this is cool? If we, ya know, do it? Fuck?" he asks, inches from my face.

"Hell yes, I am so ready."

Within a second, he's on top of me, and we're passionately making out. *Ew.*

Then he grabs the back of my head with his hand and tries to do my signature gaze back to me, but it looks like he's about to pop a blood vessel instead. *Ew.*

His hand drops to my boob as we continue to kiss. *Ew.*

Then my skinny jeans unbutton.

Okay, this is when I'll start to like it. And honestly ... it does feel kind of good. He slowly lets his hand go over my lacy black thong first, and I inch closer to him.

Okay ... Okay ... this is good ... this is fi—You probably look really fucking stupid right now.

I jerk my head to the right side at the sheer audacity of this intrusive ass thought. I press up even closer to him, hoping that feeling the sensation of his body will help me feel my own.

Okay, pants are coming off ...

Okay, undies ...

He presses his fingers into me.

Don't make him feel bad you little bitch.

I fake-moan louder and jerk my body a bit.

"Fuck yes, baby ..." he whispers, and I realize I've had my eyes closed this whole time, so I peek through a hazy gaze and see him wiggling around, trying to pull his pants down while on top of me. I wince. The fun part will be when he's *in it* with me, right? I fucking wish the process of him getting naked with me wasn't so harrowing. He looks like a fish out of water. I close my eyes again.

I hear him fiddling around with the condom and putting it on. I peek one eye open to see if he really does have a 12 inch ...

Holy mother FUCK.

His dick looks like the salami I used to have to bring over for my grandma's holiday party. Oh god. I don't want to be thinking about *her* right now. But it would be nice to be eating stuffed grape leaves instead of whatever this is? FOCUS.

Wait? How the hell am I supposed to fit that thing inside of me? It goes fucking in and out and feels nice, right? It didn't hurt the first time I had sex, so why would—

"Ready, Annie?"

Annie? Bro. This is getting fucking DARK.

But all I do is whisper "mhmm" in his ear.

He works his way halfway in before he starts rapid-fire thrusting. I picture my cervix in one of those 1980s sweatbands with boxing gloves on getting absolutely destroyed in the ring.

"OW!" I yelp after he tries to put it all the way in. Sorry, but I cannot fake that to make him feel good—his dick is the Russian and my cervix is Rocky getting knocked out.

I immediately regret my unintentional yelp of pain, because now he's going so fucking slow and gentle, which is somehow worse, all while he's trying to gaze in my eyes. Sir, we are NOT making love right now. Oh dear *God*. I pretend to roll my eyes in the back of my head just so I can close them.

"I'm gonna—" he begins, as he starts pumping furiously halfway in again.

"Ouuuauuuuuaaaa," he groans while doing sporadic, jerky, half-hearted humps.

Oh. Dear. God.

I am horrified. Not in, like, a creepy rapey way this time. That was just like ... bad. I genuinely thought I was supposed to like this? Like, he has a huge dick—don't people lose their damn minds over that?

"I've never felt anything that intense before in my life," he whispers into my ear.

I am too stunned to even try and say anything back.

"Do you wanna see something really sexy?" he purrs millimeters away from my lips.

"Um ... yes?"

He pushes himself off of me, hops up at the end of the bed, revealing that he never took his fucking socks off. My eyes bulge so wide I have to turn my head to face the wall. But that's okay, because he's turning his back towards me anyway, and I'm making eye contact with his buttcheeks as his knee socks linger in my peripherals.

He looks over his shoulder to meet my eyes.

"Girls lose their shit when I pull this one out," he says while adjusting his legs ever so slightly. What the actual fuck is happening? What could possibly be more jarring than his massive, enormous, pure Genoa salam—

OH.

MY.

GOD.

He is ass clapping. Violently ass-clapping. *Furiously* ass-clapping. He peeps over his shoulder to gauge my reaction. And ... we're making eye contact. While. He's. Ass-clapping. Won't stop looking over his shoulder at me to see my reaction. Oh my GOD, we are making eye contact while he is ass-clapping.

"Wow, that's really good! Good work!" I say in my best customer service voice.

He's out of breath. But he's still going.

"*Very* impressive!" I chirp. I'll say anything to make this ass-clapping moment come to an end.

He finally turns around and does a couple of floppy dick moves (not quite sure what this is called, but I *think* it's a male stripper move).

"Well, I am grateful, but I have to meet with my family really early tomorrow morning, or I'd invite you to stay over," I lie through tightly clamped teeth.

"Get it, girl. I get you. This was fun, I'd love it if you can meet my mom this week when she comes to visit. I can't wait to tell her about my Annie!" I try to hide the absolute shock and horror from my face as I tie up my little satin robe and open my bedroom door as he jumps into his khakis.

"Well, I gotta pee, you know how it goes after sex, so, thanks again! Get home safe!" I say way too quickly, giving him an awkward kiss on the cheek, and scuttling into the bathroom like the freaking little rat that I am. I lock the door until I hear him walk up the stairs, and then hear the front door slam.

Thank you, God.

I text Alexa, T, and Cara to come down, like, *NOW*. And suddenly I hear someone blaring that stupid "I Just Had Sex" song from SNL. We spend the night unpacking this ordeal while we try to blow up the rest of the magnum condoms and laugh about the whole thing.

Turns out, it's possible to simply **not be** attracted to someone. Which I know is a very fucking *duh* moment, but I guess I'm a slow learner? Why the fuck did I just force myself to do that? Why did I think going further would somehow make it better?

I lay my head on the pillow and close my eyes. *No harm, no foul, I suppose*. My eyes feel heavy. *Lesson learned.*

And in three seconds flat my eyes shoot open, feeling the rush of panic from my guts to the top of my head with such ferocity that my mouth flies open and I *immediately* gag.

My whole body shakes.

I frantically flip open my laptop.

"Remember when you weren't a big fucking whore? Glad I got in that before it was tainted. Remember who stole your innocence," reads a text post on Michael's Tumblr.

I run to the bathroom and put my head in the toilet and dry heave over the toilet until my whole body hurts.

THE NEXT MORNING, I'm walking to my world religions class on campus with my burlap backpack, harem pants, leather jacket, and extensions, looking like Joan Jett if she went guido and hippie at the same time. I'm playing the EDM playlist that my new friend Vita has made me. I reached out to her on Twitter over the summer during my festival craze, because she was allllll about the scene. I've wanted to be Vita's friend ever since I first saw her, freshman year.

Let me tell you about Vita.

I'm sitting on a curb off one of the sidestreets of the school, clicking my platform boots together in boredom. She walked right up to my group of friends with a cigarette in her hand, and bluntly asked, "can someone with two hands light this for me?"

It was only then that I realized she had one arm. When a drunk frat bro asked her what happened, she simply and stoically replied: "I got hungry." From that moment on, I was obsessed with her.

After that I asked her (via Facebook Messenger) if I could borrow her Sexy Little Miss Muffet costume for Halloween, even though I hardly knew her. I'd seen her wearing it the night before, and she looked devastatingly hot in it. I tried to blame the fact I was asking a practical stranger for a favor on us having similar curves ... but really I just wanted to make contact.

Then I accidentally ripped the costume while hooking up with a finance bro named Evan and never gave it back.

But I messaged her again this summer because what did I have to lose? I'm into "the scene" too—so why wouldn't she want to be my festival friend?

My calculated plan to be Vita's friend worked. We had our first official "hang" a couple weeks back, where we ended up at Chipotle. I proceeded to spill an entire bottle of diet Coke on her Chanel bag and we've been inseparable ever since.

Vita is the kind of woman who can write the world's most moving, poetic, brilliant, work-of-art essay in twenty minutes while sitting on the toilet of a Barnes & Noble. She's the kind of person who can electrify people with her wisdom and wit, while also giving her best *Simple Life* impression with the perfect vocal fry to boot.

We have been bonding over music, and not just festival music. Music, like Jimi Hendrix. We talk about poetry and she introduces me to my new favorite poet, Andrea Gibson. And, of course, most importantly, we trauma-bond over our recent, horrifying relationship experiences.

Vita gets it. She doesn't look at me like a poor little victim, or like I'm "too much." She knows what it's like to doubt everything, to give up everything, to be in the space of trying to figure out the aftermath of a soul-sucking experience.

Vita's dark relationship was with another woman, which is another reason I love her so much. I've never seen someone rock who they are or be so true to themselves before. And if she ended up in a toxic relationship—it could happen to any of us.

The other thing with Vita is that we cry together. We tremble in fear. We go deep, raw, and real. But no matter what, we always end up laughing, somehow.

Even though she's a new friend, she's shown up harder than any festival friend I've made. And I think it's time we go together. Plus, I can be my full self around her because she's as messy and as weird as I am.

Five minutes later, we're planning our first friendship festival date.

Flash forward two weeks after Tony C and we're getting ready together. Vita makes her own rave bras and we're both rocking them. Mine is black with realistic monarch butterflies all over it, which I pair with fishnets and black booty shorts that are practically undies. Vita is adorned in a bedazzled bra, bracelets I used to make at Camp Sunset (that I find out are called "Kandi"), bootie shorts, and her giant, hot pink, fluffy boots.

"Can you see my extension tracks popping out?" Vita flips her long dark hair, turning her back towards me.

"You're good, how about me?" I do the same.

"You're perfect. God, you look amaze."

"YOU look amaze!"

"WE look amazing," we say in unison, in a corny, mocking voice.

I tap her giant boobs like I'm playing the bongos and we start soulfully singing,

"Weeeee loooook ... amazing! We look amazing!" We harmonize as I clap the beat using my own tits as bongos too, it's a four-piece drum kit now!

"Weeee ... loooook ... amaz—"

"You guys are so hilarious, like what are you doing? I love it, but we have to go, we're gonna miss the ferry," Vita's friend Courtney lectures. She's a tiny little thing, shorter than me and way skinny, with thin hair and a big smile that exudes sweetness. She is also wearing a rave bra and booty shorts, but somehow she looks ... less like she could potentially get arrested for indecent exposure. Whatever, Vita and I have tits, whaddya gonna do? We're all heading there together, but Courtney is a fierce rave girl who has a strict schedule to see every single DJ she can that doesn't align with our laissez faire attitude, so we break away the second we arrive.

There are paper jellyfish hanging from trees, rolling green hills, tents and pavilions as far as the eye can see. And so. Many. *People*.

After going through security and scanning our tickets, Vita and I link arms and make our way down one of the hills. The sun is glaring down on us on this early September Saturday. Everyone is sweating even though the day hasn't even started yet.

I feel self conscious in my rave bra and undies. Probably because I don't have any molly. I also hear a whole lotta house music, and not the intense bass music that sets me free.

It's a sea of fluffy boots and neon, with no harem pants in sight, unlike the festivals I've gone to. But Vita radiates confidence, so I decide to parrot what she's doing. Head up, tits out, eyes on the prize: the music. We pop into some tents but walk out immediately after shooting each other an "ehhhh" look.

"This kind of sucks, but my all-time favorite DJ is playing in a couple hours, so it'll be worth the wait. Last time I saw them live, I peed my pants, literally," Vita declares.

"Well, then, I can't wait," I giggle, looking around.

Suddenly, the air evaporates from my body as quickly as a popped balloon.

About 100 feet away, stands a wolf-pack of Michael's frat brothers. I stop dead in my tracks. And of course, like dogs sensing fear, they all whip around and stare at me, staring at them.

I dig my fingers into Vita's arm.

"Do you want to leave? We can leave right now." She is staring at them too.

I shake my shoulders and stand up straight.

"No, I got this. I can't run forever." Why am I sweating so much in this skimpy rave outfit?

I walk over.

*I am **not** that girl in that frat house. I am **not** that girl in that frat house. I am **not** that girl in that frat house.*

I march toward them. "Hey guys, how are you?" I'm still arm and arm with Vita, who is smiling coyly next to me as my secret, silent support system.

"Ani, Sweetheart, how are you? You look great," one of the most Italian looking men I've ever seen says. The rest of them nod, clearly uncomfortable with their shifty eye contact. The scruffy Italian, big-boned frat bro is Anthony, a super super senior who Michael wanted to be just like. He is a notorious party guy, but not in the hot shot way, more in the ... nothing you say or do is ever taken seriously way.

"Listen," he continues, "don't worry, we dropped that motherfucker. Don't worry about him, okay?"

"Oh, yeah, whatever, don't worry about that. I don't care," I blurt quickly, trying to hide my visible relief. "Who are you most excited for?" I force a grin.

"I don't even know who is playing, I came here to roll my dick off honestly. Want some?" he asks, fishing into his fanny pack.

Vita squeezes my arm. She isn't into drugs. I look at her, and we telepathically communicate through eye contact and subtle facial movements.

"Okay, we're in!" I chirp.

"Okay here. Just be careful, it's strong," he warns, giving us each a capsule with the yellow powder in it.

"How much is it?" I ask.

"Free," he responds with a wink.

"No, I mean, how much am I taking?"

"0.2," he responds. Okay perfect, that's how much Ty said I took the first time.

I pop it into my mouth. Vita waits.

"Oh shit, sorry, my 1.2 ones. Someone is gonna have fun," he laughs.

Is it that much of a difference?

Whatever. I'll just dance extra hard.

We giggle and pivot away, and walk to a tent to start to dance, both pretty silent, probably due to nerves, but we're not about to talk about it and ruin our good time.

We're moving through the swarms of people, trying to figure out where to go. Eventually, I give up trying to figure it out and leave it to Vita, because everything is getting really ... wavy? Blurry? Swooshy? I try to steady myself by clinging to her arm harder. The sun is starting to set, but there is a haze in the air. Everything feels ... off.

Suddenly we are stopped by a man with LED gloves shoving his hands in front of my face, moving his fingers around like a tripped-out magician casting an illusion spell. The LEDs on his fingertips look insane. I see a camera moving around us, and I can't imagine what my face is doing.

A shot of nausea hits my stomach as I abruptly feel massively dizzy.

"She doesn't look so good," I hear someone say as the guy and his camerawoman scurry away.

It's then that I start hyperventilating. I try to turn to Vita, but I can't. I can't see. The swarm of people turn into black dots, millions of them, and everything around me turns to static TV. All I can see is static TV.

"Vita?" I gasp, "Vita? I can't see. Vita, I can't see." I panic and feel her cling on to me harder. I can't really hear her because I'm too focused on the fact that I can hear my own voice but can't feel myself say the words, like I'm a POV camera with my lens cap on and my mic volume only picking up my own sound.

I can't hear her over my own gasps for air—everything sounds as blurred together as my vision. I try to run even though I can't see and don't know what running would do for me, or where I could go. I just need to get out of there.

I don't know how far I get before crashing to the ground, shaking uncontrollably. I roll on my back and face the sky.

"V-vita? V-V-Vita," my voice is as shaky as my breath and body. "I'm ... s-s-sor ... so ... sorry," I gasp. I still can't hear. I am seeing white now, facing the sky. I think I'm talking but I can't be sure.

Suddenly, I feel her body slink next to mine. Her hand rests over my hand.

I start to pray.

God, please keep me here.

God, please keep me here.

Earth, keep me here.

I focus on breathing in and feeling Vita next to me. If I can feel her, I'm not going anywhere.

I suddenly can hear people rushing around us.

A tidal wave of shame rushes over my body. People seeing me like this. I can't hear again and my body shakes harder. I tilt my head and puke on the cold grass.

Vita squeezes my hand harder. "It's okay, I'm here. I asked for help. Help is coming."

"NO!" I scream. Or at least I think I scream. What if I get arrested?

"Vita, I need you to kiss me," I say in one quick burst.

"Really? Are y—"

"I need to feel my body," I plead.

We kiss.

And I ... relax. My body stops convulsing as much. I feel her lips on mine. Waves of panic morph into bursts of fireworks. I break away for a second, feeling more grounded after realizing I can feel my body again.

Wait ... is this like, creepy of me?

Suddenly the world starts to whoosh again.

I take the biggest deep breath in and hold it, and slowly let it out. My body has some aftershock shakes. I do it again. And again.

Whatever, my friends and I always make out when we party.

I lean back in. And we are kissing with vigorous passion.

"Sweetie, what did you take?" I hear a voice interrupt.

"Some molly," I manage to answer, breaking apart from Vita.

I sit up and see two EMTs in front of me.

"I'm fine though. I swear. I'm okay now. My friend helped me." I sing-song, feeling like the worst of it has passed.

"Drink this, okay?" They hand me some OJ and water. I realize I can't grab it because my hands are locked into claw-like shapes.

They put it to my lips. I drink and feel even better almost instantly.

"Thank you, seriously, thank you. What you're doing here is amazing. Your families must be proud of you," I say earnestly, feeling oddly misty eyed, thinking of the pride of their mothers. They giggle to each other. "She's going to be fine, we'll leave this orange juice with you. Drink up and if anything changes, the medical tent is right over there." And with that, they head towards their next cracked-out festival goer.

I turn my head and look at Vita. I can see her if I focus really hard. Vita is beautiful. She is hot.

I lay back down next to her, and we're both on our sides, facing each other. Even though we are surrounded by people at the base of a hill, it feels like there's no one else in the world but us.

"I'm so sorry ... you're going to miss your favorite DJ."

"None of that matters. I'm here."

"Can I tell you something? I think I'm bi." I press my forehead against hers. "And honestly, if I don't have sex with a woman in this life, I'll be so pissed at myself."

It's true. I'm only now really realizing it but it's *true*. I always prefer making out with girls as opposed to guys at parties. I only watch lesbian porn, and for some reason when I think of fucking a girl my whole body goes a little limp, in the best way.

"Okay, honestly, I think you're gay as fuck, but you also just took a fuck ton of molly," Vita says this like she's been keeping this in forever.

"Dude, so many people think I'm gay, I think it's because I am." I grin. "We should fuck." I giggle while moving closer to her.

"I mean, I would be totally down to fuck you when you're not out of your mind. You're hot as fuck. But you're my friend and I don't want to be the creepy lesbian porno trope who preys on straight girls."

"You're not! Watch! Kiss me again!" We start kissing.

Suddenly, there are two dudes who drop-down, laying by our sides.

"May we join?" And SPLAT. My little imaginary safe bubble bursts. I remember we are in public. I start to panic.

And without so much of a beat missed, the bigger of the two (whose face I can't make out because it's nighttime by now) rolls me away from Vita and towards me, and then we're kissing.

Ew.

"Where's Vita?" I pull away. "Vita?"

I roll around and see her making out with the smaller dude.

"I'm good," she assures.

I can't even see who's in front of me. He starts going on this long-winded story about someone trying to kill him once. I am rambling about something I'm not even fully aware of because all I can think about is Vita.

Did I just fuck up our friendship? I'm not gay ... .right? I mean, I love love love to make out with women. I love the thought of moving that further, always have. I don't know if I could ever date a woman. Vita would be amazing to be with—but

No. You are not gay. You're traumatized. And high.

TWO WEEKS LATER, I SIT on my bed and stare at the blue glitter I spilled pre-life-altering festival moment with Vita, shimmering through the holes of the crocheted, circular throw rug I bought to cover the ugly yellow puke stain on the carpeted floor. I still haven't cleaned it up.

Everything in my overly-done maximalist bohemian-dream basement bedroom is hanging up by tacks and tacks alone, which I hammered into the wall with my black platform patent leather spiked booties. I'm talking full-on floating shelves, hanging on for dear life by strategically placed tacks. Bright pink tapestries of dancing bears and dark brown and red spiral patterns draped lazily over the bed; big framed art splayed crooked across the wall; the Marshall Amp fridge door only latches on the bottom, flinging off every time I reach for some Pedialyte for my hangovers.

Since that night, Vita and I have managed to sweep everything under the rug and not talk about our kiss, but I feel crippling anxiety, morning, noon, and night. I feel like I'm in a dream now. Everything feels far away and vaguely unfamiliar. I don't feel happy, or sad, or hopeful, or doomsday ... I just feel, far.

Why the fuck did I think doing molly at a festival was going to make me feel better?

Nothing is working out the way I thought it would. I don't have a massive group of festival friends, because if I'm being honest, they probably didn't even like each other without drugs. How free are you if you're buying it for twenty bucks a pop?

Why the fuck did I try to pretend like this was it for me? It was all so contrived, so fake. I mean, I did love feeling free for the first time in my life. But look where that got me. I could have died. I could have ruined a friendship. I ended up humiliating myself and leading on a good fucking person.

I'm a bad friend—a selfish person who let my drama and insecurity almost destroy my life. Again. And while the whole group of festival friends wasn't awful, and I am keeping a few of the gals around, the rest can go kick rocks.

And I am never, ever going to do drugs again.

I grab T's handheld vacuum and suck up any last remnants of glitter in sight. It's time to get my shit together. This time, for real.

4
Sad Bitch

As messy as I am, I am a sad bitch. I've always been this way.

When I was a kid, every time an episode of *Winnie-the-Pooh* ended I'd swallow down hard, painful marbles of tears caught in my throat because I thought *for sure* they were all dead. When I was 13, I'd carve my name in trees next to the initials of hearts just so some random stranger knew that I existed. To this day, my pillow is stained yellow from all the tears I've shed in the middle of the night.

I thought having a relationship was going to be the thing that saved me from myself, but I had only ended up *more* down and out. I thought being liberated and free at music festivals would be the thing that brought me back to life, but I found nothing but cheap bursts of chemically-engineered happiness that left me the second I came down.

I thought I could mask the soul-sucking sadness with mixed drinks and jungle juice. But when the night winds down, I make my way back to my room, and there my secret lover lies: sadness. Waiting for me on the bed and spooning me until I fall asleep.

I know people pick up on it. It's like a whole other entity follows me when I walk into a room. There's the bubbly, shiny, Stevie Nicks impersonator that I am pretending to be; and then there's the sad succubus me, like in the memes with evil Kermit wearing the hood. Plus I always end up losing energy and spacing out after a while. When that happens, I do what every mental health professional suggests when what you really need is a rest—I scroll aimlessly on my phone for hours. Sometimes without blinking!

I scroll to distract myself.

I scroll to get inspiration.

I scroll to find a lick of hope.

I scroll to feel better about my life.

I scroll to find peace.

I scroll to feel connected.

When sadness wakes me up in the middle of the night, with her sister, anxiety, like a blaring alarm sounding off in my gut, I shoot open my eyes and aim right for my phone.

To scroll.

When I'm in class, privileged to be getting an education at all, guess what my ungrateful ass does?

She fucking scrolls!

When I'm with my friends, I scroll. When I'm in the club, I scroll. When I'm in the bathroom, I'm scrollin'.

I hop from Tumblr, to Instagram, to Twitter, to Google, and I scroll, and scroll, and scroll. All to not feel so fucking ... sad.

Until it is 2 a.m. on a Tuesday, and I'm scrolling on my bed in my bohemian-dream basement. My phone hangs dangerously over my glazed-over face when I know I'm going to drop it at some point and get the slap of reality I probably need. But I'll scroll to cope with it.

I'm scrolling through a spiritual page on Tumblr. It's filled with tips and tricks on how to really be "connected," "at one with the universe," and "at peace with yourself and others." Sign me the fuck up. Because on top of being an absolute drag, this sad-girl energy is *not* spiritual. And if there's one thing I learned from my festival days, it's that I want to be closer to *The Universe.*

I want to be in "my magic." I want to manifest with the best of them. And I know enough to know that being constantly miserable will only create more misery. I need God, man. But not, like, the God I grew up with, who would doom me to eternal suffering at the slightest hint that I didn't love him the most. Hmm. Sounds a bit like my ex (*ba-dum-tss!*)

I wonder what he's ...

Don't do it, Ani.

I type in Michael's username, just to make sure he didn't leak my nudes.

Stop while you're ahead!

And there, on his page, is a post stating: "You have no idea the war you started."

I fly out of bed instantly and drop to the floor, where I start dry heaving while convulsing violently. I grab my phone again with shaking hands, and I open Instagram to try and distract myself. But my eyes can't focus on anything because now I am in the throes of a panic attack. I throw the phone down and rub my hands over my face, letting little gasps of air enter and escape my mouth.

I grab my phone again and Google "chanting for anxiety relief"—a tip I saw on the spiritual Tumblr. I still can't focus on anything, and desperately click on the first video that pops up.

A woman is singing some sort of repetitive prayer in a soothing voice, while a man plays all these instruments behind her. I listen with my back against my bed, arms wrapped around my legs, head folded over and resting on my knees. I am rocking back and forth. I must look insane. I *feel* insane.

You are disgusting. You know you will lose any war you're in because you are the fakest, most insidious, ugliest human. He's going to destroy you in any way he can—online, in real life.

It's not working; I can't even hear the anxiety chant over my own thoughts.

You probably gave him all the ammo he needs. You existing is all the ammo he needs. It's only a matter of time ...

I lunge forward and gag again, my body still convulsing, unable to steady myself. I am on my knees now, shoulders slumped over, body shaking, my throbbing head feeling like it weighs a million pounds.

And I start to pray.

How come you can't just forgive me, God? How can I show you how sorry I am for getting involved with a bad guy and being a shit of a human being myself? God, please, I beg you, show me what to do and I will do it.

And out of nowhere, my dry heaves are replaced with sobs, and I lean forward on my rug. My whole chest burns so bad. I let out a huge wail, and I feel a stab wound directly to my heart.

I start to whisper out loud through my sobs.

"How could this happen, God? How could *I* let this happen? I let you down. I let everyone down. I don't want to be this selfish, this narcissistic, this miserable. I just want to be happy."

I am crying, shaking, gagging, gasping, and rocking. The only light comes from my phone, which is still blasting the anxiety chant, and the words just keep coming.

"And I miss him. I miss being loved so fucking much. It's all I ever wanted. I crave his comfort. But how can the thing that once brought me the most comfort bring me so much fear?"

I let out one more big, shaking breath.

"Please, God. Love me." I sit there for a moment in the silence. The chanting video must have ended. I feel a tiny flutter of relief. Hope. Determination.

I snake back into bed, sneak under the twisted sheets, and lay my damp, salty cheek on my pillow.

Something has got to change.

MY EYES PEEL OPEN in the morning, crusty with dried tears. I stare out the window for a moment and let my mind wander.

My relationship with God has always been ... complex.

I've always kind of had this creepy obsession with him, honestly. But the relationship feels like I'm his battered wife just trying to be good and please him, only for him to pop the fuck off and destroy my life if I even slightly step out of line. Hah, kinda like my ex! (*Ba dum tss, again!*)

As a kid, I went to Catholic school and a four-hour Armenian mass every Sunday. I knew the Our Father in English *and* Armenian. Looking back, it's kind of tragically hilarious to picture me reciting this powerful, ancient prayer when I could barely pronounce my "R"s with my thick, East Coast accent.

It went something like:

"Owah fatha, who awht in heaven, hallowed be thy name."

I would say that and the Hail Mary every single night, without fail. I wanted to be good. And ... I was not about to go to "H-E-double hockey sticks," as my kindergarten teacher liked to call it. Oh yes, *hell*. I'll never forget the first time I heard about it, in kindergarten, after getting in trouble for eating an Oreo in class.

"Ani, are you *eating* during class?" Mrs. Smith sneered at me in front of everyone.

I shook my head "no" in humiliation, mouth still packed with cookie.

"And now she's lying!" she announced to everyone. My heart was beating so hard it felt like the bass at the nightclub my dad worked at.

"I'm sorry, Mrs. Smith."

"Don't be sorry to me, be sorry to God. He blessed you enough to be here getting an education to begin with, he does everything for you, and you lie? You know where liars end up?" she raged on.

This is when I learned I could go to hell for not apologizing to God for eating an Oreo in class.

From then onwards, I would spend my days thinking about what it meant to be "good," and how to show God I was "good enough" to not get "punished." I felt solid enough—I would pray and I even learned the Act of Contrition and added it to my nightly prayers:

"O my God, I am heartily sorry for having offended Thee, and I detest all my sins because of thy just punishments ..."

But if anyone in my family did anything remotely wrong, I didn't know how to handle it. I would run to the nun's office at my school almost daily in full panic mode and blurt out questions:

"What if I do everything right and go to heaven, but my dad does something wrong and goes to hell, and then we're separated? I wouldn't be happy in heaven without him and I'd cry every day thinking about him suffering forever so it would be like two different h-e-double hockey sticks!" I would sob.

Sister Judy had a very large gullet and a stutter. She had no answers for me, and I would leave her office feeling even more distraught.

And so I would sit through class all day begging God to have mercy on everyone and everything. I would fixate on keeping the devil away from my family. I would even risk my life nightly, walking around the house to scan for demons.

Blankie over my head, dressed in my Barbie nightgown, I would go from room to room, prepared to throw myself at whatever creature from the depths of hell was waiting for me so I could protect my family.

Eventually my parents, obviously concerned, tried to soothe my fears. My dad even got me a Saint Michael the Archangel prayer card—the one where he's stepping on the devil's head, sword drawn. I so appreciated that. I started holding it out in front of me while I scanned the house for extra protection.

As the years went on, my feelings about God morphed from fear, to horror, to disgust. And now there is just sadness.

No one I know thinks about God like this. They're either big-straight-teeth "live, laugh, love" Jesus girls with two loving parents; are of the "God is scary and gonna punish you" vibe; they hate God and organized religion in general; or they just don't really think about the whole God debacle all that much.

I haven't met anyone who, like me, feels, well, *heartbroken* about the whole thing.

I kick down my sweaty '70s floral-printed sheets, grab my laptop and Google: "spiritual healers and mentors."

I scroll through a slew of bald men wearing all white, their piercing blue eyes and bare feet giving them an uncanny resemblance to Mr. Clean. If Mr. Clean meditated and traded the chemicals for patchouli.

When I was little, I had two invisible friends: Vanessa and Auntie Lulu. They lived in this parallel universe I created called "Ani World," where everything had its own land. There was chair land! Tree land! Binder land! And then there was spooky land, where everything I was scared of went.

Auntie Lulu was an older woman who would bless me and Vanessa before we ventured there. She'd give us an amulet for protection and an army of bees that I could send to swarm whatever frightened me. I would put my radio on to dead air and pretend it was my army of bees when I was up scared at night.

And now I'm scared, like, all the time. And I need an Auntie Lulu.

I add the word "woman" to my Google search and scroll.

I find a link that reads, "Heal Your Whole self, Step Into Your Power,

Access Full Love With Intuitive healer, Spiritual Mentor, Hummingbird"

I click on the link faster than the speed of light.

Oh. My. God. YES. The website features bad graphics of dolphins jumping over a lush white wave that leads to *her*. She stands with closed eyes, a serene smile, chin lifted, draped in full white garb. Her feet are planted in the sand, hands clutching a bouquet of flowers and feathers. I can tell she's shorter, and she has a round face and body, with long brown hair falling over her shoulders, and wispy bangs framing her eyes.

She can't be a *cult leader* if her graphics are that heartwarmingly terrible, right? Also, she seems Auntie Lulu-level comforting. I could *barf* with relief.

Also, her main shtick is helping people with self-love and connecting to God while developing their own spiritual gifts. Imagine if I had spiritual gifts to develop? Imagine if I didn't want to burst into tears every time I tried on clothes in the dressing room? Imagine if I didn't cry myself to sleep every night, or scroll until my last brain cells turned into those creepy Spongmonkeys from that early 2000s Quiznos' commercial?

I click through the other pages on her site. They are filled with photos of people looking completely blissed out, dancing as if they are completely content with every aspect of life. As if they could laugh at anything and didn't have to take a shot to numb the insecurity of moving their bodies, and could cry sweet tears of *happiness* over a beautiful moment at the drop of a hat.

I'm into it.

I scroll down, and in bright purple letters I am pretty sure is "papyrus" font, I find bullet points, stating what Hummingbird promises I will learn from working with her:

• Feel genuine peace and call in love to your everyday life
• Connect with Spirit, heal your body
• Express your soul's creative codes
• Balance your emotions, and clear negative emotional drains
• Stop reacting and start living
• Feel able to live with light and love

She's the one. Yes! She is the one who is going to help me become peaceful. Loveable. Able to be responsible for my life and decisions and path. She is going to help me manifest my dreams, heal my soul, and become a moved-by-the-beauty-of-nature-to-the-point-of-tears kinda gal.

Without another second of hesitation, I call her.

"Blessings, this is Hummingbird!" Her voice sounds like a freaking Disney fairy godmother and I am already ascending.

"Hi Hummingbird! My name is Ani, and I'm wondering if you have any space to take another student?" I ask while pacing in a circle, squishing my toes into my off-yellow, barf-and-tear stained carpet.

"Hi sweetheart, I'm really glad you called. I'd love to hear more about what you're looking for and how I can support you," she coos. Everything she says feels comforting.

"Yay! Okay, well, I'm a nervous wreck and I made a huge mess of my life and when I'm not scared I'm completely checked out and I think I *really* fucked things up with God; but I'm not sure if the God I believed in is the God I believe in—it's more of like, a universe situation I guess? Anyway, I ruin every relationship I'm in, I'm a huge bitch to my family, I hate the way I look and I hate that I even care, nature gives me anxiety, and I'm a nasty, gossipy, victim-y over-privileged college girl with not enough real problems so I just keep creating them." I finally remember to inhale and take a huge gulp of breath.

"How about we start with this—are you open to me doing a little practice with you right now?" I look at the time on my phone. It is 12:05pm and I'm officially late to class, but whatever, it's math and I'm a film major and isn't healing my soul more important anyway?

"I would love that." My lips stretch into a real smile, my first in months.

"I have a guitar, her name is Melody, and I'm going to play you a little song. You just open yourself up and receive this medicine." I hear some fumbling on the other end of the phone. I put her on speaker and sit on the patch of sun coming in through my tiny basement window.

Her song has no lyrics, and yet I find myself tearing up. I feel the way I did when I would see my dad pull in the driveway during a rainstorm, feeling sweet relief at the fact he did not, in fact, get struck by lightning. Is this what peace is? Relief?

Minutes later, there's silence. And we're sitting in it. And for the first time since I can't remember when, the silence doesn't feel like a blood curdling scream in my ear. It feels kind of ... nice. I can hear everything more clearly—the sound of the heater, the hum of my mini fridge—and I am seeing everything for what feels like the first time. My plants look more vibrantly green, the sun outside is a beautiful glowy orange. I can feel the softness of the carpet beneath me, the graze of my oversized t-shirt on my chest.

"What the hell ... was that? I feel more calm than I ever have and I'm genuinely not just saying that to gas you up or whatever," I blurt out in shock.

She giggles.

"Sometimes when I am with my clients in a healing session, Spirit will guide me to pick up Melody and play. Music changes energy, it calls forth energy, it heals energy. It's a gateway to the higher Universe." She hums gently and I look up at the Jimi Hendrix "music is my religion" decal on my wall. I couldn't agree more, even though I would never have phrased it like that.

"Wow, yes. Music is one of my favorite parts of being alive."

"Me too, Sweet One. What is your favorite music to listen to?"

I light up at the chance to share my faves. "I love all classic rock but especially Led Zeppelin. The Smashing Pumpkins and Nirvana. I just discovered EDM and—"

"Oh my goodness!" she laughs. "No wonder you're feeling anxiety! If music carries energy, what do you think those songs are inviting in? There is *low* vibration, and then there is *high* vibration. Our first task if we work together would be getting you into high vibration. From there, we can anchor in the light and you can start really being in your power, living your truth, and being fully open to giving and receiving love freely."

"Well, shit. Okay, yes. I get that. And yes I would love to work with you if you want to work with me. Don't worry about the music thing, I'm a quick student," I assure her.

"I hear your devotion. And I honor it. We can talk about the investment—or as I like to call it, the 'energy exchange,' because money is energy—over email. And I'll include some heart-centered musicians for you as well. Some of these musicians are reincarnations of ascended masters, and have transmitted the healing violet flame into their songs, which are actually ascension codes!" she adds, giggling, as if she didn't just start talking in *Star Trek* language.

"... Wh ... what is that?"

Another giggle.

"Just trust the process, Sweet One. You are doing a big thing for yourself today. When you do this work, it impacts seven generations before you, seven generations after, and every sentient being around you. This investment in yourself makes a massive difference in the world. Blessed be. Mmmmmm," she coos.

I feel a lump in my throat. For once, I'm going to actually *do* something about my life and take charge of myself. For once, I feel a shred of hope that I can change. For once, I feel less like a colossal piece of crusty shit, and more like a fresh one—covered in morning dew and being kissed by the morning sun—that could be used for compost or something.

For once, I think I did something right.

"HUMMINGBIRD, I CHECKED MICHAEL'S WEBSITE again and now he's saying that—"

"Ani, we're cutting the cord. NOW," she commands. I am so shocked by her tone it halts my spiral pacing. I've never heard her talk like that.

"What do you mean?"

"Every time you go to that website, you are creating an energetic chord with him that keeps you linked. It links right to your heart and your womb, where you take on his fear and negative energy. We need to sever these chords, and you are NEVER to look at that website again."

I am so stunned that I can only nod my head yes over the phone. I've never thought about my womb before; never even considered calling it a womb. I put my hand over my lower belly and feel my body relax a little. I slink down to my floor and lean my back against my bed.

"Good, okay. Visualize white light around you, and see the energetic chording on your womb and heart. Now, take your fingers, and make them like scissors, and start cutting!"

I start to frantically snip around me like the scissor-happy hairdresser who gave me a Joan Jett haircut when I said I just wanted an inch off.

"Divine Creator and Holy Spirit Guides, we ask that you protect Ani and bless her with your love and healing energy. We ask that the white light and violet flame cocoon her as she returns these chords with love and gratitude to the sender. We ask that these chords never form again and that she is cleared from this energy, wholly and permanently, in this lifetime and any other timeline, and so it is, so mote it be."

Waves of tingles wash over my body and tears pour out of my eyes. Suddenly my basement feels like some sort of temple.

"Now Ani, you are to never go on that website again or that chord will absolutely reform. Promise me."

"I promise, never again."

Hummingbird only wears white or single-color outfits designed to evoke certain "energies." I have been told NEVER to wear black, as it absorbs all negative energy, which then hangs on me like a trench coat.

I've started learning all about archangels, different deities, spirit guides, and dreamwork. Every Tuesday and Thursday at 7pm, I am on the phone with her talking and processing and learning and meditating.

And everything is starting to feel a bit more okay. I'm learning that God doesn't have to be this scary weird guy in the clouds just waiting for me to fuck up. That God can be … an energy … the Universe itself … and there's like this whole etheric team I have rooting for me and taking care of me.

Which is why I say "yes" when Hummingbird tells me a few weeks later that I have advanced far enough that I am ready to make the pilgrimage to Mount Shasta, aka the heart chakra of the whole fucking world. A place with portals and aliens and mythical creatures and even a crystal city where *the Lumerians* live (which, I find out, is not a people from somewhere off the coast, but rather these five-dimensional beings who existed with the people of Atlantis before it sank).

I am so fucking ready.

In fact, I have even bought a real freaking backpack in honor of the fact I will be sleeping in the great outdoors—and this time it won't be because I passed out on the neighbor's swing set after drinking too much strawberry moonshine.

It will be because I am fully claiming this spiritual path, and this is the moment where I will finally, wholly and truly, meet God. I have already frantically Googled stories of Mount Shasta and all the deep spiritual wisdom, massive and monumental healings, and wild sightings of mythical creatures that have happened there. There is no other option but for me to *finally* have my moment with God.

I am determined to change my sad-girl script: to get so close to God that I shall never feel like I'm carrying the weight of the world on my shoulders again, and the only tears that fall from my eyes shall be ones of "beauty."

My whole body is humming to the tune of this as I doze off, one step closer to my dreams.

THE PILGRIMAGE BEGINS WITH WHAT feels like the longest plane ride of my life (it is, in fact, only six hours).

I end up in a small hippie town, where I meet Hummingbird face-to-face for the first time. I feel bubbles brewing in my belly and I'm not sure whether they're nerves, excitement, or gas from the airplane food. Either way, I clench my buttcheeks as the taxi pulls up to her house—a small craftsman style home with a dilapidated garden and prayer flags covering every nook and cranny. There's a giant stuffed tiger on the porch, who, like me, looks like it's been through some shit. And there she is, in a full on denim-on-denim ensemble.

"Ani! You're finally here!" She is much shorter than I expected. Her brown bangs are blowing in the breeze as she rushes to the taxi and scoops me in her arms. I relax into her hug, and close my eyes dropping my entire weight into her.

"Hi! Oh my goodness! I can't believe I'm here!"

"Let's go to the healing room," she giggles, as she grabs my bags and leads me to the small room that's separated from the rest of her house by the garden. The room is bright and sunny, with wood linoleum floors, homemade artwork, and loads of angel and horse paraphernalia everywhere. There is also a couch, a big computer, and a massage table in the corner.

She begins to excitedly get into all of what to expect from my spiritual journey, as I take in the West Coast landscape for the first time out of her window. It feels so foreign and wild and uninviting. And that all makes it SO appealing—like the quiet, mysterious Scorpio at the party whose validation you need ASAP. After the pavements of NYC, this land looks ancient and untouched; there are no Dunkin' cups littering the ground by the trees.

I can't believe a place like this has existed all along; that I have spent so much time wanting this; and that I have lived most of my life without it. I can't believe there are people who will never get to see this kind of beauty.

My throat begins to clench up when I'm suddenly interrupted.

"Hey, where are you?" Hummingbird is inches from my face trying to make eye contact with me. I must have been completely glazed over, blankly staring at the mountains in the distance.

"Oh, uh, yeah just taken by the beauty here. I've never actually seen a mountain before in real life."

"Where were you actually, Ani?" she interrogates. I try to hide my smile and can't look her in the eye, like a kid being caught in a lie. *Shit*. I've been caught red-handed.

"I'm not sure," I lie, trying to protect her in a way. If I actually feel this weird sadness for zero reason, it would be like all the work we've done is a lie. I would have failed her. And she's not the problem—I am.

"Ah, you went into your cave. You have a cave in your heart. Don't get lost in there," she continues, before continuing to give me her lowdown on the epic adventure we will be leaving for in the morning. I'll confess my lying sin on the mountain and hopefully that will be enough and this new God will understand.

Apparently, we are going to be joined by two other "young people" as she so endearingly calls us.

"Well, why don't you settle in for the night. There's your bed; there's the sink to wash up. I will tell you more in the morning."

I nestle into the pullout positioned between a full-sized painting of a bear eating a wild salmon from a rushing river and a sculpture of a dragon made from dried seaweed—and think about who could be joining us, and what they will be like. Maybe I'll finally feel like I've found my people.

I look out the window again, and feel into the mystery of this land, the *deep* wildness of it. Looking around the room, I take in the altars and the offerings to Spirit, and I can't fathom how someone can have *this much* faith. I grab for my phone, which of course doesn't have service, and scroll through my photos until my eyes close. When I open them again, it's sunrise, and I'm still holding my phone, which I quickly tuck away so no one will see.

I MAKE MY WAY TO THE KITCHEN, where I find Hummingbird surrounded by potions and dried herbs. There are dirty dishes, pots, and pans everywhere. She busily packs up a box of tobacco and dried herbs. I scan the kitchen for some coffee.

"No caffeine, you are officially on your pre-fast. You'll get one meal today, and then only water from the springs on the mountain."

I shudder. No ... coffee? No ... food? Fast ... ing? She notices.

"You won't even notice it after the first day, Ani. Trust me. Fasting helps you hear God more and open yourself up to deep spiritual experiences. When your body isn't being distracted by digestion it can focus on divinity," she explains.

I now fully know I'm a sack of shit because of the pure rage I feel towards Hummingbird in this moment. *I mean, giving up coffee and food for a few days isn't such a bad exchange for meeting God and healing on every level, right? And it's not her fault. But ... maybe I should get a bagel and sneak it in my new backpack just in case? Or maybe even just some instant coffee? Or, I guess I could potentially sneak a Pop-Tart because they are more inconspicuous, and also very delicious? Why is this Higher Power such a finicky fucking bit—*

"HUMMINGBIRD!" A young couple suddenly bursts into the kitchen, making me jump so high that I completely forget about cursing God for the small print of a spiritual journey that hasn't even begun. The only other time I've heard this level of excitement is when frat bros would play "Don't Stop Believin" at a party and would all rush into the room and swarm each other like the stampede scene in *The Lion King*.

The couple are around my age, totally hippie'd out—the man bare-foot, the woman wearing *gulp* Chacos. They are both wearing flowy har-em pants with elephant patterns, and crystal wraps dangling from their necks. I pull at my little floral slip dress to try and make it longer, looking down at my motorcycle boots. I see them doing the same.

"Hi, we're Dean and Luna!" the girl sing-songs like she's on a Broad-way stage. I go to hug both of them and they clearly are not wearing de-odorant. Something about them reads as overly-caffeinated high school theater kid energy, which I tend to have a visceral reaction to. Usually I would just go silent and check out. But I'm not going to be a judgmental douchebag—at least not anymore.

"Hi, I'm Ani, it's great to meet you. Oregon is so cool so far, you're lucky to live here!" I belt back, channeling my inner theater kid. They both dart *a look* at each other and start cackling.

"Or-e-gon?" Dean mocks.

I'm genuinely confused ... *is this not where we are?*

"Sorry, we've just never heard it pronounced that way. We say Or-e-gin."

Sick Luna! Yeah! That's funny! Thanks so much! Dean, you're kind of a fucking dick but okay!

We talk about Or-e-gin for a while longer, making small talk and ni-ceties. I'm trying to bond with them. Honestly, they are vaguely insuffera-ble, always petting at each other and laughing at the end of every sentence, which I then *have* to mimic to be nice. They also smell like ass, but like a very specific kind of healthy ass. Never thought I'd meet God with this particular crowd, but I'm not questioning it because they are the ones laughing while I'm sitting here in my vaguely dissociated judgmental state.

"You've all prepared for this in your own ways. And although we are going up there alone, we are connected." Hummingbird's stern and seri-ous tone breaks me out of my thoughts.

*Wait. **ALONE**?! What in the ever-living fuck do you mean, alone?*

"I'll be around in case of emergencies, but you'll have to find me as there's no cell service and we are leaving technology behind. We will be meeting at the base of the mountain for our last meal, and then hiking to the top in the morning where you will stay for three days and two nights. Use this time to be in prayer, and be open to what comes your way. This is a vortex, remember, and wild things can happen. Your one job is to tell the pain story you are ready to release before we go up. We will witness each other in our shedding, and then you will let the medicine of the land heal you."

Nervous diarrhea pains sweep my system and my buttcheeks clench yet again.

What the ever-living FUCK is happening. No food, no coffee, and now I'm going to be ALONE?! First of all, what the fuck is up there? Can bears live up that high? Are there snakes? What if I get anal probed by aliens that abduct me? Like, really though ... is that a possibility? And honestly, do I even believe any of this shit? Is this whole going-up-on-a-mountain-to-heal thing just me being dramatic again? Are these the people I want to be following? Is God even real?

The thoughts continue to hound me on the two-hour drive to the base of the mountain. Hummingbird plays her "Sounds of the Ocean" CD the entire way in her tan Subaru. I am so hungry my stomach grumbles and I can't stop picking at an ingrown hair on my leg.

"There, on your left, that's Mount Shasta. Up at the top you can literally see a face!" Hummingbird goes on to point out more features of the mountain, and I stare in complete awe. It is beautiful. I can feel some sort of *magic* beaming off that mountain. I expect to see angels and aliens soaring to and from the peak, and fear begins to be replaced with wonder.

We finally pull into the base and I see Dean and Luna already setting up for our last meal. I plan on savoring every last bite knowing it'll be my last for a while. And as a Taurean Italian/Armenian whose closest encounter with divinity thus far has been after eating a perfectly executed penne alla vodka and whose love language is cheese, this food needs to last me.

What we get is little pellet-like things in a bowl, mixed with some raw broccoli and tomatoes. A rush of horror washes over me.

"Wow! Thanks!" I fake. "What, uh, what is it?"

"It's a quinoa dish!" Luna beams, totally stoked on her creation. "It's protein!"

I knew I should have brought the *fucking* Pop-Tarts.

As a hot girl with digestive issues (every hot girl has digestive issues) who does not know how one poops on a mountain with no toilet—and who does not trust people who wear baggy harem pants to wash their hands before preparing a meal—I take the world's smallest portion and pretend to eat it.

Next, it's time to tell the pain stories we're ready to shed. We all sit on a large rock in a circle, the creek in the background making sounds like a comforting mother soothing a baby. I am curious to hear about what Luna and Dean are releasing—what their *pain* is.

Dean goes first. He closes his eyes and takes a deep breath: "I am releasing my former self: the one who partied, the one who drank, the one who smoked, the one who had loads of sex. I am releasing him NOW."

Everyone hums and haa-s as he keeps his eyes shut and lets the moment linger. I stare at a bush and hug my knees in close.

Luna's turn. She closes her eyes. "I am fully releasing the pain of hating my body. It has destroyed my life in so many ways." She pauses, as tears stream down her face. "I have spent years trying to fix something that is not even broken. My poor body ... I am scared ... I am sad ... I am ready to release this pain and let this go." She is fully breaking down and sobbing now.

I start to choke. My eyes feel wet. I *see* her pain as I look into her eyes, and a rawness bellows out of her being and grabs each one of us by the heart and shakes us. I look over at Dean, and he is crying his eyes out, too. "I love you, you're so strong, you are so amazing, baby. I am right here for you," he comforts her, as she falls into his arms.

And that is the thing that breaks me.

I've never seen that before: someone so loved, even in their moment of immense pain. I've never seen that kind of support before.

Now I am sobbing.

And now it's my turn. I feel like I just got the shit kicked out of me; my body hurts and I can't catch my breath. My face is hot and I feel the red shade of my cheeks. No one has ever really asked me to share my pain like this. I can't look at any of them. I trace my leg with little hearts to try and distract myself from crying. It doesn't work.

"Um," I exhale sharply to try and calm myself.

What do I actually want to release? What do I want God to take from me? What is ready to go that I've been holding?

"I am releasing the pain of feeling so fucking alone. I am releasing the pain of fucking up my life. I am releasing the pain of ... him. And all that happened there. I'm releasing the pain of realizing that I've never been loved like what I just saw ... not like that." I look up and see Dean's arms still around Luna.

"... Not like that," I repeat to finish.

Not like that.

Not like that.

Not like that.

Nobody wraps their arms around me. No one is there crying with me in my pain. The sharp knife twists itself in my gut even deeper and I focus my gaze on scratching big Xs on my leg.

"And with that, we release it to you, Great Spirit. We ask that you guide us in our own separate journeys. We ask that you give us the healing and medicine we need to be our truest, most empowered selves. And so it is." Hummingbird grabs her little tin box of tobacco and sprinkles some on the land.

Well, I have never been more ready to hike up a goddamn mountain. We part ways, I grab my stupid backpack, and set forth on the designated path while everyone else takes a moment to decompress.

The pain ceremony dredged up what actually feels like raw fuel in my body now, as I replace all my fear and sadness with desperate determination. I fix my gaze forward and I don't break it once.

I start walking faster.

I walk through a desert-like landscape, not a patch of grass in sight, just broken red rock everywhere. This is supposed to lead to some kind of a meadow? I am also quickly finding I'm ill prepared, even with my backpack. My Led Zeppelin water bottle is already empty and my boots are causing blisters. I stop to rip them off, throwing them in my backpack before I continue on the hot ground, barefoot and breathing heavily, licking my dry lips the whole way.

I climb up a steeper part of a hill and the landscape changes from desert to woodsy terrain. The moss is almost fluorescent green, and the ground is softer and more forgiving than the orange-brown crumbling rock I have been pummeling through. It is alarming how quickly the landscape has changed, and I wonder for a moment if it's one of those dehydration mirages you see in cartoons. I power on through the trees and pass little streams of water. I splash some on my face and keep going down a little dirt path, letting sheer determination be my guide.

Finally, there's a clearing. A huge clearing. There is warm, soft grass, and more bubbling streams running down the mountain—even some butterflies (again, *could* be a mirage).

But—*I did it. I'm at the meadow!* I purse my lips and do a sly "I told ya so" smile to no one. My feet are bleeding, my mouth is parched, my body is on fire, but ... *I fucking did it.*

It is stunningly gorgeous up here. As I slow down I realize how out of breath I am, and the more I breathe, the more my mouth feels like that desert I just walked through. I plop down and set up my backpack next to one of the running streams of water. Hummingbird said this is the purest water around, and to drink plenty of it. I notice there's a bird happily chilling in it, with its butt in direct flow of the trickling water. I can't fully imagine the water here being *that* pure, and so I hike up a little higher before I fill up my Led Zeppelin water bottle and chug. I lay down next to the bank.

I did it.

But like ... *Now what?*

I take some breaths as I realize ... I didn't really think this through. *Am I supposed to like, do something?* I guess I kind of thought I'd be aided by angels, and that God would be waiting up here for me with a bottle of Champagne and a magical amulet I could wear that would finally make people love me.

I guess I'll wait.

And wait I do.

I sit there for hours, trying to clear my head. Trying to pray. Sitting in silence by the creek, looking out for signs in nature, asking God to come to me, again and again.

I am aware that I'm starting to sound like a woman in denial about being stood up by her Tinder date.

Hey! Yeah, it's me! I'm just checking in, I thought we were meeting today and I just wanted to make sure I didn't mess up the time!

Nothing. Just the hunger pangs screaming inside of my empty stomach.

I'm not even sure what I'm expecting. Like, how would I even know if God was here? What the actual fuck was I thinking would happen? Christ coming down from the cross and high-fiving me? Inter-dimensional beings entering through a time-space portal and braiding my hair while I braid their tentacles? Angel Gabriel coming down to bring me a message that I rock? *Am I like, seriously this delusional?* I close my eyes harder and frantically pluck at a random chest hair I have found. Then I put my hands on the ground. The sun is setting. It's time to get real serious.

"God please, I know I haven't been, like, great. But I have a lot riding on this, please come to me. I am actually begging you. Please, I did all of this for you. I am trying to prove to you how ready I am. I am begging you. Please, come to me. Show yourself to me. Let me feel you."

More stomach rumbles.

"Okay, okay ... I get what you're throwing down. This is a test. Well, if I didn't prove myself already by attempting to eat quinoa and hiking up a mountain with my bare feet, I will just sit here till you come. I get it!"

Nothing.

The sun is really setting now, and so I lie down. It is freezing. I pull out my baby blankie from my backpack and drape it over my head to get some of its healing powers. Maybe I'll meet God in my dreams.

I WAKE UP AT DAYBREAK and my limbs are so cold that they feel frozen solid and won't move. My whole body hurts. I am famished and my stomach churns. I look around and cannot believe I just fully slept on a mountain, on the ground, with no tent, *all alone*. God *had* to have seen that.

I hobble up and stretch my body as best as I can, and begin to walk around. Maybe I have to go *find* God instead. I walk through the meadow. I look into the rushing water. I pray, and I pray, and I pray some more. I spend the whole day fighting the feeling of deep broken sadness (and hunger) with the aggressive hope that God will pull through for me.

Still nothing.

Night comes again. Well, maybe this time God will come in my dreams.

I wake up on and off the whole night, freezing, hungry, frustrated, and reeling through the stories I've heard about how many people have these epic spiritual experiences on this exact mountain.

I watch the sun rise. Again.

God?

Nope.

My biggest fears are coming true: God *isn't* real. Or, God actually wants nothing to do with me because I'm actually as shitty as I believe myself to be. Or, I'm just not trying hard enough. I'm down for God being a being, or a feeling, or a literal passing sign.

At this point, I'll take what I can get.

I sit up and pray again.

"I'm still here. Ready when you are."

I look up to the sky once the sun has fully risen, and see these big, white, fluffy clouds.

And they look ...*familiar.*

Something about them stirs something in my stomach—a good feeling. A feeling of peace. I watch as the clouds begin to move and shift, like they are breaking from one another, but still connected. It reminds me of something—something beautiful. The feeling in my stomach intensifies.

I watch as the white cloud stretches across the sky in a way that gives me goosebumps. *This is it! This is the moment! This is God!*

But nope. No. I consciously realize this is me fully thinking these clouds look like the mozzarella on Chicken Parmesan.

Maybe I did all of this and I'm no fucking better off, and God isn't something that's going to come down and love me.

Maybe God is reserved for certain people and I'm not one of them.

Maybe life is just *fucked* and magic *isn't* real and I'm so mother*fucking* alone and sadness doesn't leave just because you ask her to.

This mountain is supposed to be the place where all the work pays off. And all I'm seeing is Chicken Parm in the sky.

I take a deep breath in.

And I cry my fucking eyes out.

And this is the *other* moment that breaks me.

I don't think I've ever cried this hard. They are the fattest tears, straight out of a Japanese anime movie. I let them fall on the ground by the rushing water. I cry because I've been trying so fucking hard to be good enough for divinity to find me, too. And I'm not good enough.

I cry for the times I opened my heart and had it used as a rag to clean up someone else's mess and then tossed aside.

I cry for the time I feel I wasted, because I felt so alone and sad, when I was supposed to be having *fun*.

I cry for the nights spent praying to God that I would feel okay one day, only to be ignored.

I cry for all the other people in this world who feel this way, and have it way worse than me.

I cry for all of the times I've shoved down my pain so that I could feel normal.

I cry. And I cry some more. My head pounds. I keep crying. Even after I feel like I've run out of tears, my body is still wrenching and moaning.

All of a sudden, the reasons *why* I'm crying no longer matter, as all the thoughts leave my head and all that's left is the experience of crying. I haven't cried this hard since I was a kid.

Wait.

I haven't cried this hard since I was a kid.

I feel just like her at this moment. And there is sadness herself, turning into that little clingy 3rd grade friend who sits next to me on this mountain.

I don't push her away. I sit with her for a moment, and let tears stream down my face. Then I take a series of deep, steady breaths.

"What do you want from me?" I ask this sad little girl, gently but desperately.

A flood of emotion takes over my body. Intuitively, I lay down in the fetal position and feel the earth hold me as I hold myself and let myself melt. This time, I don't run. Instead, I grip each part of my body: my feet, my calves, my thighs, my belly, my chest, my shoulders, my arms, my face.

If God wasn't going to be there, and no lover was going to be there, then I guess I would have to scoop this sad little girl up, bring her inside of me, and hold her.

I sit up and hug my knees, placing my forehead down on them, holding my whole body as if I'm holding this sad little girl who I've ignored my whole life. I breathe. I feel the dense earth under me. I let the tears fall. I don't run. I don't scroll. Instead, I hug, I hold, and I even sing her a little song under my breath.

And suddenly, I feel something land on me: a little bee. It crawls across the skin on my leg. I feel this little girl working through me, except this time, she feels *different* ... I can see this bee through her eyes.

I watch this bee move on me.

And then another bee lands on my leg.

And then another one.

And another one.

And all these little bees are not stinging me. They are simply moving and grooving, *just like Auntie Lulu's swarm of protector bees.*

I watch in awe. Actual awe, not the *forced* awe where you put on a show making your eyes and mouth into big "OH!"s to add to the drama of a situation.

My body feels a billion pounds lighter, and it's not because of the lack of food.

As I watch the bees move, I begin to wonder:

What if God wasn't breaking my heart, but was trying to crack it open?

And maybe some people just feel more than others do. Maybe some people carry the whole world in their hearts until it gets so heavy it explodes. Maybe some people have experienced more hurt than others, and what if the tears shed were the holy water that cleansed you not of *sin*— but of the weight of it all?

What if the tears shed were not a sign of weakness, but were the holy water that carries away what's too big for you, just like this stream on this mountain? What if the sadness, the pain, isn't always because something *bad* is happening, but because people who feel this much are also built to feel earth-shattering, heart-quaking love?

What if God is in every tear shed for the hardships of the world?

What if God is in every holy moment of heartbreak?

And sitting on this mountain by the flowing river—covered in dirt and bees, feeling the sensations in my body for what feels like the first time—my once sore, tense muscles are now relaxed. My shoulders are softened. My face feels puffy and soft.

For the first time in years, I feel a warm, glowy feeling of what I guess you could call magic. A feeling that life is worth living. This is a cleanse they don't sell at juice shops.

This is a medicine they can't market and advertise.

In this moment of pure elation, I do what any gal would—I wrap my blankie around my shoulders and sniff it while I process this magical mountain moment some more. I watch the bees fly off, one by one, and my moment ends pretty abruptly as my stomach makes a primordial growl. I take it as my divine cue that even the most metaphysical moments must come to an end, and I pack up my blankie, leave a little offering of herbs and a crystal, and strut down that mountain like I am on a mystical catwalk, with all the confidence of Tyra Banks.

Back at the base of the stream, I see the crew waiting by the previously agreed upon meeting spot, wearing huge smiles and cheering me on. We hike all the way back down the mountain together, through the woods, through the desert, through the rocks, and to our cars. I beam with pride thinking that I must smell like healthy ass now, too.

Then we immediately head to the Black Bear Diner in town.

I don't know if it was the crying, the fasting, the epic epiphany, or the fact that this mashed potatoes and salmon is one of the best meals of my entire life. Hearing everyone tell their stories, light up while listening to each other, trying bites of each other's food, feels just as magic as the moment on the mountain. And I realize ... God is right there, sitting at that divey diner table, sipping on lukewarm coffee with me, as I watch each person at the table come alive.

5
Raging Bitch

I'm sleeping in my room in New York.

I am woken up by a man.

A naked man.

Pulling the covers off me.

Trying to get into my bed.

The tapestries and velvet covers are replaced with cold air on my bare skin, as I stare into the eyes of this tall, skinny man. He flashes me a slasher smile and meticulously moves his body over mine. He slowly, steadily peels the covers off of me and scans my body, which is illuminated by the overhead twinkly lights I left on.

My body is frozen, my brain is foggy, confused and sleepy. But my heart is surging, pounding so hard I feel like it's going to bust out of my chest and run out the door; my limbs are paralyzed but vibrating with electric distress.

"What the fuck?" I manage to whisper.

My heart pounds against my rib like a cop to the door.

"WHAT the fuck?"

POUND. POUND. POUND.

My legs are broken tree stumps, heavy and unmoving.

"WHAT THE FUCK?"

The surging energy in my body escalates as I become clearer about what's happening.

"What the fuck? What the fuck? What the FUCK?!"

The voltage dials itself up. My torso shoots up, but my legs are still unmoving stumps — like Uma Thurman in *Pulp Fiction* after they jab the shot of epinephrine in her chest. The strange naked man smirks. He's getting a kick out of this.

I throw the rest of the covers off of me, slide under his arm, and dart/flail past him and all my newly opened and rummaged-through drawers. I fling myself into the hallway of my new home in New York and scream to my eight other housemates. My whole body is shaking but I still can't feel it, my mouth is completely dry, and my eyes are gaping wide like a runaway bride.

My roommates jump out of their rooms at the sounds of my shrieks, only to see me leaning against the closet in the hallway, pointing to my open door, unable to properly form words. Inside my room, the man suddenly pretends to act intoxicated, stumbling around clumsily when mere seconds ago he was painstakingly precise.

He stumbles back, I watch in horror as stumbles closer to my bed, moving in slow motion, and sits his naked fucking ass down on my beautiful bedding. Like, direct butthole to comforter contact. This is arguably the most traumatic moment of this whole incident: his butthole on *my* bed.

His name is Lucas. He's a frat bro who goes to my college, and he's been hooking up with Sam, who lives down the hall from me. But I guess he also has another agenda. I look over at Sam, who quickly replaces her worried grimace with a clearly forced, unsure smile, and meekly puts her arm around him to usher him into her room. He is still very naked and clearly *pretending* to not be able to properly stand, leaning all of his weight on her.

The rest of us are still gathered in the hallway, and no one really knows what to do or how to react, including me. There is some uncomfortable laughter and shifting of gazes, but after about five minutes, everyone retreats back to their rooms without saying a word. It is as if, deep down, we know that talking about it will mean that scary things actually *do* happen sometimes—even to us. I'm like a kerosene lamp constantly attracting creepy, scary moths. We keep our mouths shut to protect our peace.

I go back into my room and look at the drawers he went through: underwear and bras on the floor, crystals, and incense tossed around. I look at my bed, which is now completely messed up. What was once my vibe-y orange dream space has been tainted by fear, confusion, and literal butthole. I shut my door and lock it. I lean my back against the wall by my door in order to feel some sort of support. To calm the shaking. I slide down to the ground and stare at my torn apart bed as I try to process what happened.

My thoughts race: *Did this just happen for real? Was it serious? What was he trying to do? I saw him looking at me funny earlier, was he planning this all along? Why was he going through my drawers? How long was he in here for?*

I feel like a fallen power line, with severed, live wires sparking on the street.

What if he comes back? What if I didn't wake up? What if this is just the beginning? What's going to happen now? What if he does this to someone else? What the fuck do I do?

My body shakes uncontrollably, teeth chattering. I can't catch my breath, and I can't focus my eyes on anything in particular.

Then comes pure, unadulterated, pungent RAGE as my gaze focuses on my bed again. My fists clench and I try my best to get my nose to stop twitching by curling my lips tight. Rage. I'm feeling *RAGE*. And I swallow that poison and shove it down like a harrowing shot of tequila. It burns. I clench my jaw and replace the intensity with a loop of doubtful thoughts. Like, come on. I'm so fucking *dramatic*. Maybe he is actually just really drunk and simply made a mistake. I'm too fucking much sometimes. Get over it. Just. Let. It. *GO*.

I eventually pass out on the floor. There is no way in hell I am getting back in that bed.

I WAKE UP THE NEXT MORNING with a kink in my neck. Everything looks like it is shaking when I look around my room. Or maybe it's me that's shaking. I try to ground myself by feeling the floor of my room underneath me. Hummingbird taught me this trick; it's supposed to ground me and bring me back into harmony. I glaze over my Fender-inspired mini fridge and the boxes of unused smoothie supplies sitting on top of it. I look at the little seaweed dragon Hummingbird gave me. I feel a wet drop on my leg. I've been picking at a cuticle so hard that I'm bleeding. I'm filled with the desire to punch something (or *someone*, honestly).

But here's the deal — I am a "spiritual" bitch now. I found God in the shape of a fucking bee on a fucking mountain! Gone are the days of drunk Ani punching an innocent rain gutter because she's "hurt." Gone are the days of calling my friends to shit talk about something I won't address to the person but need to vent about. I am determined to not go back there, because a) it sucked for everyone, and b) it is *so* not spiritual. So that means I must devote my life to *not* being a fucking raging bitch.

I look down at my bloodied thumb. Let's be real: my months with Hummingbird haven't prepared me for this. There are no creepy naked frat bros in Lumeria ... right? What I'm sure of is that I'm in what Hummingbird would call a "low vibration state." I peel myself off the floor. Why do I feel like I've just been hit by a bus?

I throw my leather jacket over my jammies and silently slip out of my house, tiptoeing to my blue Rav4, my only safe haven in this God-forsaken place. I have this boho embroidered steering wheel cover that is wildly impractical and falls off mid-turn every single time. The second I hop in I slam the doors, lock them, and rip the stupid wheel cover off. I fumble with the key and start the engine and am quickly reminded of my car's weird glitch where it starts playing "Boombastic" by Shaggy whenever I turn it on. I slam off the radio and throw my bag of shit on the passenger seat.

Then I peel out of the driveway and drive up the road to a parking lot outside of my school building, where I park off to the side of the gate. I can't drive far. The quaking of my limbs is so intense, I feel like I'm driving on drugs. I need to call Hummingbird. Hummingbird will help. I desperately scroll through my contacts list, click her number, and pray that she answers.

The hanging crystal I have in my rearview mirror looks like it's vibrating.

"Good morning, wonderful Ani!" she chirps.

"HUMMINGBIRD!" I croak. "Something scary happened—there was a man. A frat bro. A big frat bro. And he was naked, I mean fully naked. And his butthole was on my SHEETS—I mean before that he was trying to get into my bed—and he was about to be on top of me—his eyes were so intense and he wouldn't stop even when I was yelling—my body stopped working ..." I'm blubbering and babbling, sounding like I have done seven lines of cocaine, feeling rage bubble up like hot magma from the depths of me.

"Ani," she cuts me off, "STOP. You need to control your temper, NOW. You know how powerful you are. You know your energy has ripple effects. And those ripple effects impact everything and everyone around you. I KNEW something was happening with you—your anger is destroying the Earth as we speak! There is a wildfire in California today and it is being energetically fueled by your rage! Anger is fire, and our planet reflects our emotional states. You've been working with me for too long to be here again, you're too powerful at this point. Control yourself, NOW. You are better than this. Do you know this? That this is your power? That this is what you are doing because you cannot control yourself?"

My throat closes up, and I silently stare forward as she goes on about the harm "my energy" is causing. I let fat tears drop from my eyes, the kind of tears that don't even run down your cheeks—they just fall right into your lap.

"... No. I didn't know tha—" are the only words I can manage to squeeze out.

"Yup. You are too powerful to let your fire leak like this. You have got to work on this. There are animals perishing, trees that are hundreds of years old are being destroyed. You know how to do this. Call on your guides and release this and pray for the Earth."

I don't respond. I slowly nod. My head is heavy, like lead. I stare into the oily, brown puddle and Slurpee cups littering the ground and tune her out as she calls on my guides and angels. Eventually, I manage to mutter out a dispassionate "thank you." I hang up the phone before promising "to do better."

Have you ever used that photobooth filter that makes you move in slow-mo? Have you ever felt that filter in real-time? I start my car without moving my head, staring at a raindrop roll down my windshield, collecting others as it makes its way down. I slowly pull out of the parking lot and start driving away, still unable to turn my head, the traffic noises sounding like they are very far away.

Listen—I don't fully believe that my energy is causing wildfires. Right? I mean, that's insane. I'm not that egotistical. But I have been doing "the work." And maybe my unrest *is* contributing to the general unrest in the world? I don't know. All I know is that rage is wrong. Toxic. Scary. I've seen what it can do to people, never mind the planet. Rage is one of those dangerous stress emotions that do horrible things to your body, like cause cancer. What's wrong with me? I'm doing all this work on myself and yet I'm still the same little brat poisoning everything else by leaking my stank-ass energy all over the place.

That rage magma begins to bubble again in an attempt to fight back against my rationale. I clench my jaw, sit a little straighter, and exhale to try to relax. My body is still so tense it's hurting. I never break my forward facing dead-inside gaze as I try to make myself feel okay again by driving—my once heal-all salve. But it's not working. Everything feels ... far. Like a dream. In an attempt to go back to some sense of normal, I go through the Dunkin' drive-thru to get an iced hazelnut coffee that I don't drink. I go to a bookstore to try and feel some sense of safety and familiarity, because the smell of books comforts me and always makes me have to poop immediately for some reason, but I can't get my gaze to stop glazing over and moving like I'm a glitchy Wi-Fi connection personified.

So I listen to my favorite 1970s music as I drive around the empty streets. I still feel nothing besides the occasional twinge of rage and fear, which I repress immediately. I scroll recklessly through Instagram at every red light. I know I have to go back to my house at some point, but the thought makes me want to vomit. I'm lowering my vibration and I'm just going to keep attracting more of this shit if I don't stop indulging in the absolute warzone that is my internal landscape.

So I bite the bullet, roll up to my house, and pretend I don't feel like a loaded gun. I park my car out front and I don't even bother turning it off; the running engine will motivate me to just get my shit and come right back down. It feels like being dared to go into the dark, scary rat-ridden basement as a child. You can't be a wussy, so you just suck it up and do it, and then sprint right back to safety.

...1... 2 ... 3 ... GO.

I sprint upstairs because I'm not even sure if he is still here, shove random clothing from my floor into an overnight bag, and grab the blankie that I can't sleep without (which was untouched by his butthole, thank

GOD). Then I run back to my still-running car. When I drive off, my tires even make that screeching noise you hear in movies, which I think is cool for just a second before all the feeling leaves my body again and I stare into my deadpan reality. *Now what?*

I need to sleep somewhere but I can't burden anyone else with my shit. Not to mention I literally hate everyone and everything about this place. Fuck them. Fuck my roommates and fuck that guy and fuck the lack of anything comforting and FUCK I'm raging out again. Deep breath in. Find your center. Bitch.

Before I know it, I'm in a Motel 6 parking lot. I check in with my blankie on top of my head and I realize halfway through signing the paperwork how weird I must look. I follow the dark red carpet and fluorescent lighting and enter my very own room, number 106. It feels like a sanctuary with its crisp, floral bedding and cable TV; a space far away from the chaos that awaits me back home.

I'm staring at myself in the mirror, looking into the barrel of my expressionless gaze when it hits me: I don't recognize myself. Where is that girl who just had a fucking beautiful epiphany on a fucking beautiful mountain? Where was the girl who found God at a roadside diner? I decide that I'm going to grab this whole situation by the horns and toughen up if it's the last thing I do. If I can't be angry, I'll funnel this unsteady emotion into looking hot as fuck. Hot girls don't get angry. And honestly, all this spiritual shit is feeling a bit too much tonight. I want to let go of the pressure to be enlightened or have a high vibration.

Suddenly I know exactly what to do and where to go. I grab my straightener out of my bag with a newfound purpose. Then I begin to doll myself up from head to toe, painting my lips with fire-engine red lipstick, flattening the kinks of my wild mass of curls. I perfectly apply my cat-eye and douse my lids with glitter. I squeeze into the tightest black dress I own. I finish the look with black tights and motorcycle boots. Then I power walk out the door of the motel room.

And I do what any girl would do to get rid of her rage on her healing journey.

I go to fucking Benihana.

Alone.

WHEN I ARRIVE, I APPROACH the communal hibachi table in my clingy slip dress. There's a chaotic family at one end. The exhausted-looking mom is trying to hold one baby while barking commands at her crazy toddler son, all while her husband sits silently, stoically staring ahead. In between us, another family sits. They look like the kind of family that has vacuum lines in their carpet at all times. They don't speak or laugh, they just stare at the menus in heavy, disciplined silence.

And then there's me. I peel off my studded leather jacket; for some reason I think it might be scaring out these nice, normal families. Immediately, the stoic dad starts devouring my cleavage, a look of horror in his eyes. I look down. My boobs are so out they look like they're about to start doing the hibachi tricks themselves. I slide the jacket back on, my cheeks as red as the grill.

I find out real quick that there are few things darker than being dead inside while sitting alone at a communal hibachi table dressed like a sultry Vegas lounge singer, while excited suburban families clap and howl as a chef flips shrimps into his hat and wows everyone by making an onion volcano.

No amount of billowing flames or steak chunk flips can bring me back to life. I'm sitting next to the vacuum-line carpet kid, staring blankly at a burning piece of rice that's stuck to the corner of the grill, when I realize everyone has gone alarmingly quiet. I lift my heavy lids to see everyone *staring* at me in anticipation. What the fuck just happened? Was I supposed to be, um, doing something?

"... What?" My voice is as vacant as my eyes.

The chef dumps some steak on my plate and the blond-bobbed, perfect carpet-line mom trades seats with the kid who was sitting next to me. Oh, now I get it. Everyone thinks I'm high out of my mind. Which sucks because for once I'm actually not. I try to eat a few bites of said steak, but I can't. Chewing feels foreign. I have also forgotten how to hold chopsticks and a piece falls on my lap. I only look up once more to see the nice, sweet families staring at me bewildered and horrified, trying to distract their kids from me.

I pay the bill and am out of there before I do any more damage to these poor kids. Then I speed all the way back to my seedy motel room, where

I immediately have explosive diarrhea. Apparently heavy emotions and hibachi don't mix.

I sit on the bed, peering at the tacky mid-century mass-produced prints on the walls. I lay back and stare at the popcorn ceiling, praying to a God I am no longer sure even exists.

"Please God," I whisper, "let me be okay, please make my life not this way anymore. Please take away these fucking heavy emotions. Please don't let me go through life completely dead inside, either. Please stop letting me attract any more of these situations." Tears stream down my face. Mascara stings my eyes. I keep going, "Please make me stop being a messy, dramatic bitch who makes everything so big. I'm begging you. I know I can do this, but I need your help. Remember the mountain? Please just make these feelings go away. I want to be happy. I want to be okay. Please."

Eventually, I pass out in my red lipstick, cat eyes, and too-tight black dress, over the covers, motorcycle boot feet dangling above the off-putting bold and dated carpet that only motels seem to have.

When I wake up it is at 6 a.m. and there is no feeling in my legs. Fire trucks blare outside. Somehow I make it to the bathroom. I run a shower with water so scalding hot it could boil a lobster. Then I crouch down in the tub, not willing to fully sit but too wobbly to stand, and I let my mind wander.

I think of all the times in my life I've been told to "get over it" and "be good." The times when Sister Judy would tell me to just "give it to God." Or all the times my well-meaning friends have tried to remind me that everything "happens for a reason." I think of all the wellness influencers on Instagram that talk about how "your vibe attracts your tribe"—how you'd better keep the vibes high, or you're going to be a "lonely bitch for the rest of your life, babe!"

And I would do anything to feel like I felt on top of that mountain again. Fuck this.

I launch up from the hot water like a pinball being fired from the machine. I see black. I lean my forehead against the cool tiled wall to balance myself. I stay there for a while just feeling the heat of the water kiss my naked back, partly showering, partly comforting myself, and the cold of the bathroom tile presses against my forehead, steadying my breath, try-ing to mute my anger.

"You know what?" I say to the unkillable cockroaches of rage skitter-ing against the cold tile floor. I close my eyes. A small smile creeps onto my face.

"I'm moving to fucking Oregon."

6
Run, Bitch

Three months and dozens of Hummingbird sessions later, I am fully committed to moving to Or-i-gen. For now, it is January on Long Island and it is freezing cold. I fling my sheer floor-length merlot-colored duster out of the way as I crouch down by the IKEA dresser that I've painted with stars and symbols to make up for its bland simplicity. I catch a glimpse of myself in the mirror with my painted crimson lipstick and smirk at the irony.

I sweep up piles of the burnt herb I used in a protection spell I did the week prior. My room finally feels like mine again. It took me a while to reclaim it after that frat bro bullshit, but enough prayers, salt, protection spells, offerings, and cleansing, and the energy in here is as smooth sailing as the sound waves gently playing from my record player. I feel closer to okay than I have in what feels like forever.

Everyone in the house is buzzing. I can hear my roommates in the hallway venting about how stressed they are about school, furiously gabbing about getting ready for graduation this spring, dreaming about "what's to come." I'm quietly putting little prehnite crystals in the herbs I'm growing to make healing sachets. I crank up my floral-printed record player. Stevie Nicks drowns out the excited chatter of my roommates and I'm honestly grateful that I will not be graduating this year. Having dropped out for a while after Michael means I'm behind. All I have to do is finish this one last semester, watch everyone *else* graduate, then I'm transferring to a college out west. Truly, I can't wait to get the fuck out of this hell-hole.

I picture the small, craftsman-style homes that litter the land in Oregon, and wonder where I'm going to end up. If I can take this dilapidated room with her tainted bed and walls covered in whispered words of self-hatred, and somehow manage to transform her into a beautiful star-painted sanctuary ... imagine what kind of aesthetic magic I will be able create in an untainted home in a charming hippie town? It'll be so magical, I'll probably ascend from the porch swing I'm sure I'll have.

Chills (the good kind) skip down my spine like long-haired Woodstock goers. I'm going to live in that small, stunning hippie town and do as the mystics do, damn it. I'm going to be the kind of spiritual bitch who sautés organic veggies for dinner and hugs strangers in the broad daylight. Most people might say the responsible thing to do would be to finish out my courses here, graduate, and then go; but they would be underestimating the urgency that is a soul awakening just waiting to happen.

BOOM.

"AYYYYYY!"

I scurry over to my door and lock it. A flock of people has just come flying through my front door, squawking like crows in a feeding frenzy, and I am not ready for all that. I am over this scene. Yes, I found some pretty impeccable friends here, but we are on different paths. The only one who seems to really get me is Joni, but since she's been going to school in California, all we have is phone calls when the timing aligns.

If anything, since my epic mountain trip and working with Hummingbird, I've become like the old witchy woman who lives in the woods that curious youths turn to when they're desperate to believe in themselves and seek the creepy old hag that everyone makes up rumors about. And honestly, it's the most "me" role I've ever been cast in. All this time trying to be young and vivacious and Tumblr-famous hot, only to find I'm happiest living like a grandma. Oh, life and her curious little mysteries, amirite?

Every time a girl has taken too many shrooms and is freaking out at a party, or is having a full-on breakdown about the pressures of school, or feels like she can't live up to the shitty standards of her shitty boyfriend, or is paralyzed with fear over what the fuck she's going to do with her life—I hear a little knock on my door. I leap to open it and welcome the anxious entity into the womb of my bedroom with open arms. I always have oils diffusing and candles lit in my room. Little pockets of crystals and magical herbs to ease every alignment possible are tucked into my dresser, and I never fail to play the perfect song for the most harrowing of moments. I mean, can you blame any troubled human for wanting in? It's been a "build it and they shall come" kinda thing. The irony being that this environment was born from my own need to heal. Now, others starved for the TLC I so craved at my lowest, feel it, and flow my way.

I should also mention that my housemates throw a party almost every evening, so plenty of distressed drunks or curious coke heads come to find me too. God, I get them. And I love that people feel like they can come into my space and be real for once. I love that at the end—after the bad trip subsides or the tear ducts have dried—we always end up laughing. It reminds me of my music festival days.

But listen: I'm not the "mom" of the group—I'm not organized or gentle enough for that role. Me? I'm more like the your chainsmokin' forever single Great Auntie from the Deep South who loves her whiskey as much as her herd of obese cats and has a raspy, wicked cackle, multiple chin hairs she never seems to notice or care about, and a filthy sense of humor to boot.

That's what I'm working toward at least. I'm still basically a total chode, but a chode who is doing her healing work. A healing chode, if you will.

Tonight is a party at—shocker—my house. While I'm over partying just for the sake of getting plastered, I haven't gone full bathing-her-crystals-in-the-moonlight-on-a-Friday-night yet. This is Lawng Island, after all. And I'm hungry to connect! And college kids on Lawng Island connect over four lokos and menthol cigarettes in basements at house parties, not in fields of wildflowers next to the majestic mountains under the unpolluted glow of the stars. After I'm done cleaning my room, literally and energetically (this healing shit is working!), I doll myself up with my signature sparkly cat-eye, slink into my shiny black harem pants (the elephant-print ones were a little much—it's called balance, babe), and grab my obsidian necklace for, you know, protection!

"I am safe, I am protected, I am connected to something higher, and I am exactly where I need to be always," I whisper to the stone before slinging it 'round my neck, a ritual that has replaced the vomit-inducing "slap the bag" game before partying with a big group. I douse myself with a yummy oil blend I made myself to "attract love." I'm kinda killing it if I do say so myself. I mean ... livin' it. Hummingbird told me to watch my words because they are all spells and carry energy. I'm LIVIN' it!! I swing open my door with Led Zeppelin's "Since I've Been Loving You" playing—which just so happens to be the sexiest song of all time.

Maybe it is the super-sexy song.

Maybe it's my spell.

Maybe it's my hand-crafted Love Oil.

Or maybe—just maybe—it's fate.

I don't know. I don't care. 'Cause right outside my door, melting into the soiled brown couch that haphazardly sits in the center of our living room, is a unicorn. A unicorn in a sea of testosterone-fueled frat bros. By which I mean a man so motherfucking sexy, I feel like my vagina could drop out of my body, thud against the floor, pick herself up and run off to get whipped at a Brooklyn play party.

But seriously. Who in the ever-living hell is that?! I've never seen him before and I know just about everyone at this point. He is FAR from a frat rat. He's wearing a vintage orange button-down with large lapels totally unbuttoned. A regal puff of chest hair swells from the folds of his open shirt. He's serving a "Christ-on-the-Cross" level skinniness that's strangely enticing. His lanky legs are stretched open wide and his slim fingers are rolling a joint with great focus and intention. He looks like a 1970s dream machine. Like if Jim Morrison from The Doors had a 1990s pretty boi haircut. You know the kind: bleach blonde and tousled, falling into sleepy sexy stoned eyes that break your heart but also piece it back together?

I beeline towards him, my body buzzing. Every other human in the house has metamorphosed into a blurry blob and the only thing I can hear is Robert Plant's voice wailing about the pain of seduction through muffled speakers.

My eyes smolder. "Who are you?" I ask.

The mystery Christ skinny boy looks up at me. His eyes are half-closed. "Johnny," he smiles. "And who might you be?" He lights his joint and inhales slowly, pressing his back into the couch, looking me right in the eye, waiting for my answer.

"I'm Ani. And you're going to want to remember that name. I can guarantee it."

Johnny hands me the joint he took such great care in rolling. He stretches out a free arm and slouches it over the back of the sofa. I haven't done this in a while, but when a man this hunky is asking, ya tell your shit to shove it and ya take the damn joint. I sit on the coffee table across from him, cross my legs, and lean to the side, sexy like a Raquel Welch breed of bombshell. I inhale slowly, and pray to my guides that I don't make an ass of myself choking on the smoke.

"Ani." His voice is hazy and slow, like the thick clouds of smoke emerging from our lips as we pass the joint back and forth. "Ani. I heard your name before. I've been told we should meet. You're the witch and this is your house, right?"

Through sheer, unprecedented determination, I suppress a hack of a cough. I try to say something but I actually can't or a lung will fly out of my chest, so I just squint my eyes and smirk in a way that says: "you heard right."

He leans forward and grabs my hand. He presses his soft lips against my fingers and kisses them lightly. "The pleasure is all mine."

My pussy starts belting an aria from *Madame Butterfly*. I am too stunned (or too stoned) to speak.

I remember the words of wisdom from the hot icons (well ... just my mom) who came before me: Leave 'em wanting more, bitch. Which means it's time to get out of there.

I stand from the table and gently guide his chin up until his eyes meet mine, then crouch down so we're inches away from each other's faces.

"What's my name?" I hover dangerously close to his face, my eyes darting from his dark blue eyes to his full soft lips.

"Ani," he breathes.

"Nice to meet you, Johnny. Find me later if you want to talk more." I stand up and walk away, not quite sure where to go because I didn't exactly plan this pussy-singing encounter, so I just walk to the kitchen and pour myself a vodka cranberry.

After the whole Tony C ass-clapping incident, I've been repulsed by the thought of another college hookup, and no one has inspired me to challenge that. But Johnny's voice sounds like it's making sweet, sweet love to my eardrums. And he also looks like that rare creature that could pull off saying "sweet, sweet love" without seeming like a serial killer.

Four hours go by. The party is ending. Couples are either fighting or getting ready to fuck. Singles are sealing the deal on their hookup situations. I make it a point to not be within eyeshot of hot n' hunky Johnny—to, you know, keep the mystery going.

But then he appears from nowhere, and we're locking eyes. I take a sip of my third vodka cranberry. I'm ready. I nod my head at him. He excuses himself from his friends, very gentleman-like, and walks toward me. Tall. Smooth. Strange. And did I mention sexy?

I grab his hand and lead him toward my door, following the strong scent of smoky incense and sandalwood oil. We enter my little oasis. "Woah," he says, taking in the twinkly lights and salt lamps and the art deco sculpture of a woman draped on the moon.

"So this is the witch's den? I've heard good things."

"It's a labor of love, but this is my little magical space. It's like a safe haven in the chaos, you know?"

He zeros in on my record collection. "Fuck, you have the original *The Song Remains the Same* album?"

I feel my pussy inhale to belt another aria. What? Any man who gets my music just does it for me! I sit on my bed and cross my legs. "I do. I got it at a garage sale for a dollar, can you believe it?"

"I can't believe any of this." He pauses. "You intrigue me ... big time."

Success.

We spend the next few hours talking about music (there's a huge chance he's the illegitimate grandson of Pete Townshend from The Who!); our backgrounds (he's from upstate New York, no siblings, and his parents are still together—talk about a unicorn!); and our majors (me, religion and English; him, business. Purr).

By 4 a.m., I am perfectly lucid. Everything is flowing. He's on my bed and his face flickers in the candlelight as he waxes poetic over his hatred of music festivals and all those who attend. Do I need to make the pussy aria joke again or do we get it? His back is resting on the wall behind us, one leg sprawled out, one knee bent so he can rest his arm on it. He looks like the cover of an album I would've played on repeat in high school.

"This song is called no quarter," Robert Plant announces from the record player, and the eerie intense keyboard blasts from the speakers and swirls through the incense heavy air. I crawl onto the bed across from him and he motions his head, as if to say, come closer. I take his cue and inch toward him. "Closer," he softly commands aloud this time. Before I can move he pulls me on top of him. I'm straddling him. Our foreheads are touching, but we're not kissing. Or speaking. The sandalwood-scented air, as thick as the felt tension, cocoons us. He traces his fingers across my arm. I feel like I'm in an altered state of consciousness— like we're underwater on a different planet. There is no hesitation and our movements are flowing into each other wordlessly, thoughtlessly, in perfect sync. He sits up and grabs my hips, thrusting me in closer to him, kissing my shoulders. Then my neck. He guides my face to his lips. We are kissing. Everything is heavy, a good kind of heavy. Like the warm feeling in your body after consuming the perfect amount of red wine.

The record ends and my speakers connect to my Bluetooth and start playing my angsty playlist, beginning with TOOL's "Schism." He takes off my shirt, then his. Slowly. By the time my shirt is off the Deftones are playing. He kisses and softly bites my neck, my shoulders, my lips. When a brooding Nine Inch Nails song makes its way through the speakers, I am kissing the length of his body.

I feel like my soul is two inches in front of me, leading everything I do, and so is his. The electricity in my body is powerful, but steady and deep.

And finally, he pulls his mouth from my flesh and looks at me expectantly. I know what that look means. I'm down. I nod my head, yes. He reaches into his jeans and unearths his wallet. He pulls out a condom, rips it open with his teeth, and slides it on. I lay down and start shaking slightly. I chalk it up to it being cold without the heat of his body pressed against me.

"Are you ready?" he asks, leaning over me.

"Mhmm."

He kisses me deep. "You okay?" He gently pushes into me.

I smile and nod and pull him in closer and kiss him.

He leans in more and goes a little deeper.

My shoulders tense and he pulls me closer. I am okay. He thrusts himself all the way in.

And then a lightning bolt of fear strikes me harder than Jimmy Page's guitar solo. I feel like I have been electrocuted, but I pretend to be feeling electrified by forcing a moan. I will not ruin this.

I probably look so ugly right now, what is my face even doing? Suck in that gut, Ferlise! Ugh. He's going to notice the scar tissue on my nipple from my piercing. You look terrifying when you have sex, your eyes roll in the back of your head and you look possessed.

Michael's voice pierces through the dark cloud of thoughts in my head. I feel loose flesh jiggling. I hate my body. Ugh. Fuck this! I can't believe I'm letting him win. My cheeks are hot and I bury my face to the side, hiding as much as I can in the pillow. I try to pull Johnny in closer to me so he can't see me.

"I like making your legs shake," he whispers into my ear, blissfully unaware that I'm trembling with anxiety, not pleasure. I make sure he's fully convinced by faking another pornstar level moan or two.

I just want this to be over. The thick scented air that was so romantic thirty minutes prior is now suffocating me. I feel like I'm deep throating sandalwood.

I know exactly how to make it end. For fuck's sake, here we go: "I'm gonna cum," I growl in his ear.

Thirty seconds of sped-up thrusting and another Oscar-winning performance from me, and he is rolling to the side, breathing hard, finished.

I kiss him quickly, roll over, and slide into my floral mini robe for protection. My trusted satin shield, preventing him from catching a glimpse of my naked body. I don't want him to see me once the lust hormones have dissipated. I can't take it. I try my best to slip seductively out of the room. The second the door clicks closed, I dart to the bright fluorescent bathroom where I immediately book it to the toilet and gag. I stare at the overflowing trash, a mountain of used up God-knows-what pouring over.

"Same," I whisper to no one.

ME BEING ME, JOHNNY BECOMES my new boyfriend. Yeah, I'm 10000% sick of my own bullshit, too. Or at least, I tell him that I'm moving to Oregon, very soon, but that I'm down to keep sleeping with him. Then our hookups turn into hangouts, which turn to me once again isolating myself from my friends and spending all my time with him.

Before long, I've made his baby blue room at a house he rents a few streets over into my safe haven. I leave only for class and then take the pilgrimage back there immediately. I tell myself the reason I'm spending so much time there is to "get away from all the annoying parties." Then I start to hang out with his wholesome mom and dad in their suburban upstate home. They have a golden retriever and love Yankee Candles and Thanksgiving. It's sweet. In the baby blue room, we watch *Bob's Burgers* and eat Thai takeout every night. And it's like. Fine? I guess?

Except that I just want to feel the way I did on that mountain. I just want to find my path and finally move on from all my hurt and traumatized boring bullshit. I want to feel okay. I want to heal. I am also convinced that this will happen in Oregon, and so I keep my sights set on the move.

Eventually, Hummingbird finds me a small house to rent in a tiny hippie town called Ashland, Oregon, where I'm going to become the powerful bitch—*ahem*, I mean *woman*—I've always been destined to be. I send in all the paperwork before I even see it in person. And it is *exactly* what I pictured: a wood-shingled house with a porch covered in wisteria. A massive rosemary bush gorgeously frames the front gate. The living room is bright and sunny and even has a sprawling view of the mountains. Johnny has to stay in New York to finish out school, so we're going to be "long-distance" for now.

And then suddenly, Johnny is helping me pack up my records to take on the plane. The morning before I leave, in the name of "passionate goodbye" sex, I let him try the pullout method for the first time. It's nice. I guess. When it's over I practically backflip out of the room with my new orange cat Patrick Swayze in his kitty carrier, and catapult to the airport. I'm *so* ready to start my new life.

Hummingbird is waiting for me on the front porch of my new home. Her eyes are closed and she's drumming a big white hand drum. Large bowls of cornmeal rest at her feet, along with a feather wand, and a whip made of horsetail hair (to cleanse and bless the house, I quickly find out).

God, I already love it here.

My first month in my new home passes and I am comfortable in a way I didn't know was possible. I'm finishing up school at the local college, setting up my house, and learning basic human things like how to properly recycle? I always have my little Sirius radio playing in the kitchen, tuned to a 1970s cheesy easy listening station. It matches my mood: Simple. Sunny. Wholesome. I've also officially gone vegan because my body is a fucking temple. I flip through recipe books and jot down neat grocery lists on lined paper. Sometimes I hit the YMCA and work out with the local 60+ crowd.

My absolute favorite part of my comforting new life? Food shopping, babe. The local market also sells crystals and incense and clothes that, well um, look organic? And the cast of characters in this spiritual little market, is *wild*. There's the naked old lady who isn't technically breaking the law because her bush is so big, she's technically not showing her genitalia. There's a group of people who dance to—get this—"the sound of nature," in the parking lot. There's even a man with a "rainbow maker," which is basically just a giant piece of plastic with rainbow film over it, that he directs over people's heads, dishing out healing rainbow therapy for free. What a gent!

I feel like I'm in an episode of *Gilmore Girls* meets a sci-fi movie meets a documentary about Woodstock. I don't know anybody yet, but I exchange many friendly smiles with the kooky/sweet locals. Also, Joni and I speak on the phone daily, which keeps me feeling connected to humanity.

I also haven't really felt the need to talk to Hummingbird all that much. I've just been feeling so grounded and so *calm*—I don't need our sessions the way I once did. I just want to relish in the magic of this beautiful place. I want to figure things out for myself.

One Tuesday morning, I'm loudly gabbing with Joni on my porch, lounging on the patio and telling her about the naked grocery store lady while sipping coffee in a Barbie pink satin robe. Patrick Swayze is sleeping next to me, flopping his tail every so often to signal that he's still alive.

BEEP. BEEP. BEEP.

Hummingbird is calling on the other line. I ignore it for now.

"Hummingbird keeps calling me but I need some space," I yap to Joni. "She's been really invasive recently. But anyway! The naked lady—she's not even breaking the law, right, 'cause her bush is so fucking intense and wild, it's like, furry undies, you know?"

Joni ignores this and goes in for the kill, as she is wont to do. "Wait. Ani. Did you just say Hummingbird is being invasive? Like, what do you mean?" Her concerned tone pierces the bubble of delusion I've been try- ing desperately to keep intact.

I'm not ready for it to deflate; "Honestly? It's probably just a 'me' thing."

Joni's silence is so loud that it POPS the bubble.

"Fine, she's driving me fucking nuts!" I blurt.

"ANUS!" Joni bellows into the phone. "How are you *just* telling me this now? Like what's she doing? I'm, like, actually shocked. She always seemed so comforting?"

"I don't know. But she's giving me severe anxiety. I told her I want to switch to seeing her on an 'as needed' basis. But she's being really intense."

"Enough with the cryptic sentences! Just tell me what's happening, exactly?"

I stand up and pace around the eggshell blue coffee table on my porch, making patterns with my fluffy slippers in the fallen pine needles carpet- ing the floor.

"Okay, well, I don't *know*. Her creepy boyfriend with the low pony who uses big words on Facebook messaged me and, like, asked to take a bath at my house? It weirded me out. Also if, like, I say I feel connected to a deity, she'll say things like it's because she's a direct descendant of them." I sigh. "Honestly, she sounds absolutely batshit."

Patrick lifts his head and shoots me an annoyed look and I realize I'm sitting down again, bouncing my leg so much he looks like he's on a mas- sage chair. I start picking at my cuticle instead.

"Are you kidding me? Ani—that's really, *really* strange."

Pick. pick. BEEP. BEEP.

Hummingbird is calling again and I ignore it. Again.

"Yeah, and she also keeps reprimanding me for everything and telling me what to do. She'll bark commands at me like 'get my drum' or 'cleanse this stone' and I'm like, 'okay a simple please would be nice,' you know? And she also said this thing that like, I will take on men's DNA forever and it will never leave my body even if it like, wasn't consensual ... weird right?"

BEEP. BEEP.

IGNORE. *Get the hint!? For fuck's sa—*

BEEP BEEP.

Stored-away memories of Hummingbird acting in ways I fundamentally disagree with and refused to unearth begin to spin through my head like a Rolodex.

The floodgates are officially open.

BEEP. BEEP.

"Ugh. She's calling me. Again. Joni Linea I'm about to *SNAP*." My head is so hot I picture my spirit guides lighting their cigarettes with my crown, attempting to calm themselves before having to deal with my colossal cosmic cracking, and face the conversation I know I have to have with Hummingbird, which might turn into a Jersey-Shore-meets-Rainbow-Gathering moment.

I slam my thumb on "send to voicemail" five times until I almost throw my phone.

BEEP. BEEP.

IGNORE.

BEEP. BEEP.

"JONI I'M—"

BEEP. BEEP.

"Anus, tell her right now. This is *INSANE*."

BEEP. BEEP.

"Okay I'll call you right back." I click accept.

"Hello?" My voice is so shaky I sound like the old lady in *Titanic*.

"There you are! I've been really tuning into you and you *need* a session." Hummingbird exhales loudly. "I feel it."

"Actually, I'm really doing really well. Like we discussed. I don't need a session, but I'll let you know when I do."

"But I think you do. I can feel it."

Suddenly, an unhinged smile stretches across my face and my desire to "please her" disintegrates, as does my respect for her. I may not know a whole lot about spirituality, but I do know a whole hell of a lot when someone is trying to play me.

"Where are you?" I ask, smiling all ax-in-hand, "here's Johnny" from *The Shining* style.

"I'm on a road trip, actually."

I keep my creepy smile intact, as I stare blankly into a rosebush.

"Well, my car broke down and I'm waiting for Simon to transfer some money into my account."

And there it is, kids. There. It. Is. There's a mark on the wooden fence that looks like a face. I smile at him. Her words blur together.

"Since-you-pulled-back-from-our-sessions-I-just-don't-have-the-funds-to-cover-it-myself."

"I'm sorry you're stuck. But I'm sure you'll get it sorted out—you always do," I slur, dead inside.

"How about, when I'm back, I will discount some sessions for you. I think you need to go back up to at *least* two sessions per week, but three would be best." Her forced chipper nature makes me even more unhinged.

I slide back on the couch and pick up Patrick, letting him melt on my lap.

"Hummingbird," the lump in my throat is so big it hurts. I can actually feel the weight of the words I haven't said to her. "I know what you're doing," I whisper softly.

"What? Honey, you need to sit with your shadow and NOT project it at me ..."

I tune her out and stare at the mountain I see from my porch. I wonder how many dead animals are on that mountain right now. It's totally creepy, just these decaying animals being fed on by maggots and vultures. It dies, and then it gets swarmed. Damn, nature is not magic; it's dark and harrowing. I wonder what my grandfather looks like now, after five years of—

"You have darkness inside of you. It's YOUR shadow. I refuse to take it on. REFUSE." She sounds like Veruca Salt bitching to her daddy in *Willy Wonka & the Chocolate Factory*.

I squint my eyes toward the mountain, trying to see any vultures flying or any bit of truth in anything we did together. "Okay. I'm gonna go now." I take a pause. "If you really need the money for your car, I can send it to you. But after that, I'm feeling complete with our journey together."

"Your money is dark to me. Keep it."

CLICK.

"Pat, that was like, a lot, huh?" I pick him up and kiss his head, his orange fur catching a rogue tear I didn't even realize I'd shed.

Then I stand up and kick open my front door and look around the living room that not one person has visited yet. The light green record player has been playing the same record since I moved in— *Billie Holiday's Greatest Hits.* The cute glassware from Anthropologie I ordered for special occasions and girls' nights has thick rings of dust on it. The pretty pink roses I bought for myself are swimming in murky brown water. I dart to them, grab the stupid ugly Goodwill vase they're decaying in, and march outside to dump them out. I end up dropping them, vase and all, from the porch. It cracks and the water spills out around it.

TWO WEEKS LATER, I'M STRUCK with the dark realization that I actually have no one to talk to here. I don't even open my mouth most days. No more Hummingbird and her nutty musings. Joni's slammed at her new job. Everyone at my school is way too into anime and musical theater which—whatever, good for them. Even my lanky lover Johnny is abroad in Amsterdam. When we *do* talk, we don't really have much to say, anyway.

It's time to make some friends and build some community.

So I straighten my hair in my giant bathroom, slip into my floor-length peasant dress, and paint my lips with Lime Crime "Wicked" lipstick.

All just to walk through town to see if I can have a main character moment and meet a friend or mentor by chance. Or just get the tiniest hit of attention or validation, for fuck's sake.

As I walk to civilization, I do my best mystery girl saunter toward the lone street in this tiny town. The stores are either very old lady chic or way too "far out" (even for me). I pass by a shop that exclusively sells unicorn paraphernalia. I check myself in my reflection in the window and then look poetically into the distance, as if I'm in deep thought. I have to *show* my depth. You know how it goes.

"Ey, wanna help the bees?" a transient barefoot bald guy yips from the street corner. He's with his two buddies and a dog that looks like he's seen better days. They all look like they've seen better days, but *bey*. Maybe the bees are a sign? Maybe these are my new friends? They could turn out to be—dare I say it—cool?

"Yeah, I'm in, I love bees!"

"Amazing," the bald guy jeers, "and I'm sure they *love* you!" His friends do the most "Dazed and Confused" style stoned laugh I've ever heard. I force a giggle.

"Well, what are we doin' here! I want to help in any way I can!"

"Bust your tits out for the bees, babe!" a long-haired, way-too-old-to-be-doing-this guy blurts.

"Are you fucking kidding me? Oh come *ON*, that is so fucking embarrassing you're like 45," I groan and stomp away.

"Fucking bitch," he hisses under his breath. Little does this dick know, I've got WEEKS of pent-up rage to let loose.

I metaphorically crack my knuckles as I pivot on my little black booties and swivel around. "Hey? Do you think you're any less of an asshole because you don't wear shoes? You're joking right?" I sneer, feeling slightly aroused by the idea of tearing the whole lot of them a new one.

"Look at you all done up with your dress on and shit. You're chained to your looks! Chained to consumerist bullshit!"

Herrreeeeeee's ANI.

I grin. Calmly. I crouch down to meet their eyes.

"You are more chained to your boring, cliché lifestyle than I'll ever be to my looks. And I'm not going to let you live in the delusion that you're free, or that you're 'helping the planet' or whatever the fuck bullshit story you try to tell yourself. You're wasting your life and pretending it's fulfilling by trying to recreate a movement that died decades ago because everyone realized it fucking. SUCKS. So if you're going to suck, just suck, but don't try to fool yourself. And don't bring the bees into your bullshit fucking pseudo-enlightenment. Not only is it boring and tacky, but you're smearing your shit on something actually worth defending." I half expect a forked tongue to slither out of my mouth.

"Wow, you're, like, really mean," the silent friend responds, as they all look at me with horror.

I get up and turn around, the blood rushing to my cheeks as quickly as my steps.

Welp, so much for making new friends. This healing adventure is NOT shaping up to what I thought it would be. Like, not even slightly. But I need to put a pin in that planning because Johnny is coming to visit in three days anyway.

Knowing I'll be having sex again soon, I have also become obsessed with my body. In my bathroom, I lift my shirt up and look at my torso, which I've never been able to do without bursting into angry tears. After a lifetime of getting made fun of for my weight, I did a big spell before I left for Oregon to help me finally love my body. And it's *working*. I feel kind of ... amazing? Even my tits feel like they are growing and my stomach feels hard as a rock. Probably because all these veggies are making me emit so much gas that I'm scared I'm singlehandedly contributing to global warming.

I'm actually excited to see Johnny. I miss him, even though he broke six of my most sacred vinyls while he helped me pack them. And I want him to see what a beautiful, wholesome home I've made. I can't wait to cook him dinner and, strangely, I can't wait to have sex. I've been really horny lately. Maybe it's all the hormone-balancing herbs I've been sucking down. I've become obsessed with hormones, do you know they control, like, *everything*? And my stomach has been weird AF—I only can tolerate Indian food and the sight of most things makes me ill.

The day he is due to arrive, I throw on yet another floor-length peasant dress, hop into my car, and set off to the co-op to get a probiotic to settle my stomach so I don't fart my way to the airport.

And with every step I take, my tits are KILLING me. I hold them up for a minute as I walk past the buskers and through the doors of CVS.

I head to the health section, and my eye catches a display of pregnancy tests. I feel a pang in my gut. No. There's *no* way, but just to be safe, I grab one. Then I check out, sprint to my car, and race to the airport, to claim my Johnny. I literally *run* into his arms.

"My girl!" He picks me up and flings me around.

All I can feel is the hard rocks that are my tits, which feel like they are about to fall out of my chest.

"Whoa ... my ... *girls*!" He backs up to get a better look.

"Seriously. I got a pregnancy test just to be safe even though I know we're fine," why am I telling him this? "But if for some reason I am pregnant, I'm leaving your ass," I joke, kissing his lips.

There is no time like the present, right? When we get home, I leave him to get settled and unpack some of his stuff. Then I head to the bathroom, squat over the toilet and recite my pee chant. I can't actually start peeing without reciting my pee chant. It's from some late '90s Disney movie: "si se puede, si se puede, si se puede."

Works every time. I dutifully pee on the pregnancy test stick and gently place it on the counter. I sit back on the squishy old lady toilet seat that came with the house. I wait, and it feels like I'm about to go dance on stage but don't know any of the moves.

I scroll through Instagram to distract myself, and am looking at the benefits of putting onions on your feet for detoxing when I realize the time.

I pull my pants up and rush to the test to get my hit of relief.

"PREGNANT" reads the test.

This can't be right. I take the other test in the box. Same routine.

"PREGNANT" reads the test.

"JOHNNY?!" I scream, collapsing onto the bathroom floor.

The door bursts open and Johnny cannonballs inside. He picks up the test and peers at it. "Positive? Is it positive? Ani?! What does it say?" I have NO room for this. It literally spells out the word: POSITIVE.

"LOOK AT IT JOHNNY. DO YOU THINK I'M ON THE GODDAMN FLOOR SOBBING FOR MY FUCKING HEALTH? I push past him and squeeze out of the bathroom.

I text Joni.

PLEASE CALL ME. THIS IS AN EMERGENCY. I AM NOT OKAY.

"FUCK!" Johnny yells into the ethers.

My phone rings.

"Joni," I sob.

"What is it? What happened?"

"I'm such a fucking sack of *shit*." I close my eyes and wail.

"What did you do?! Ani?!" Now she's crying, too.

"I'm pregnant," I say, then bury my head back into my knees.

"... Oh Anus. Oh my God. Listen, are you listening? We're going to get this all situated and figured out. Do not panic. I'm right here, and I'm not leaving your side, no matter what."

"Joni, the ONE time I had unprotected sex, and he pulled out, and I did it out of obligation because I was leaving and he was sad, and now I'm PREGNANT."

Saying it out loud like this, I feel it inside of me for the first time. An alien invasion of my body. Like a parasite I didn't even know was there has been dictating my moods and what I eat. Is this why I've been craving Indian food for the first time ever? I picture a little fetus eating paneer particles in my belly like a goldfish eating flecks of fish food.

Oh my god *EW*—is that why I've been so horny? I cringe thinking about how I masturbated with a fucking *child* in my belly.

"Joni. What am I going to do? I can't do this. I need Johnny away from me."

"Go to Planned Parenthood, make sure the test is accurate, get your options. And remember: I'm right here."

The rest of the day exists in flashes of more confirmations that this is really happening and pamphlets telling me what to do about it. I avoid touching my stomach at all costs. I sob on the phone on calls to Joni and my Mom. Johnny silently drives me to Planned Parenthood and back. He doesn't open his mouth once. Apparently, I have one week to decide to either get rid of it—or have a baby. A. *Baby*.

There is no running from this one.

THE NEXT MORNING, MY MOM convinces me to go see her friend, who lives thirty minutes away. I've never met this friend, but apparently, she and my mom have been close since I was a kid.

Her name is Brigid. Turns out Brigid lives on the very mountain I've been staring at from my living room window. Johnny and I pull into her long winding driveway, past a field of majestic-looking horses.

Her home is jaw-dropping. Floor-to-ceiling windows cocooned in gorgeous bushes filled with the most stunning, fragrant roses I've ever seen. Wisteria climbs up the walls. A cluster of plump rocking chairs sits pretty on the giant porch, which overlooks the mountain range. A hand-mosaicked fire pit stands between them.

Brigid emerges from the French doors and glides onto the patio, waving us in. She looks like an off-duty model: Tall. Thin. Clad in a moss green sweater and the skinniest of jeans. She's got a real-life Celtic-chic vibe. Witchy, waify, and ageless, with long, raven waves framing cheekbones as high as the sky. Her blue eyes are both plush and piercing.

"My darlings, I heard you've found yourself in a little kerfuffle." Her voice is honey. I melt. Who knew those were the exact words I needed to hear? She opens her arms for a hug.

I collapse into her, and she hugs me with so much presence I feel like she is strengthening my body with hers. I start sniffing so I don't snot on her sweater.

"It's nice to meet you," I mumble into her shoulder, refusing to break what may be the best hug I will ever receive, ever.

"I've been waiting for this day for a long time, sweet one. I've been watching over you since you were a wee one. That's why your mom was so down to have you move out here, you know; she knew I'd be right here if you needed me. And here you are." She beams, breaking the hug to look me in the eyes. "And you did good, coming here," she says more softly, her eyes piercing mine as if she's trying to telepathically tell me something.

"And you must be Johnny." She pulls him in for a hug. "I have a special day planned for you. The ladies need their time. Johnny, you'll be hanging out with Max, my partner. He's down the way there, past the garden. Big, burly man with curly hair. If it feels okay to you, he's going to teach you how to use a backhoe, and you guys have a lot to talk about, I'm sure."

"Yeah, that sounds perfect. I'll let you ladies ... uh ... do your lady thing? The boys will go be boys, as they say." He moves his arms around like a weird praying mantis and I can't help but shoot Brigid a "this is what I've been dealing with" look.

"Well, whenever you're done, Johnny, I have some enchanted spice

cake in the oven. It will heal anything from a broken heart to the flu and make you believe that magic is real. It will be waiting for you." She winks at Johnny, who nods his head and starts down the rose-bush-lined path.

Then she wraps her arm around me and starts leading me to the kitchen.

"You—" she gleams "—get spice cake now. And some tea. Let's talk, my love. Then, we go see Dagda."

I don't even bother to ask who or what the fuck a "dagda" is, I'm too relieved.

"I really can't thank you enough for taking me in. I sort of feel like the biggest burden of all time right now."

She stops right before we swish through the French doors.

"Turn around for a moment, and look at the land. Feel into it. Breathe it in. Let the roses get into your field, let the mountains sink you into your body more." I close my eyes and, like magic, the most perfect, soft wind licks my hair, planting cosmic kisses on my cheeks.

"I've been waiting for you," Brigid continues in a gentle tone. "This land has been waiting for you. This is where you can come and rest your head and fill your heart, whenever you want, whatever state you're in."

I take the deepest inhale of my entire life and whip around to smile at her and fully expect the *Full House* theme song to start blaring from the heavens. This is it. The reason I moved here, in plain sight looking at me in the eye.

Then she guides me inside, which is every bit as magical as the outside. An ornate grandfather clock ticks tocks; tendrils of thriving hanging vines are vibrant against the yellow walls of her kitchen, which are hung with actual oil paintings of chickens, Joan of Arc, horses galloping, and a village in celebration. Her giant stone hearth has a little fire going, surrounded by dried roses. And the whole damn place smells like smoldering herbs and magical spice cake.

BABOOMBOOMBOOM

I hear something TUMBLE down the stairs and turn around to see if she's scared.

"Oh, here we go," she giggles, "Calidore's been waiting for you, too. Brace yourself, baby." She moves out of the way as the biggest gray goof-

ball of a wolfhound dog barrels into the room and runs up to me.

"WooooWWOOOOOOwoWOOOO," he sings so loudly the windows shake, wagging his whole body as if we haven't seen each other in years.

"Oh my God, he looks like a horse!" Calidore wraps his whole body around me like he's hugging me, and then collapses on my feet, staring at me to solicit cuddles. I plop on the floor next to him.

Then, while sitting cozy on the floor, the hot spice cake is in my lap (it *is* magical!), and I'm talking to an almost perfect stranger, feeling more comfortable than I have in years.

"I just ... don't know what to do. I can't have a kid, and he can't be the father. I can't be tied to him for life. But I also ... I can't believe my body actually did this. That I'm capable of this. And there's a little thing inside of me just chilling and I think I'd actually be a really good mom," I croak in between open-mouth chews of spice cake.

"My heart, there's no doubt you'd be a good mom. Right now, you just need to be in the bewilderment of it all. There are no wrong choices—just different life paths. Think of it like a 'choose your own adventure' novel."

I just sit there in stunned silence.

"Brigid, who is Dagda that you said we have to talk to?"

"Let's go see him, we'll hop in the car. I think you're gonna like him. And we'll see Carrie, she's a trip."

With that, we head back outside and hop in Brigid's old pickup truck and start making our way to see this sage soul, Dagda. I place my hand on my belly and I feel a kind of electricity going from my hand to my lower belly like I'm warming the little thing up with love, the way Brigid is doing with me.

"If I keep this kid, I want to move to Scotland," I say, unsure as to why.

"Tell me more!"

"I don't know, when I think of home, that's what comes to my head. Even though I'm not even slightly Scottish."

"Pay attention to that desire," she says.

Okay, I am in the bewilderment.

We pull into yet another long driveway, with fields of horses on either side of us. A tiny woman with a ponytail past her ass is waving furiously at us.

"And there's Carrie. I told you she's a riot, and really good medicine at a time like this."

"Gals! Park here and hop out, I gotta show you the new tanning bed, too!" For such a tiny human, Carrie is LOUD.

Brigid shuts the engine off and I'm barely out of the car before Carrie scoops me up. "Alright, I'm so glad you're here. Dagda's all ready for you. I'll show you the tanning booth after, just go see him." She's actually just as loud up close.

"Thank you for having me and setting this up. I'm sure he's busy. Is he in the house?"

She looks like I just spoke in full-on alien language.

"*In* the house?" She turns to Brigid. "What does she mean, *in the house?*"

"What do *you* mean in the house?" I ask back, genuinely confused. Do I have pregnancy brain already?

Brigid comes to the other side of the car, giving Carrie one of her signature hugs. "She doesn't know who ... or what Dagda is yet."

Carrie smiles a Cheshire Cat smile: "Let's go."

With one hand pressed against my stomach, I strut behind them down the dirt driveway, through the mud, beyond the barn, and right up to a pen.

.... There's no fucking way ...

"Dagda!" Carrie makes clicking sounds with her tongue.

Then a giant, chocolate brown horse comes cat-walking leisurely to the gate, not blinking once, stopping right in front of us.

"Dagda, Ani. Ani, Dagda. Dagda, please do your thing with her, we'll give you some space." Carrie talks so fast that I think I must be hearing her wrong.

This is Dagda? A FUCKING HORSE?! How the fuck did I get myself here? I am barreling downhill for absolute fuck's sa—

"Be in the bewilderment, Ani. Nothing that crosses your mind is an accident," Brigid whispers from behind me, squeezing my shoulders. Then she walks off with Carrie as she yammers on and on about her new at-home tanning bed.

Okay, let's try it. What do I have to lose? *Stay in the bewilderment, bitch!*

"Uh ... hi. Do I talk out loud or is this, like, a telepathic thing?" I ask the horse, puzzled. Is the horse okay? He still hasn't blinked. *Whatever.* "I am scared and confused, so um, if you could, like, help, that would be cool." I feel insane.

The horse stares at me. Maybe he's dissociated? Can horses be dissociated? For fuck's sake I'm trauma dumping on a dissociated horse and expecting answers. Have I REALLY stooped this low?!

I stare at the little baby hairs peppered across his soft pink nose.

I wonder what my baby would look like. I envision a little girl. Brown hair and eyes, rosy cheeks, and a powerful gaze with thick brows.

I'm having a miscarriage tonight. I quickly ignore the strange thought shooting through my brain.

"Dagda, what do I do? Have the kid and go to Scotland? Terminate this and live my life here? What do I do?"

You won't make the choice, you'll miscarry tonight. The thought comes flying through my brain again.

After what feels like an appropriate amount of time to be communicating telepathically with a horse, I awkwardly curtsy to Dagda and walk back to Brigid and Carrie, not sure of how I feel about any of this. For now, I'll chalk it up to me still trying to convince myself that this *spiritual* shit is real.

I don't even have a single cramp or anything.

"Be in the bewilderment" I repeat to myself over and over as we make our way home and I get Johnny.

That night I wake up in the middle of the night and gasp. I reach my hand down my pants.

There is blood everywhere.

7
Witch Bitch

I wait a few days to make sure Johnny is being supported by his family, and then I break up with him. The last day we are together, he tries to have sex with me, as if I wasn't wearing pads so big they were practically diapers. Once he has left for New York, I barely leave my house, but I can't go anywhere near that bathroom. I'm pretty sure those tests are still on the counter.

Meanwhile, Brigid has fully become my actual *fairy godmother*. A few weeks later, I sit in her kitchen, staring into the fire, getting lost in my mind. I am twenty-two years old and I know I'm not going to do anything with my English degree. I mean, I came to Oregon to do what? Sit on my ass and be in my shit? *I don't think so*. It's time to go ALL in. But I don't know what the next step could even be. I don't know what I'm going to do with myself, period. We're getting down to the wire here in terms of me making a living and becoming a functioning member of society—I have to figure it out. I came to Ashland to become more spiritual or something, and I haven't. I've just been putzing around and eating my body weight in sautéed kale, which, as it turns out, is not half bad when you add enough garlic. But really, is anything bad if you add enough garlic?

"You need to remember your connection with plants," Brigid interrupts, psychically picking up on my thought spiral. "You should study herbalism. With the best of the best of the best: *Diana Deonyssia*. She's an old witch and she knows plants better than any other teachers out there. She does apprenticeships where you learn how to actually communicate with the plants, not just herbalism."

An old ... *witch*?

Apprenticeships? That sounds ancient. What even *is* an apprentice-ship? I stare at the flames dancing and become even more consumed. Come to think of it—that word is kind of ... *sexy.* I can't help feeling, dare I say, "turned on" by the idea of being an "apprentice." Done! I'm in! Who knew finding your life path was such a piece of gluten-free, sugar-free, dairy-free, low glycemic, paleo-friendly cake.

With that, I bolt home and begin furiously researching this Diana character. To say she comes off as "intense" would be like saying Anna Wintour is just a tad "particular."

First of all, she looks like she would literally sacrifice me with, like, zero qualms or hesitation. Maybe it's her frizzy hair that she lets run completely wild. Maybe it's her unapologetically saggy boobs that are so low they practically reach her stomach (not gonna lie, this is kind of amazing and I love it #goals). Or maybe it's the fact that her eyes are so intense, one look and I could turn into the missing wart from her nose.

I scroll down and see a video of her. Cute! Let's just hit play and get a feel fo–

"HELLOoOo."

"AHHH!" I jump so high that I choke on my own spit and slam on the pause button.

Her voice sounds as if a chain smoker and the primordial sound bellowing from Earth's inner crust came together and greeted me. If the whole look didn't sell her witchiness her voice just did.

It's like lightning is coming from her eyes, even though she's smiling and trying to sound nice. I take a deep breath to ground and center and press play.

"I am Diana Deonyssia. I am an herbalist, a witch, a crone, and a fierce, fiery, angry teacher. If you want to be an apprentice with me, you must do one, simple task. Write me a letter as to WHY you want to study with me, even when you know I'm going to yell at you, I'm going to make you work, and I'm going to push you to your limits. You will study with me for 13 weeks time, and your life and you will never be the same. Are you ready?"

Hmm. Bold. But, hey Diana, real quick question—*what the fuck?* Seriously, this is crazy, right? I mean, why would I want to study with an old witch in the middle of nowhere and get screamed at 'till I'm scared shitless every day? My eyes dart around my room. Well, perhaps the woodstove I only use as decoration could be lit for the first time. Maybe I would actually use the jars of magical herbs I have neatly organized on a bookshelf. And perhaps all these crystals I've collected will actually, ya know, start working? I sigh. I have been *cosplaying* spirituality. And ya know what else? Diana seems fucking strong, unapologetic, smart, powerful, connected—all the things my self-indulgent ass is not.

I run to my desk, light my Cher prayer candle, and start writing to her:

> Dear Diana,
>
> Thank you so much for an opportunity to study with you! Thankful is an understatement when I think of being on your land and learning under you. I know it sounds like I'm sucking up but when I picture apprenticing under you, I envision a space where I can be the woman I am supposed to be. I feel the strength and support of the land, the fierceness of your wisdom, and your divine understanding of the magic and medicine that surrounds us, always. I am excited to wake up to the ancient and sacred knowledge that I believe is in me. My heart has guided me to your space, and if you'll have me there, I can see me expanding and connecting so deeply to the plants and land with the love and respect they deserve. Thank you and many blessings,
>
> Ani Ferlise

I stare at my letter with pride, the blue light blaring from my laptop screen illuminating my face. There are very clear instructions for what to do after you send Diana your letter. But instead of reading these, ADHD decides that I actually need to Google where the cast from *Degrassi* ended up, and how they feel about Drake's subsequent success. Instructions are my worst nightmare to be honest; I always check out after "step one." Once I've finished fake reading them, I send in the full payment for the apprenticeship with my letter, just to be safe. There's no chance ADHD can win this round. The entire cast of *Degrassi* cheers for me in my mind.

TWO MONTHS LATER, I'M IN Vita's apartment in New York. I haven't seen her since I lived here, so naturally we went on a rager the night before. I am deathly hungover. It reeks of pizza (even though there was never pizza but for some reason when you wake up in the house the party was at it ALWAYS smells like pizza in the morning) and I'm trying not to vomit. Then my phone buzzes with a call from a random number from Oregon.

"Hello?" I croak, my voice sounding as crusty as the crescent moons of flaky mascara under my eyes.

"This is *Diana Deonyssia*," croons a deep, brooding voice.

"Oh, hi, what's up?" I try to not vomit from the non-existent pizza stench.

"I am *aghast—aghast*—that you think you can just pay me and come here without reading the instructions. **You clearly didn't read the instructions**. I have not accepted you yet, nor do I think I will," the voice booms down the speaker.

"Oh, okay, I'm so sorry, and I understand."

"What's your excuse?"

"I don't have an excuse. I just sent the money. And I shouldn't have."

She pauses. "Fine. We can discuss this later. But the only reason— THE ONLY REASON—I am still considering you as my apprentice is because you didn't give me an excuse."

My pupils dilate. *This must be what people in sports feel like when they make a goal!*

"What if I give you chores to do?" Diana pries.

"I'm coming to stay at your house. You wouldn't even have to ask me to wash the dishes! You are letting me stay with you and are teaching me," I chirp, my hangover forgotten.

"What if I YELL AT YOU," she yells.

"Well then, I'd probably hear you better."

I'm like Serena Williams to her Maria Sharapova, with this witchy back and forth.

"Fine. I do believe you are ready for this. But follow my instructions CAREFULLY this time or you are NOT to come, am I clear?"

I collapse to the ground as if I've just won the US Open.

"YES!" I cackle, momentarily forgetting my "good apprentice" persona.

"Here are your instructions for when you arrive, and I'm only going to say this once so listen closely. You will pull up to 545 Blue Water Drive. You will make your way down the long road and you will NOT park AN-YWHERE close to the wild plants. You will get out of the car, walk up to the front door, and knock, but you will NOT enter. You will wait until you are greeted for the next instructions. Am. I. *Clear*?"

"Yes. I will see you then and won't let you down. Thank you!" I blurt while frantically typing these new instructions into my Notes app so as not to forget.

Okay, *THIS* time ADHD won't get the better of me.

DIANA'S PLACE IS CALLED *Wild Water Farm*. I envision a lodge and a fireplace with a bunch of cool witches huddled around the flames. How epic! And I could be one of them!

What does one wear to Wild Water Farm? I wonder, weeks later, as I at-tempt to pack for this voyage. I have no idea what I'm going to be doing there. I have no idea what to expect about anything, really. All I know is that I'm going to (hopefully) live out my apprentice fantasy. Sick!

Oh.

And there's going to be some plants involved. Yeah. Cool.

I pack a bunch of those linen elephant-printed-harem-pants things, intuiting that my celestial-embellished dusters are not going to cut it. I throw in some t-shirts and a pair of combat boots for walking in the woods. I also pack my blankie, a journal, and some essential oils to give Diana as a gift.

Two weeks later, I'm driving with Carl, a friend of Brigid's I met at a dinner, who generously offered to take me to eastern Oregon with his wife. I am the size of his bicep. Carl has done a stealth amount of jail time and doesn't have any fear. His wife, Linda, is quite possibly the nicest, kindest, most beautiful human. We chat warmly the whole way up about their love story.

After a five-hour drive, we make our way down a long, winding dirt driveway. Wild plants line the gravel road. Deer prance awkwardly. Then we pull up to a small, blue house with a dilapidated old car out front, shattered fencing, and a lime green lake completely blanketed with the thickest layer of algae you've ever seen. Also, I realize the deer aren't deer. They're fucking goats.

My heart pounds and the saliva in my mouth has evaporated. Knock. Knock. I am so proud of my ADHD brain for remembering to WAIT to be greeted before ENTERING. I picture the witch from Snow White slowly cracking open the front door. Several minutes go by before I realize that no one seems to be answering. Is this my first test—

or—

did she forget?

For twenty-two minutes I stand by the front door awkwardly, like a teen outcast in a high school cafeteria clutching her lunch tray, unsure of where to sit. Right as my inner teen is emotionally preparing to eat lunch alone in a bathroom stall, a bald man walks out the front door. When I tell you bald, I mean *bald*, bald. Every ounce of his body is bald. No eyebrows. No armpit hair. The shiny kind of bald that gleams like Mr. Clean in the sunlight. He wears nothing but short shorts and knee pads. His naked (very hairless) chest reveals a giant, gold, glimmering nipple ring. The thick hoop is pierced through one of his (very hairless) nipples.

"Uh, hi, I'm looking for—" *don't say nipple ring, don't say nipple ring ...*"— Diana? I'm Ani, the apprentice." I extend my hand for a shake and he just stares at it.

"Ahh! An apprentice." I awkwardly put my hand down, cringing.

"Diana isn't here yet. But you're going to go live up at the Motherwort Nest. Go. Get set up there, that's where the apprentices live. There's only one other apprentice this year," the bald man drops casually.

There's only going to be two of us? My palms break a sweat.

I make my way to the Motherwort Nest with Carl and Linda where I see the other apprentice and her boyfriend who is dropping her off. He looks like a stereotypical gamer who survives on a diet of Cheetos and Mountain Dew (and who doesn't wipe his hands after the Cheetos).

The Motherwort Nest itself is a rickety ranch duplex covered in so much foliage I can't actually see it until I wrestle through the leaves and vines right up to the door. I have to duck and shimmy my body in order to get to it, but when I finally do, I lightly push it open.

And ...

For fuck's sake.

It looks like Keith Moon and the rest of The Who had a stay right before I arrived. The place is fucking *trashed*. The (yellow ... brown? *gulp* ... once white?) wall-to-wall carpet looks like an even more lived-in version of the bile-stained carpet from my college room.

I whip my head to Carl behind me who looks like he is about to start recording himself snot-crying, *Blair Witch Project* style, as his eyes dart around in horror.

Okay, okay ... woman up Ani, *you got this*. I walk in with my head held high, and go into the first room.

A twin-sized mattress pad sits on the filthy floor. There are cobwebs so massive and intricate they look like they've been created by a set designer for a "spooky" Disney movie. But no, they're very real. I walk to the next room down the hall with high hopes of finding an actual bed. Instead, I'm met with a wall filled with dozens of pictures of women spread eagle, vulvas just out and proud, Scotch Taped to the walls.

I wince, and look behind me again to see Carl about to go into full-on cardiac arrest. I smile at him reassuringly but my face drops when I see the wall behind him.

"What? Ani? What?" he asks, like Brad Pitt asking what's in the box in *Seven*.

Behind him is a giant mural of a hairy, gaping pussy that looks like it's about to suck the soul right out of his body.

He turns around slowly.

"Oh, Ani, oh no, no. Oh, Ani ... I can't leave you here. I can't leave you here," Carl panics.

"It's good, Carl! This is all good, I can make it work! I'll clean it right up no problem!" I panic-promise in response, hoping I can make good on it.

I continue my walk through the "house." When I cautiously peer into the kitchen, it's covered in mouse poop. Good *GOD*. I open a door and the stench of old piss and Lord knows what else punches me square in the nose, almost knocking me out. I stand there, gasping for air, while simultaneously trying to hold my breath. The bathroom looks like a fucking crime scene, with rust on the shower that looks like old, dried blood. Above the toilet hangs a sign, crafted with crayons, that reads, "if it's yellow let it mellow, if it's brown flush it down."

BARF DUDE.

I slam the door shut. Carl cannot see this.

Okay, so what? I was expecting a lodge and a beautiful cabin in the woods. I am in a dilapidated hoarder's house with pussies-a-plenty watching my every move.

O-FUCKING-KAY! Woman up, bitch! Witches, like, high-five spiders and collect eye-of-newt. It's *not* a pretty profession. Stop being a prim and proper broad, and claim your space!

I head back to the first room, the furthest away from the bathroom, drop my bag, and claim my new digs before the other apprentice gets any funny ideas about taking it. I will make friends with the mice and spiders like Cinderella, and they'll become my trusted allies and encourage me when I am riddled with self-doubt.

I'm about to get down and (literally) dirty with the glamorous mattress pad on the floor, when Carl appears at my doorway looking like he's got nothin' left to give.

"Where's Linda?" I fake chirp.

"She's not coming in here. She's crying in the car. I can't leave you here, Ani," his eyes are misty, like the sweat emerging from his forehead.

"Carl, I have to do this." I grab him by the forearms and barely get my hands around them. "I'm going to be okay."

"Just call me, call me. I will be here in two seconds."

"Carl, I love ya. I appreciate ya. You are my knight in shining armor, really. But don't worry—I'm like a witch now, or a bitch at the very least. I got this," I joke, only to see a tear roll down his cheek. He turns away and marches to the car and I walk with him outside. He revs up the engine, and I watch my last chance of escape begin to pull out. He pops his head out of the window one more time, looking back at me worried eyebrows raised high, just to make sure.

But I am sure. I smile, nod a "yes," and wave goodbye.

I head back into the Motherwort Nest to see what I can do to spruce this place up.

"Um, Hello. Hi. Uh, Hi," a voice from my doorway starts, tripping over her words like a 15-year-old in stilettos.

I see a short woman in light blue gauchos, a white button-down, and a pink crochet beanie standing at my door.

"I'm Sheila, I'm the other apprentice, I-I-I got here two days ago. I am staying at the end of the hallway." Sheila needs like, ten Klonopins. STAT.

"Hey, Sheila, nice to meet you! Do you do hugs?"

"Uh, well, yeah, I mean, yeah hugs? Yes." I go in to hug her and she lightly pats my back and sticks her entire bottom half of her body out so it doesn't come near me.

"Well, wanna come talk to me while I unpack? I'd love to hear why you're here!"

Yes, she would like to talk. I start organizing my space as she stands, back against the wall, spewing out facts and stories about Diana. Turns out she is her *biggest* fan. I suddenly feel *extremely* unprepared. I didn't even read any of Diana's books, and this girl has studied the ins and outs of her entire psyche, for fuck's sake!

"Fuck, you really did your homework, huh?" I finally interject, looking at her fully for the first time. Sheila, as it turns out, is in her forties and her face bears a deeply furrowed brow and wildly intense frown lines.

"Well, uh, yeah, well, homework? Yeah, I do my homework, was there any actual homework? Did you get assignments?" She's so nervous, she makes me seem like I've reached Buddha levels of enlightenment. It suddenly dawns on me that for the whole summer, it's going to be me, Sheila the nervous wreck, Diana the witch, and the bald man. At this point? It just *has* to be OKAY.

"No, I don't think so. But I did get Diana these beautiful essential oils," I meow to Sheila, proudly pulling them out of my bag.

Sheila's beady eyes transform into flying saucers. "DON'T DO IT. DON'T DO IT. DON'T GIVE THEM TO HER." She flings herself off the wall and slaps them out of my hands.

"What the actual fuck, Sheila?" I snap, genuinely in shock at the speed of her reflexes.

"No. No. *No*," Sheila shrills, frantically picking them up and shoving them back in my hands. "Diana is *so* against essential oils. She says they do awful things to you. She says she'd rather take *antibiotics* than be *near* essential oils. Get rid of them! Now, before she sees them, she's going to freak out!"

I've never seen such raw fear in a person. It's not even human fear. It's *animal* fear. I soften my gaze hoping to calm her the fuck down. "I promise I won't give her the essential oils—"

KNOCK. KNOCK. KNOCK.

We both jump. I shove the oils into my suitcase, zip them up, and throw my blankie on top (just in case).

We stand there with our hands behind our backs like we're teens who just successfully hid the weed from our overly-strict mother.

As the door creeps open slowly, the dusk light creates a familiar silhouette.

Wiry grey curls held down by a straw cowboy hat. Un-held, bra-less tits kissing the top of a belt loop. Faded blue tie-dye wolf shirt and dusty denim.

Diana.

Shivers shoot down my spine and twirl around with the lingering adrenaline, forcing me to start clenching the muscles in my legs. The long-titted lady lingers in the doorway.

I'm in awe. No one is speaking.

Then she approaches, circling us like a vulture over prey.

Her face is inches from Sheila's and I'm watching from my peripherals, not daring to intervene, even though I can practically feel Sheila about to erupt with fear. Then she walks over to me, and I open my mouth to say "hi." But right as I inhale, she grabs my wrists and looks deep into my eyes. *What the fuck is in the water at this place?*

I stare intently back at her to let her know I'm here. Then she grabs one of my fingers, still not breaking eye contact, and smacks it. Hard.

"We have to do something about *that*," she hisses, gesturing to my finger. The tip is buzzing.

"I'm down to do whatever you want, Diana. It's nice to finally meet you," I say.

I'm experiencing such an unabashed bout of main character syndrome, the finger-smack doesn't even bother me all that much. *Oh my God. What could this mean? There MUST be big magic afoot.*

"I am honored to study under you!" I squeak, and quickly regret it as her face turns fiery.

"Do not EVER say you study UNDER me, or UNDER ANYONE. Do you think I would every say I study "under" someone? You are studying WITH me. Not UNDER me. Get in your power." She smacks the wall while still looking me in the eye and I just nod my head in agreement. She's right. That was a bit much, but she's right.

"Tonight is your initiation. Meet me at the cedar house when it is completely nightfall," she croaks, hips swishing out the door.

Well, shit.

Thank God Sheila knows WTF the "cedar house" is. Once the sun has set, Sheila and make our way there in the dark.

Inside, I see Diana sitting in a rocking chair. Without pause, we sit on the floor beside her.

Without looking at us, she opens up the book in her lap.

"This is the story of Baba Yaga." She goes on to dramatically tell a story about this girl, Vasa something, who has this evil family—wicked stepmother and all, the whole spiel. The wicked stepmother wants her gone, so she sends little Vasalisa to the home of Baba Yaga to collect some fire as one of her chores. Baba Yaga forces her to do all of these crazy, impossible tasks, like sorting every poppy seed out of the dirt, or otherwise she will cook and eat her. At first, she doesn't know what to do; she's being challenged with tasks that it is simply not possible to complete. But somehow with the help of ~magic~ she gets them done. And then Baba Yaga gives her the fire in the form of this flaming skull, which not only guides her back home through the darkness of the woods but also turns her wicked stepfamily into ash. As a bonafide slut for drama, I'm covered in full-body chills.

"I am Baba Yaga." Diana slams the book closed. "Your life will never be the same after this. You will not be able to run away from yourself ever again, and I will incinerate your whole life." She looks at us. "Thousands of women have attempted this apprenticeship and only a couple of hundred have graduated. They leave and flee in the middle of the night. And of those couple hundred, only *seven* have been successful."

Oh, I will be successful—get ready for number eight, Baba, I think to myself, getting charged.

"I will find your greatest weakness and I will use it against you," she continues. "You might think this is mean, but any woman making a change in this world will be crucified and criticized. When I am done with you, you will never be fazed by criticism again." She then hands us each a necklace with a little turtle charm on it.

"This is a reminder of this conversation, because you won't remember it in a few weeks. You're going to want to leave. And if I *don't* make you want to leave, I have failed you." She pauses and leans down, her voice getting slower, softer, and deeper. "But if you *stay* and keep your commitment to me, I am yours forever."

I'm not sure if my goosebumps and belly grumbles are out of excitement, or if the nervous gas is quickly approaching.

"There will be no running to mother. As of now, consider your mother dead. That's how all good fairytales start, remember. You're on your own journey now," she adds, before leaving us in the dark.

The drama and theatrics are better than an episode of RuPaul's *Drag Race. Loving it.*

That night I lie awake on my lone mattress on the filthy carpet watching as a whole damn community of spiders crawl around me. I wanna scroll, or at least like, cry to my mom for a minute (damnit, Diana). Everything is starting to feel real. But cell phones are forbidden, along with all other contact with the outside world. Television. Music. Podcasts. I get up to distract myself, making my way across the hall to a little closet with no door, which has a landline inside and acts as a makeshift phone booth. There are letters from prior apprentices taped all over the walls. I scan them the way I do gravestones in a graveyard for the dates, the oldest one going back to the 1980s. Then I read the messages:

Don't leave—you got this!

Stay here. It's worth it.

You can do this, Goddess! Love yourself, invest in yourself, don't run.

Stick with it.

What the actual fuck have I gotten myself into?

I WAKE UP IN THE morning to explosive diarrhea and a toilet that barely flushes.

Then Sheila and I make our way to our designated morning prayer spot. A circle of cow bones and a fire pit mark the space, and we wait in silence, military style, for Diana to arrive.

I can hear her angrily yelling at Andy, the bald guy, in the distance, and then she is huffing and stomping toward us. I hold my breath and stand up taller, making sure to not look at them, pretending to meditate.

"Let's PRAY," she yells, sounding like she's the MC announcing a metal band. We join hands.

"THE EARTH, THE AIR, THE FIRE, THE WATER, I WILL RETURN TO THE SACRED MOTHER," Diana sings, sounding like a troll that lives under a bridge. I open one eye to take a peek, and she's actually baring her sharp, grayish teeth, her mouth forming an "o" shape as she sings. Sheila and Andy know all the lyrics and are completely unfazed.

FUCK. Diana's eyes shoot open and she looks directly at me. I slam my eyelid down. She knows. *Fuck.*

I pretend to mouth the lyrics.

And suddenly her groan/singing stops dead.

"Sit!" she barks.

We sit.

"Today we are starting chores. You will be paid for your chores because women's time is WORTH SOMETHING." She stomps her foot and the cloud of dust she creates is like an energetic exclamation point.

"Your time is valuable, and you should ALWAYS be compensated, no matter what."

Wow, that is actually so true! Women *are* always asked for free labor, when our time is worth something!

"The pay is $2 an hour that you will get at the end of your apprenticeship should you decide to stay."

Okay. *Um*? Okay. Well, I came here to learn, anyway.

"I talked with the Goddess last night, and she told me that Ani needs to be in the witch apprenticeship, not just the herbalism apprenticeship," she continues.

Oh. I hadn't signed up for the witch apprenticeship because it was five months long, which had sounded like *way* too much of a commitment for me. Also, I could make a living being an herbalist, but a witch? I gulp.

"And we both agreed that you are ready, Ani—we can do it in a short amount of time because you're already open."

I try to hide the fact that I feel like I just won Ms. America, my main character syndrome swelling to new heights. Okay, now I am excited. I am writing my acceptance speech in my head when Diana interrupts.

"Ani, your first task will be goat watch. Five hours per day, every day." Oh.

"You will herd the goats, you will milk the goats, you will take the milk to the kitchen and you will make yogurt and cheese from their milk," she recites, busy picking seeds from her teeth as she talks.

Okay, Babs, but what about the *learning* part?

"You will need to get in your power, and you will command the goats with my energy. It takes no technical training. Just power. Stand up, Ani."

I hop up like I am being flung by a slingshot. She reaches behind her, and pulls out a giant stick.

"Because you've acted weak your whole life, you'll need this."

Nice. I am not about to beat these goats, right? A gal's got limits ...

"If you want these goats to listen to you, you have to be LOUD," she yells, jumping up and slamming the stick on the ground, scaring the ever-living shit out of me.

"AND, you must be in your body," she smiles, beaming with pride for successfully scaring me enough that I have become present. "You cannot be a people pleaser and succeed in this work, Ani. You have got to take up space. You have got to make your 'no' LOUD and CLEAR. And, if they still don't listen, slam the stick into the ground and yell even louder. Don't be afraid."

I just blink.

"And I walk through the day while the goats all play. Goody, goody, goody, goody, goo!" she sings to the goats. Without hesitation, they dutifully line up in a straight row behind her and obediently follow her down the trail to the woods.

"LET'S GO!" she yells to me, and I rush toward her in an attempt not to appear more stupid than a goat.

The goats look at me. I look at them.

Okay, well, the singing thing seems simple enough. I take a deep breath, shake my head out, and hold it high.

"Goody, goody, goody, goody!" I sing to the goats, sounding more like Mandy Moore in *The Princess Diaries*. They don't budge. *Okay—what the fuck are they just staring at?*

I lower my voice and try again.

"Goody, goody, goody, goody, goody, gooo," I croak, trying to sound more witchy. I'm now creeping myself out.

I feel wildly insecure.

Get in my power. Get in my body. Deep breath in.

"... Goody, goody, goody, go—" I am IMMEDIATELY cut off as a mother goat named Cindy Lee (for real) charges me from behind and triumphantly runs ahead. Like she *actually* flips me, ass over backward. *Cindy Mother Fucking Lee that little beady eyed son of a—*

The next few hours are torture. Like actual psychological warfare. For hours and hours and hours, I sing "Goody, goody, goody, goody!" their stupid little ma-a-a-a noises sounding more and more like laughs, mocking me.

Five hours per day, every day. So this is my life now. I am covered in dirt and bruises from falling and wrangling the goats. But, ya know, it's all worth it.

Because I am a witch in training.

And the days tick by. In addition to goat watch, every morning Diana gives me strict instructions on what my duties will be for the day. But she will say them only once, and I am not allowed to write down the copious, hyper-detailed tasks she assigns me. "This is how the spirit communicates with you. They say it once and you listen because they won't repeat themselves," she clips.

Okay well, Spirit also gave me ADHD so ...

I am not allowed to ask questions, either. If I put something down in the wrong spot in her hoarder-level, jam-packed house she gets in my face and screams.

"If you put this ingredient in the wrong place, I'll die!" she shrieks. "You're trying to kill me, aren't you?"

A week or so in, we're making yogurt from goat's milk. I have washed (we aren't allowed to say "clean"—as a fuck you to purity culture and whatnot) the measuring cup. "Wait, the measuring cup hangs here, right?" "And that bowl goes on top of the fridge?" "Oh and after this we're going on a plant walk to forage for dinner, right?" I make the mistake of asking.

She stares at me for a long moment. "You know, Ani, you sound like a big, fat *baby* when you ask so many questions," she sneers. "A big, fat baby whose ass needs to be wiped for her."

Now, my inner Snooki wants to throw hands. But I've done enough self-work to realize that she's simply reflecting back a piece of me that I don't like. And I'M the one I want to punch, not her for pointing it out.

However. I still can't remember a goddamn thing she's instructed me to do. And I can't ask questions because I'm not a "stupid baby." Or am I?

Hmmm, time to get creative. "Okay, I'm putting the washed jug on the counter here!" I peer over my shoulder to see if she winces. She doesn't. *Check!*

"Here I go, putting the yogurt on the second shelf of the fridge!" I slowly turn my head and check her from my peripherals. She's not even flinching. *Sick!*

"Alright, now I'm going to take this big jug, and tuck it on the side of the fridge here, nice and organized," I say, not turning quick enough to gauge her reaction.

Suddenly, she pushes my back from behind me and I am face against the wall. She grabs a towel from the rack to our left and aggressively starts to wipe the outside of my pants.

"NOW YOUR ASS IS WIPED. YOU BIG BABY!" she cackles.

I should be shocked, but I start laughing hysterically. I don't know why— I'm probably a masochist or damaged or both—but I happen to think this is the funniest shit I've ever seen. I hear Sheila sobbing in the background.

"Next time, to stay in your power, you say 'I'm going to do this unless instructed otherwise.' Or you SHUT UP and do it and face the repercussions without shame, blame, or any excuses. Am I clear?" she belts from the next room.

Crystal clear, baby.

WEEKS INTO THE APPRENTICESHIP and the days are the same, but growing harder. Goat watch. Cooking. Foraging. Washing. Getting screamed at. And I'm left wondering when the witchy shit is going to go down. Where are the plush velvet cloaks? The crackling bonfires? The rituals?

I mean, the New Moon is approaching. We must be doing *something*, right?

That night, Sheila and I meet Diana by the unlit fire pit at nightfall. Finally, something that's not chores. Magic is afoot!

Diana begins to preach. "You must learn to embrace the darkness. Take off your shoes. Drop your flashlights for the rest of your time here. The darkness is not bad, it's the place of the Goddess. The mystery. The unknown parts of yourself and life. To think of the dark as bad is everything that is wrong with our culture. We need to stop focusing on ascending, cleaning, detoxing the body and mind. YOUR BODY IS NOT DIRTY. The light is no better than the dark. The dark is the womb space, the place of rebirth. The most fertile ground. Yet we've been taught to see it as bad. BULLSHIT!" She screams and slams down her foot.

We are too stunned to speak. I think of Hummingbird, who wouldn't even wear black, and picture her internally combusting from the sheer power of Diana's words.

"So, to get comfortable, you will walk through the woods in the dark sans shoes and flashlights and find your way back. Alone. The only thing you need to know is to walk fast, don't look down, and keep your gaze forward. Now GO!"

I'm pretty sure Sheila has passed out. I, for one, am shitting bricks.

"GO, I SAID!" Diana screams. So I hop up and walk off in the woods. And guess what? It's not that bad! Not scary at all, and I don't hurt myself once.

Just kidding!

Every click and twig-break makes me jump out of my skin. Within five minutes I have lost my route. I have no fucking clue what I'm doing.

Nothing looks familiar. I step on something slimy that also crunches. I gag, my foot is wet. I am failing miserably. This cannot get any worse.

And right on time, it starts pouring rain.

"REALLY?!" I shout to the darkness "THIS IS A LITTLE CLICHÉ, NO?" I keep going.

I pause for a moment and close my eyes. I can't see a foot in front of me, so it doesn't make any difference. And the rain kind of feels nice. It actually feels really good. I sit on the ground and tilt my head to the sky, letting the rain fall on my face.

And I start to laugh again. Hard.

"Wait, what the fuck—how did I even get here?" I say to the darkness.

"Like … how the actual fuck did I get here? I was living in a frat house like, a year ago. Now I'm milking goats, getting my ass handed to me by an unhinged witch, and sitting in the mud in the woods?!" I am laughing so hard I can't catch my breath.

"You're a sick fuck and a wickedly funny genius, whoever you are," I say to the sky. "A creative fucking mastermind." I stand up and look forward, and start walking.

"What the fuck," I cackle again, looking forward and continuing on.

I saunter out of the woods, wet and wild but unscathed, ending up back at the Motherwort Nest.

Sheila is already back and she just scurries into her room. It's the closest I've had to a shower in a fucking minute. Did I mention we have to bathe in a creek? I sleep like a rock that night.

AND THE "LEARNING" KEEPS ON COMING. But it's all more Mr. Miyagi from the *Karate Kid* than Hogwarts.

One day, I am sitting and reflecting during goat duty, when Diana stomps onto the scene, her bare feet slamming into the earth like a prison guard's steel-toed boots on cinderblock. "I found the garlic scapes in the *compost*. GO GET THEM."

I do as I'm told, power walking to the compost and back. "Here," I hand her a bunch of gross compost-y, garlic scapes that smell like rot and ass.

"Eat them," she orders.

"I'm *not* eating them," I fold my arms in defiance, no amount of people pleasing and wooing a witch is worth that.

"EAT THEM," she demands.

I look her in the eye. "I'm *not* eating them," I say quietly.

She stares into my soul. "You know *what*? When you're around, I have to constantly look over my shoulder because I don't trust you. You're not trustworthy. And you're a nasty little girl who blames others for her bad behavior," she taunts. "I don't trust you as far as I can throw you. You don't listen. You can't do this, *Annie*."

My blood boils. I've been here for weeks by now and she can't even get my fucking name right? For real? I grin and take a deep breath.

"My name is Ani," I say, dropping the garlic scapes onto the floor. We are locked in an arm wrestle of stunned silence. "Not Annie. Ani. You should know it by now. Ani. I will NOT be called by the wrong name."

And for the first time, a look of pride beams from her wicked face, until she grimaces and starts yelling at Andy about the chicken run being too big.

Who's the baddest witch in town now, *Diana*?

After that, it's like the floodgates have opened. I have officially Found My Voice. One day during a "talking ceremony"—basically a circle where we each get to talk without being interrupted while holding a stick—I finally open up about Johnny and the miscarriage.

"And I found out right before I got here that he immediately moved on and is already engaged to his best friend. It's like I didn't even exist, and none of that mattered. I just don't get why I—"

"STOP IT! STOP!" Diana screams, ripping the stick out of my hand, and breaking the cardinal no-interruptions rule.

"You are NOT here to think about the past. ***Burn your bridges***. Burn. Them. Let the light from the fire guide you back to yourself. Did I invite you here to be stuck in your past? Did I invite you here to tell me about your problems? NO! BURN YOUR BRIDGES." Her face is stone.

I don't respond. This doesn't make sense—I don't get what the rules are. She needs to see that I'm not weak. That I'm a tough bitch. She needs to know the full truth.

So a couple days later I corner her in a field while we are picking snow peas, and spill it all. Michael, my awful introduction to sex and love. The stalking, the violence, the abuse. Partly because I want her to see what I'm made of, and partly because I want to see how someone like her will respond. "And I stared into his eyes, and I swear to you there was no one even in his body. He was catatonic, covered in my blood, staring right back at me."

Diana is silent, staring at me, totally deadpan. Then she just goes back to picking peas and plopping them in her basket. I'm used to getting a teary-eyed "I'm *so* sorry," look. I am used to being treated like delicate glass that could shatter at any moment. Diana's silence is a first, and I'm not sure which reaction makes me more uncomfortable.

I leave the field humiliated and spend the rest of the goat watch with my eyes fixed on the dirt. Just before dinner, I'm foraging some wild mustard greens on the side of the road for my salad (yum?) and I wipe the little bugs off and plop them in my basket. My thoughts are slow moving and heavy like the humid air. I don't cry. I don't feel angry. I just feel ... embarrassed.

Then: "ANI!" Diana's voice booms from her screen door.

I do a loud turkey call toward the sky in response, and begin making my way over to her. (Not my choice—I was told to NEVER yell back, but I need to let her know I heard her—hence the weird gobble gobble into the void).

Her, Andy, and Sheila are all sitting at the fire pit circle. Diana and Andy stand up as I sit down next to Sheila, unable to look anyone in the eye.

"Andy and I would like to perform for you the moment we met," she smiles.

And without missing a beat, they begin a dramatic reenactment of their love story.

"Now, listen here Andy," she acts, very theater kid-esque.

"Promise me that you will honor me just as you would if I were the Goddess herself?" They lock eyes, and Andy gets on one knee, and kisses her hand as if she's knighting him.

"You have my word, I will always see the Goddess in you."

Then they dance, they smooch, and they continue their show. I've never seen Diana lit up before. I've never seen her jovial, playful, and happy like this. It is very sweet. And very weird. They turn towards Sheila and I, and take a bow. We clap, and I can't help but grin.

"Ani." Oh shit. Mean witch Diana is back at the steering wheel.

"The first way you give up your power on a very primal, animalistic level, is when you look up at someone. Never, ever tilt your chin up and look above you at someone, that's how you show submission in the animal world," she looks me up and down. She exhales. "You are short." She studies my length. "So when you meet people, stand far enough away from them so that you never look up to anyone. Ever. That's your first step to making sure what happened to you never happens again."

"And get yourself a sweetheart that promises to honor you right off the bat. And hold him to it. He'll still piss you off while honoring you, make no mistake. But when that happens, just shave your pubic hair, let it grow back stubbly, and then *really* screw him. Perfect revenge," she advises with a wink and a smirk.

Oh my Goddess, magic is real! Did Diana just make a joke? Holy shit!

IT ALL SORT OF COMES together when Sheila and I are instructed to meet Diana in the Motherwort Nest for something called "a release." Thomas is coming, and Sheila told me he's the "energy" teacher who teaches us all of the mysteries of energy mastery. It's about damn time for some blatant magical lessons! I walk through the Motherwort Nest doors, and Diana is sitting there, spine straight, groaning as she exhales.

We sit next to her in silence, close our eyes, backs straight, and breathe with her (but I'm not making that god awful noise I'm SORRY).

Suddenly, the door flings open, slamming against the wall. I practically start levitating I jump so high, and my eyes shoot open. A portly man who definitely loves steak, with a big cloud of marshmallow hair, a broad nose and face, wearing blue jeans with a checkered button down, enters the room.

"CLOSE THOSE EYES," he commands me.

Tell me this is fucking Thomas.

He does a light karate chop to the back of my neck. I don't understand his cue. Is he trying to distract me?

"SIT UP STRAIGHTER," he barks again.

Okay, this shit is only okay when Diana does it.

"Ani, open your eyes. Look at me," he instructs. I do.

We gaze at each other.

"What did you notice about your body when I burst through the door?" he asks.

"Uh, I was scared and I jumped."

"Your eyes. Your eyes were open, round, alert. It's to help you see. Fear opens your eyes so you can really see if there's any actual danger. What else did you notice?"

"Uh ... I got nervous and jittery?"

"Yes, fear gives you adrenaline, to help you run away if you see danger. Your body knows what she's doing. But you have to reset the body. Sheila, Diana ... let's get to it."

They lay me flat on the disgusting carpet of the Motherwort Nest. Diana and Thomas hold down my head and Sheila holds down my feet. Am I like ... about to go through an exorcism? What is going on? I wonder, as they begin to maneuver my body.

"Open your eyes up as wide as you can," Diana orders. She starts to breathe heavily and makes a guttural sound. "Go on, copy me. Do that same breathing." Within ten seconds I have no control of my body. Like none. I start kicking and flopping around, almost demonically. I hear them in the room but I can't make out what they are saying, my body is just convulsing.

"SLOW YOUR BREATH. Breathe with me." I feel Diana's hands on my head, I look up and focus on her eyes.

I try to steady my breath. My hands are lobster claws, locked up and against my chest.

"The fuck?" I ask, starting to panic but also in awe.

"We're going to do it again. But this time, listen to my direction." She presses into my head gently but powerfully, letting me know she's there. "Do not lose my voice."

They do it again.

And again, within ten seconds I am kicking the air like a deranged demon.

I feel like my head is about to spin as I start spewing green bile.

"Stop it. Stop kicking, Ani. Stop kicking. Ani, hear my voice. You did it, it's over. You got away. Stop kicking," Diana repeats over and over.

I'm finally able to hear her. Not just listen, but actually hear her. I stop kicking and I cry. I cry and cry and cry and cry. I don't even know at what. I have no thoughts.

And then it just—

stops.

"Go look at yourself in the mirror," Diana whispers.

I pull myself to my knees and scoot over to the mirror. I look into my eyes and greet the reflection of myself like I'm meeting someone new. Like an alternate universe me—my eyes seem rounder maybe ... something is different, but I can't fully place it.

"What do you notice?" Diana's voice coos behind me.

"I—I look like a kid again," I stammer.

"You look soft. You're soft now." She pauses. "And now is the time to cry. Let it all flow out, now. I'm here."

THERE ARE JUST TWO WEEKS of the apprenticeship left when Diana informs us that Sheila and I will be assisting her on a Wise Witch weekend, when a group of other women will be coming to learn from her.

"Ani, you are to teach the new students how to forage this weekend and show them how to clean up after dinner," Diana informs me during our morning gathering.

"But I don't know how to forage, like fully! We haven't really gotten that far yet!" The same feeling of being unprepared for my finals in high school sweeps through me.

"We haven't even learned about plants yet," I panic-whisper to Sheila. She's the Type A kind of girl I used to try to copy off of in school. "I'm barely hanging on here myself. All I know is that weird shit is happening. Do you know what's going on here?" My eyes are pleading with hers, and she averts her gaze, just like the annoying brown nosers in high school.

That morning, I spend all of the goat watch studying a field guide to the local plants, so I don't accidentally poison these women.

"Apprentice, oh, hello!!" I hear a friendly voice break my study session.

I see an older woman with long, wavy hair, a snaggletooth, pink lipstick, and a round face with a body to match walking toward me from her car, carrying a little suitcase.

"I'm Mara, the guest teacher for the weekend. I am a priestess of the Goddess, a devotee of Venus, here to bring beauty in all that I do," she says with her chin held high. The warmth in her voice melts my insides.

"Wow! Well, it's nice to meet you. I'm Ani. I'm ... well, I don't know yet, which is why I'm here I guess." I go to help her with her bag, as we walk toward the Motherwort Nest.

"Well, you certainly are in the right place then, Ani. I met Diana forty years ago now, and she helped me get here—a priestess of beauty and a lover of grief."

"What?" I practically drop her suitcase. "Grief?"

"It's the only way to see the beauty." She winks.

She starts telling me her story and I listen carefully. She isn't what society would deem "traditionally beautiful," she says, but beauty is her absolute obsession—and not in the alter-yourself-to-fit-the-male-gaze way; but in the see-yourself-and-everything-as-beautiful-because-it's-all-worth-celebrating way.

"I like this whole thing—your whole thing," I tell her as we reach the wooden deck to the Motherwort Nest.

"Want to try something?" she asks through pink smiling lips.

"Hell yes, Mara. I'll try whatever you got goin' on."

She gently pulls my arms toward her, we're facing each other, and our forearms connect. She grabs below my elbows and I do the same to her.

"Close your eyes if you can," she instructs. I do as I'm told. She starts to hum a tune. It's like her voice is a musical instrument. Her voice carries so much pain. It's beautiful and I can't help but sway along, even though I'm baffled and truly have no idea what's going on, and am also afraid that any minute she's going to ask me to join her.

"Join me," she whispers, in between her now full-on wails.

"Woooooooaaaaaaaaaahhhhhhhhhhhhhhhhhhhhh." She sounds like she's mourning a death. We're still swaying.

"WoooAAAahhhAAahhhhhhAhhhhh." Good god.

"Come on, Ani, you have to grieve to see. Let's do it together."

Fucking. *Christ*. I inhale.

"WOoooAAAAAAHhhhhHHHHHHHHH" I wail with her. And with that, I begin to sob, the tears like a broken dam of rushing water. Mara holds me and continues to sway me as I calm down.

"Life just ... hasn't been that beautiful, ya know?" I sniffle as she just holds me, swaying away.

By the time dinner arrives, I hear Mara and Diana cackling together as I walk up to the kitchen. They are stirring a giant vat of something in a literal cast iron pot; you can't make this shit up.

"We think you need to watch this." Mara slips me a hot pink VHS tape from 1996 with a porn star—apparently named Cherry Saunders—on the cover. "Sex, healing, and the Goddess," reads the title.

"Um ... what?" I can't pretend to hide my confusion. "Is this ... is this a VHS? And like ... a porno?" I can't tell which is more shocking.

"Just this once, you can go watch this upstairs. The Goddess said you need some Cherry." Diana winks, and she and Mara cackle again. "Wait! Take some popcorn!" Mara laughs, scooping some out of the cauldron. Really?! It's like Christmas morning, except pagan and several cardinal sins are going down! I take the video and the popcorn, and book it to the super secret second floor, which OH MY GOD has had a motherfucking TV this whole time!?

I pop in the tape and some really cheesy wakka wakka sex music starts playing. My pussy smirks.

"Did you know the Goddess LOVES sex?" Me and my pussy gasp, as the voluptuous brunette Cherry whips the screen with her leather nipple tassels.

"Did you know that every time you delight in pleasure, the Goddess smiles and an angel orgasms?"

I just shove popcorn into my mouth like a heathen.

I devour the VHS that night, as terrible 1990s graphics tell me how to love my pussy, be "sex-positive," and how to actually enjoy fucking (whoever you want, whenever you want, as long as everyone is down!).

Watching the tape, part of me is lit up, and part of me feels sick and sad. I know I can do this. I know I can have sex like Cherry. I know I can be free. I get on my knees and give the sky a wink before I pray.

"Hi God ... dess? Goddess? God? Whoever—please just don't take sex from me. I wanna be able to just have sex, to fall in love, to be ravished, to be wild! I have literally only felt free at a music festival dancing to bass music on drugs. I wanna get fucked into ecstasy instead of taking it. Y'know? Show me the path. Okay ... do I end this with Amen or are we past that? Thank you, I love you, goodbye for now."

Two days later and it's time. A motley crew of middle-aged women arrive for the retreat, and all I can talk to them about in our opening session is sex. We don't spend more than five minutes on the plants. Diana screams at me, but I am in bliss, because I, Ani Ferlise, am going to be able to have sex one day and not just lay there, but like actually love myself and my body enough to really go for it. I just know it.

The first night, all the women are gathered around a fire. I haven't talked in front of a group in, like forever, so you best bet I'm giving them the ol' razzle dazzle like I'm the host of a 1970s variety show. I've been ranting for about twenty minutes about the magic of masturbation (It can be a form of prayer! How wild!) when Diana walks up to the fire.

"It's time to discover our Goddess archetypes. Each of you is to do this quiz, and then embody your result in a piece of ritual theater. Get creative. You have two hours until we meet up to perform."

"Perform?" I mouth to Sheila whose brows are so furrowed it looks like they fainted.

"Perform!" Mara catches me and smiles.

Sheila and I go take a break from being witch camp counselors, and head back to the Motherwort Nest to take the quiz. It is fifty-three questions long but I know who I'm going to get. The love-magnet, sex-driven, all-around beautiful Aphrodite—Goddess of LOVE. As I'm taking the quiz, I dream about how I'm going to perform a whole skit as Aphrodite where I saunter into the room in a clam shell or whatever.

I tally the results at the table, Sheila across from me, busy doing the same. PERSEPHONE—GODDESS OF THE UNDERWORLD.

Uh ... *What*?

I calculate the numbers again. Same answer.

I retake the whole quiz. Same answer.

"Sheila!" I bark, breaking the silence and making her jump.

"Sorry, Sheila? I'm getting Persephone. Isn't she like, the girly grim reaper?"

Sheila's brows relax, her whole body looks like it wakes up, and a smirk stretches across her face. "I knew it," she sneers mischievously. "I am also a Persephone. You reek of her. Think about it. Persephone was this young maiden and had to go through extreme darkness. But she didn't crumble. She became the Goddess of the underworld." I've never seen Sheila so ... smooth. She's transforming in front of my very eyes.

"I mean think about it. Your first experience with sex was just like hers ... let's say it wasn't, well, great. And you know, she gets stuck in the underworld because she was tricked. Hades offered her the pomegranate seeds, knowing if she ate them she would be stuck there with him. We ate the pomegranate seeds. And we trudged through the darkness of those next few years. We're still in the darkness now. But we aren't maidens in distress, we are Goddesses of the underworld." She beams.

"I have something for you. There's a modern-day Persephone I've been dying to show you, and you share a name. Do you know Ani DiFranco?"

"Not really, should I?"

In yet another shocking twist of events, Sheila busts out an illegal fucking laptop.

"Sheila, you sneaky sonofabitch, I am in love with what is happening right now!" I feel like I'm actually high, and she smiles even more smugly and lovingly.

"This is called 'Not A Pretty Girl'—it's always reminded me of you. Of me. Of us. Our little team here." She lays on the gross carpet with her knees up. I lay next to her and we close our eyes. Taking it in.

Ah yes, the Goddess of the Underworld. I start to rehash my relationship with death. I remember that when I was a kid, I was all about helping people cross over. How I often dreamt of mass shootings and natural disasters the night before it happened. How when I would go to music festivals, I was the one who was there when people went over to the dark side and freaked out. How I'm the first one on-site to car accidents. If there is a hint of death in the ethers, I seem to find it. A death even happened inside my body.

All this time, I've been trying to fix this—thinking I must be bad luck, or that my shit energy is just attracting more of it. But what if ... *what if this is my path?*

For my performance, I take the one candy bar I've been saving since I got here. I lay on the floor in front of everyone, just like Sheila and I were doing. And I simply eat the candy bar, enjoying every morsel, melting on the wooden floor of the creepy cabin, surrounded by strangers looking for hope and a taste of the sweetness of life.

"Ahh, Persephone. You've made it." I can hear Diana's smile through her raspy words.

8
Jealous Bitch

I'm back in Oregon and back on my bullshit!

It's time to settle into the town after being MIA with no contact with the outside world. If I can make it work at Diana's place, I can make it work anywhere, right? The truth is, I need some *friends*. So I do what all logical, lonely girls do in their twenties: I Go to the Bar and Get Drunk (a memoir).

Listen, it's been fucking lonely in Ashland. And this is the only way I seem to be able to meet people. But I don't want shallow low vibe connections—I want a real one! And now here I am, apocalyptically hungover, housing a breakfast burrito at Anne's Burrito Joint.

My heavy-lidded eyes first catch a glimpse of a flier advertising a "Priestess Communion Weekend." I read it again because my brain feels like it's sludging through mud. *Priestess Communion Weekend*. Beneath the headline, a cluster of otherworldly beauties sit in a circle. Straight spines cloaked in decadent red attire, delicate hands gently pressed into re-laxed-yet-perfectly-flat lower bellies, serene eyes closed, spirits cracked wide open to deep Divinity. My eyes drop down to my own belly, which is neither firm nor relaxed, just burrito bloated and anxious about the room-clearing gas I'll be battling for the next forty-eight hours.

I'm hit with a flash from last night. *Was I flirting with* ...? Oh, *god*. A flashback of me doing my Judy Garland impression to a group of unconsenting strangers hits my gut harder than the greasy burrito. Why am I such a hot mess? I learned how to "be in my power" and be a bit more fearless with Diana, but I feel like it isn't translating the way I hoped it would in real life.

I look back at the priestess flier. Didn't I move to this tiny little hippie town in Ashland because it's supposed to be this portal for deep spiritual healing? I mean, I walked away from everything I'd ever known so I could be the Spiritual Bitch I'd always wanted to be. Yet here I am. The same ol' messy, nightlife lovin' Ani I've always been. I stare at the poster again, and notice that the magical Priestess Weekend is only six days away. My eyes scan the text. And. Oh. My. *God*. It's being held at a Goddess Temple. Oh, hell yes. Fuck it upppp! This messy ass bitch is going to the motherfucking Goddess Temple where I will find my people.

The day before I am set to leave, I stare into the mirror as I clip in long, silky hair extensions, so I can embody the flowy, effortless, boho, spiritual bombshell bitch of my dreams. I make sure to apply *just enough* mascara to enhance my eyes but still give me a chill "no make-up" girl look. I run to my closet and quietly apologize to the sequin and velvet blazers I'll be neglecting for the time being, and grab a white silk vintage slip that's stuffed in the back. It's pretty much the only thing I own that is just one solid color.

Then I pack my Barbie-pink leather duffle bag with all of my magical items: a leather-bound journal, a few haphazard crystals, a tangle of necklaces, and of course, my blankie. Yeah, I'm not over blankie yet. I've had him since the moment I stumbled out of the womb, which means I'm either co-dependent; stuck in some unearthed childhood trauma; or it's got magical healing powers. I don't know. I don't care. I love it. Then I strap motorcycle boots to my feet. I'm self-aware enough to know that combat boots are probably not the vibe, but I'd rather die than wear Birkenstocks (gag!).

I sloppily shove my duffle bag into the trunk of my little car, put on my adventure playlist, and head off in the direction of the Temple. I teeter between dry-heaving wondering what the fuck I'm getting myself into, and feeling flutters of excitement as I envision a sacred, sensual version of Hogwarts awaiting me. What if it's a cult? Where do I even get off going to a priestess weekend when I've never been initiated as a priestess?

As I drive down a long, windy, dirt road, all alone, I do my best to imagine myself basking in t*he beauty* of the *Earth* as I walk barefoot and dainty through a field of wildflowers. I cringe. The crescendo of "You Can't Always Get What You Want" by the Rolling Stones blasts my eardrums as particles of dust fly everywhere. I'm here.

I lower the volume and park next to other the cars; every single one a Subaru. No, really. Every. Single. One. I get out of the car. My eyes lap up a sea of bare-faced, lanky women. It's all soft smiles, headpieces draped across dewy foreheads, and pore-less faces peeking out of long gorgeous hair, like two silk curtains framing a sunny window. Flowy white and red cotton dresses cling tightly to tall, slender bodies. Words gracefully ooze out of hydrated lips. I am a meatball. A round meatball in a world of sinewy strings of spaghetti. I take a deep breath and pray my hair extension tracks aren't showing.

I stomp in my motorcycle boots over to the skinny spaghetti girls and announce myself boldly, "Heya gals!"

Heya?... Gals? Fucking really?

Through soft gazes and smiles, I am met with a collective whisper of a "hi" and that's about it. I find myself standing on the outside of the circle, not quite sure how to interact. Dreaded scenes from middle school flash through my mind. All the popular girls showing off the new Hollister jeans I could never fit into; me desperately trying to show off the purple sparkly belt I proudly but poorly crocheted myself; the cool girls rolling their eyes and walking away in that Victoria's-Secret-body-spray kind of way.

Sweat droplets emerge on my upper lip. This is a new low. I am NOT about to be the weird kid with lip sweat in gym class. You know the kind. Always smelled like tuna salad sandwiches and loved Linkin Park?

Mean Girl Ani quickly takes control of my brain. She chews gum. She says: "Listen. You're cool now, bitch. You came here from **New York**. You've gone to warehouse parties in **Brooklyn**. You've seen poetry on the *Bowery*. You've gotten your damn ass wiped by an old terrifying witch— you're good."

"You're right," I whisper back at her. I feel relieved—until Self-Hating Ani comes flying into the scene so aggressively that she knocks Mean Girl Ani into the dirt. She puts her hands on her hips. "Listen," she taunts. "You're a chunky little meatball mess. Everyone here is so much skinnier than you. And that big ass mouth of yours? You're already freaking everyone out, coming on so strong, with that loud ass East Coast fog horn of a voice."

A stage appears in my mind. Mean Girl Ani stands to stage left, Self-Hating Ani to stage right. In perfect unison, they walk to the center. The lights dim. The show is about to start.

Mean Girl Ani: Okay I might be shorter and curvier than these gals, but I'm not, like, the ugliest. Plus, this shit they're listening to? IT FUCKING SUCKS.

Self-Hating Ani: Keep complaining about the music. Doesn't eradicate the fact that you're by far the fattest, ugliest troll here.

Mean Girl Ani: Fine. I'm ugly! At least I'm funny. Funnier than these wet fucking blankets.

Self-Hating Ani: Your humor is only relatable to Tri-state trash and you know it.

Mean Girl Ani: You're a dick. I'm a badass bitch who has more personality in my left pinky than these granola ass bitches do in their entire 95-pound bird-boned bodies.

The one act play between my two selves is interrupted by a drum playing a steady beat. I realize I've been staring intently into a patch of dead grass for several minutes. To the beat of the drum, the girls gather around the fire. I guess I didn't get the memo that drum beats mean "flock to the fire" in Priestess. Oops. A large circle is forming and I awkwardly wedge my meatball body between two ethereal women. My head aligns roughly with their shoulders. I am suddenly painfully aware of how coffee-stained my dress is. How loud the jangle of my bracelets is as they CLANK CLANK CLANK against each other. How *toxic* my anxious BO smells.

"Welcome sisters and beloved daughters of the Earth," muses a cloaked, beautiful-in-a-serious-way woman who I recognize from the flier as the hostess of this "experience." "I am priestess Maeve. I am not a high priestess, because I don't believe in hierarchies here. We are equals. All of us. Let's join hands." I wipe my sweaty palms on my coffee-stained dress real subtle before joining hands with my fellow Sisters of the Earth.™

She continues, "Please speak your full name out loud, and your intention for being here."

The first person up is named Kale. No really—*Kale.*

Kale takes a very, *very* breathy pause between each word to sound more intentional. "I (BREATH) am (BREATH) claiming (BREATH) standing (BREATH) in (BREATH) my (DEEP DEEP DEEP BREATH) power" (EXHALE). Next is Star Cloud. Star Cloud also makes the same breathy proclamation of power, taking her painfully sweet time between each word. I think I might be hallucinating when a girl introduces herself as Love-Grace.

Every intention is pretty much the same — a very slow, very breathy, pause-between-each-word-to-sound-more-intentional, eyes-closed claim to stand in their power. I wonder what the fuck that even means for some-one named *Kale*—like, telling the vendor at the farmer's market to make sure there's no gluten in her raw veggie bowl? Shit. It's my turn. My fin-gers tremble theatrically like I'm an extra in the background of a made-for-TV movie about Why Drugs Are Bad. I clamp down on the hand I'm holding, hoping it will quell the DTs. I straighten my spine. My tongue is large and dry in my mouth. *Fuck it.*

"Hi, I'm Ani. My intention is to, ya know, see what's up and connect!" I sputter quickly.

I know that I don't fit in here. I know that I don't want to fit in here. Seriously ... *Kale*?

As the sharing continues, I feel myself mentally checking out with each breathy declaration of some spiritual cliché or other. Then I see a woman with her eyes closed, dirt covering her bare feet, suddenly stand-ing in the center of the circle, breaking "the flow" of the introductions.

"I ... am ... Mary ... Magda ... LION!" She sucks in a gallon of air, holds it for thirty long seconds, and then releases a "RAWWWWR" from the depth of her guts. She is clearly going for "primal lion" but she's actually serving a more ten-year-old-boy-cannonballing-into-the-condo-pool vibe. She proudly makes eye contact with every single person in the circle with forced ferocity while *growling* under her breath.

I feel a switch flip from within.

A *sinister* little switch.

I am nasty and I am going to spend the weekend being a total asshole. Why? 'Cause this is fucking weak and bullshit and fake. Literally, no one needs to breathe that deep and anyone who claims to like the taste of salad is a fucking liar, anyway. Diana would tear this place to shreds with her barely human teeth. I mean, come on. Diana might be an unhinged witch with anger management issues, but at least what you see is what you get.

THE NEXT MORNING BEGINS WITH a laughter therapy session in the Goddess temple dome, where we are instructed by the head priestess to laugh on command. "Laughing heals the body and mind," she lectures. Everyone begins to force giggle. The forced giggle turns to a real giggle which quickly progresses into genuine rip-roaring laughter. Some of the group begin to press their foreheads together and rub noses whilst howling. The rest start dramatically jumping up and down in hysterics.

"Let your inner child be SEEN and silly!" Maeve bellows over the side-splitting laughter, to which everyone gets even *more* turnt and forcibly giggles LOUDER, until they're rolling on the floor in their unsoiled white dresses. Then someone purposely and abruptly lets out a loud, long, harrowing (yes, *harrowing*) fart, to which everyone howls even harder. My body tenses aggressively at the twisted Darren Aronofsky-esque movie I am suddenly in. I sit and try to force a small, uncomfortable laugh. I feel damp stains forming a ring beneath my pits.

Then I picture myself at brunch with my friends in New York, entertaining them all with my stories about this cringe shit that only *I*, their hilarious, spiritual friend, would dare to participate in. This is all the fuel I need to get into it.

And the day goes on. And shit gets even darker.

In an "intimacy sister share" (during which we are taught that intimacy is actually "in-to-me-*I*-see") we pair up and stare into the eyes and see the soul of the beloved sister before us. When I stare into the eyes of the woman I'm paired with, I feel a twinge of disgust towards myself. I actually feel *bad* for her. She has to eye-gaze with me—the one person here who can't seem to get it together enough to hold her eye contact—instead of one of the evolved, clear-eyed women of Spirit. I am stuck in a vicious loop of holding back restricted laughter, then darting away and trying to choke back tears.

In the devotional dance session that evening, I feel wildly isolated as everyone just whips off their tops and dances with their tits out like they don't even care. But they have perfect fucking bodies, so why would they? The real kicker is that they don't even really seem to know they all have perfect, perky tits—they seem like they're just having fun. What the fuck is *that*? They're not even drunk; they apparently know how to connect without it.

By nighttime, my head hits the pillow in my tent harder than the sock in the gut that was this Goddess-forsaken day. What the fuck is wrong with me? Why am I judging them so hard when they're just being spiritual and free? It's because I'm not a pretty girl priestess with pretty perky tits. No matter how many places I run to, I will always be way too dramatic, too blunt, too loud, too obnoxious, too bold, and too saggy-titted for the soft, sacred, spiritual world. And you know what the worst part is? These girls aren't losers. Not at all. I'm just a jealous ass bitch.

And it's always been this way.

When I was a kid, it was the kids in my class that sucked. They were mean as shit and couldn't possibly understand my complex seven-year-old brain. When I was a teen, it was the adults that sucked. They were out of touch, symbolic of everything that was "wrong with the world," and trying to repress me. In high school, I decided all the guys were fucking stupid dicks with chili dog brains and all the girls were just vacant try-hards, too air-headed to understand the sophisticated pain of being *alive*. Even in college, when I thought I was becoming exactly who I'd always wanted to be—a *real* rock 'n roll woman, eye-catching in her red lipstick, vivacious in her recklessness—I would still spend every night hate-scrolling people who appeared to be "happy" on social media.

That's just who I am now. And everyone LOVES this bitch, too. She's fucking *fun*. And powerful, and cool! She's palatable and makes people feel good and definitely doesn't remind people of why the world sucks.

Until this weekend, that is. At the Goddess Temple I'm back to square one, feeling a little nervous wreck of a chode who will never have a place in this world. The *drama*.

THE NEXT DAY IS THE water rebirthing ceremony. I shoot my eyes open, realizing I'm late when I hear the drum to gather. We're meeting by the headwaters, a natural, warm mineral spring that comes out of rocks in the shape of—you guessed it—a vagina!

"These are the amniotic fluids of the great mother. As you enter, know you are communing with the Goddess herself. But you must remove all adornments, just as the Goddess Inanna did at the seven gates, to mark your death and rebirth," Maeve instructs us.

With that, each pussy-empowered priestess starts to take everything off. I mean ... everything. *NO.* I frantically dart around, trying to find at least one other person who looks uncomfortable. But everyone has gathered around the small pool, naked and holding hands. There's no escaping this, nor do I fucking want to because there is NO reason why I should feel self-conscious, right? WHY am I SO chained to my shit, man? Who cares if I look like the little green dude from *Monsters, Inc.* I'm just as worthy of entering the amniotic fluids of the great mother, right?

I rip off my dress and kick my undies to the side while I join everyone else in the circle.

One by one, each priestess immerses herself into the sacred water, dunking three times. And when they come out, they look even *more* beautiful than before. Long hair shiny wet and untangled, makeup-free faces bright and refreshed by the minerals in the water, svelte bodies perfectly crystallizing the water droplets held by beautiful tiny goosebumps on beautiful, tiny bronzed limbs. *Every single girl here looks like a flower petal in the morning dew.* I suck in my stomach.

It's my turn. I take a step into the water. I feel like a tadpole, and I want to swim away forever. I can't imagine what I look like. I can't believe I'm doing this. None of this is worth it. I dunk right in, hot angry tears and all, and emerge looking more like a frizzy pube than a priestess. I can feel my not-so-discreet mascara smear itself down my face. My "long" "straight" hair is already kinking and curling and matting, wildly juxtaposing against the pin straight clip-in extensions I've even been *sleeping in.* I look down to see my water droplets resting on the nipple hairs I meant to tweeze before the trip. I have no goosebumps. Just razor bumps.

The drum beats. We dress and dutifully file into a line to head back to the temple. It's time to connect over "the power of our sexuality." AT LAST! My favorite topic. I can add to this, what with everything Cherry's porno taught me. I listen intently as each Goddess takes her turn sharing what epic, surrendered sexual experiences she's had. Each story seems to top the last, with how potently and deeply they claim to be able to express their sexual energy. I quickly realize that me watching Cherry talk about great, empowered sex isn't the same as me actually experiencing it. A woman shares the story of her fifteen-minute-long sacred squirting "Amrita" orgasm. *Well, one time I opened my eyes for a whole second while having sex, so yeah, I totally feel you.*

When we finally sit down to eat, superfood smoothie bowls are placed before us. I listen to the other women gabbing over how AMAZING they are and how ALIVE they feel with every bite. Meanwhile, I'm struggling to keep mine down because the texture is both slimy and chunky at once, like puke. It tastes sweet, but not in like a cake way. In a dirt way? Is dirt sweet? I wonder. My mouth waters. I am suddenly ravenous for my usual breakfast of leftover Spaghetti Bolognese.

Afterwards, while everyone else starts singing Goddess chants around a bonfire that the fire priestess built, I sit far away, sweating with dry mouth. I run to the bathroom. After I blow up the toilet, I rejoin the Goddess circle. The scene around the fire is fucking weird: someone tells the most PG, unfunny anecdote, and everyone laughs like they're at world's most provocative stand-up. It's time to show 'em what they've been missing! I dive right in when I sense my chance to interject, knowing that if nothing else, your gal here? She knows how to get people laughing.

"Alright, you wanna hear a REALLY wild story?" I purr with big glittery eyes. "So this one time, I decided that I *really* needed to get laid, and my friends hooked me up with this guy who literally only went by 'Flame.' And if anyone dared to call him any other name, he would go on a rant about respecting his firefighter uncle because he was his name-sake or some shit," I cackle. "Anyway, despite his greased up guido hair and bedazzled True Religion jeans, I went home with him and he ended up fingerbanging me while he was simultaneously singing an Alice in

Chains song a cappella, not breaking eye contact, AND getting all the lyrics wrong. Mind you this is on a loop." I pause triumphantly to wait for the reaction. The Flame story *always* kills.

"Wow," mutters a woman in a stain-free white dress.

"Yeah, wow," pipes up a girl with boobs that are so high they start singing Creed's hit song to me.

"Yeah ... That's intense ... Has anyone ever used a rose quartz yoni wand?" inquires a woman with hair so long she can sit on it.

A wave of heaviness descends on my body. Mean Girl Ani and Self-Hating Ani are back on stage.

Mean Girl Ani: Yeah, so you don't have any of these wild spiritual sex stories to tell. Or any sex stories that aren't vaguely traumatic or horrifying, apparently. But, you are by far the most *interesting* one here. All these girls are the same. They're losers.

Self-Hating Ani: Whatever. They're more evolved than you, notice how they don't even care about it. And by the way, we all know "unique hot" is just another way of saying "ugly with a personality."

The curtains fall to the floor. The scene is over. For *now*.

But as the weekend wears on, the story builds. I seethe with jealousy and judgment. If these soft, silky creatures are "spiritual women" then what the fuck am I? If *this* is who God loves, if this is how to receive and connect to the Divine, then where the fuck do I stand? Is the reason I've never felt protected or loved by this God force because I am too messy and sexually tarnished to be loved by something so pure? My relationship with Divinity mirrors every other toxic relationship in my life: frizzy-headed me trying so hard to belong, only to realize that I am too weird and creepy and should just crawl into a hole and hide forever.

By dusk that evening, I'm sitting by the fire alone with my questions and self-doubt. I stew on all the times I've felt "other" in my messy life.

My mind is dark. I start picking at the mosquito bites on my legs until they bleed, letting my eyes glaze over as I stare into the flames.

"What's alive for you, Ani?" Maeve sits down next to me and I cringe at my bloodied shins.

"Eh, ya know, just feelin' sorry for myself and melting into a pool of self-hatred and despair. The usual."

She turns her whole body toward me and looks me in the eyes, holding my gaze. For some reason I start to chuckle.

"I'm here, I can hold space."

"Just ... why am I like ... this," I croak, vaguely gesturing at myself.

"And what may that be?"

"A fucking mess. I've literally sang to goats and I still can't seem to get it together. I don't feel powerful or like the Goddess of the underworld. I don't feel 'cool girl' broken like young Angelina Jolie. I feel just—unpleasant." I have officially cracked. "I am constantly in chaos and if I'm not, I create it. I feel like I'm always hanging on by a fucking thread." Boom. I plop on the floor next to this mystical stranger and sob away, which, if you couldn't tell, is very out of character for me.

She holds me and rocks me like the giant needy baby that I am. "Look at me," her stare is so intense it's like her soul reached out through her pupils and is hugging mine.

"You are not broken. Nothing needs to be fixed. Do you think everyone here doesn't feel everything you're feeling? We all carry this wound. The 'not enoughness,' the unworthiness, it's designed to take you away from who you really are, and our culture sets it up this way."

"But what if I'm like, *actually* not enough and not worthy? Like I'm a huge sack of shit. I've been tearing everyone here to shreds in my head—including *you*—this entire time."

"That part of you — the part that tears everyone to shreds? That part of you has kept you safe your entire life. Notice what happens when that angry, upset, competitive, or jealous voice comes out. What happens next, Ani? Think about all the times you've felt this way. What happens next? Let your mind float." Maeve reaches into her basket and pulls out a small rattle and begins to play it.

I gaze into the fire. The flames dance like a snake charmer.

And I'm thirteen again. Looking at the confident, funny girls taking up space in the cafeteria, as I remain chained to my nice, shy girl identity. I seek comfort by ruminating over how obnoxious and overbearing these stupid sluts are. I talk shit about the stupid sluts all the time. Snicker about their blowjob lives behind their backs. But deep down, I wish more than anything that a boy wanted me to give him a blowjob.

I am fifteen again. Making snide comments to my friend Rachel about the popular girl who gets any guy she wants. "She's not even *hot*," I hiss, so desperately wanting to get any guy I want, or at least a lick of attention that wasn't me being made fun of.

And now I'm watching a highlight reel. It spans through several ages and stages of my life and replays all the times I've bashed the passionate and opinionated people for speaking their minds in class or online.

The crackling fire in front of me suddenly illuminates a *holy shit* kind of truth. The jealousy, judgy side of my nature has actually been showing me every single thing I've ever wanted to have or to be.

I wanted attention! I wanted to be seen! I wanted to be wanted! The confident, loud, funny girl? I wanted to be able to express myself and break free from being fucking nice all the time! I wanted to sprawl out, speak up, and take up space! The slut-shaming? Holy fuck, if being a slut meant claiming your sexual desires without apology, I wanted to be the biggest slut on the planet. The passionate, opinionated people I scoffed at? I wanted so badly to SCREAM my opinions from the ROOFTOPS, but I was too afraid of being laughed at or sounding dumb. Yet staying silent was making me feel like I was going to explode. And even though I would literally *never* wear Birkenstocks or talk that slow, with that many breaths, I do, now—more than anything—want to be *spiritual*.

I wipe the snot from my nose. "Fuck." I turn my head and face the priestess.

"Yeah, fuck," she smirks and we both start cackling.

"I want to be all the things I'm making everyone here out to be. I want to feel beautiful in my body. I want to feel free in my sexuality. I want to be comfortable changing my name to fucking Kale if I damn well please!" I cry-laugh, finally able to meet her eyes. "I want to be spiritually connected. I want to be uncomplicated. Less fucked-up. Less aggressively me. More okay with myself!"

"Ani," the priestess laughs, "I'm from LAWNG ISLAND. I used to dance on the bar at Zachary's and I was a go-go dancer at Limelight. I'm aggressive, abrasive, AND soft and gentle." Suddenly, Maeve looks like she's sporting sharp liquid lines with huge hair sprayed hair.

"ZACHARY'S?! My dad used to be a bouncer there!" More cackles.

"But Maeve ..." I lean in closer. "From one Long Island girl to another ... this is, like, a little bit cringe, right? Like it's beautiful but a tiny bit, like, contrived?"

"Listen," she starts, ready to dish the tea. "This is a special weekend. An honoring of the priestess. 'Cause lemme tell ya what," her Long Island accent really starts showing now and I can feel my pupils dilate. "Being a priestess is NOT being a princess," she grins. "It's not about the flowy dresses and the flowery words. It's chopping wood, carrying water, and being in service not just to yourself, but to the community. This isn't a princess school, it's a priestess school. This isn't playing dress-up, it's about going into the depths and seeing how you could show up."

Goosebumps. I sit up taller, remembering when we talked about making sure everything is more beautiful than when we arrived, down to public bathrooms. And making sure the elders are taken care of in the community, keeping them company, cleaning their homes, making sure they are well fed. And making sure parents are supported and have meals and childcare.

"And guess what? You don't have to be perfect. Outside of the retreat, we get to work. We are the bees, a hive. You think people don't annoy the shit outta me? No one knows how to sweep a damn floor! My Italian mother would have a heart attack if she saw the way some people around here work."

Something in the loud cackle and critical nature toward household cleaning sparks something deep and familiar inside of me. It's as if all of my ancestors came through my body. And something clicks. Why not apprentice with Maeve?

"Hey, Maeve ... do you think I can help out and just, like, clean every week?" Maeve shoots up and stretches her hands to the sky.

"YOU ARE THE ANSWER TO MY PRAYERS TO THE YONIVERSE! BLESSED BE!" she yells, her voice way too loud to be bellowing out of such a tiny being. The red flames moving behind her delicate silhouette make her outburst seem all the more dramatic.

There's one more day of the weekend to go, and I decide to give it a real whirl. Every time Mean Girl Ani sneers inside of me, I commit to breathing into her. I let her know that I'm listening, then I ask her the golden question: Bitch, what do you *really* want?

I walk over to my hot pink suitcase and look inside. Sitting at the tippy top of a messy pile of wrinkled slip dresses is a spiritual tool I'd forgotten I even owned, let alone packed: Curiosity. I crawl out of my tent, clutching it like a healing crystal.

And I begin to ask these women about themselves. I ask questions about shit I truly want to know more about. Curiosity becomes the referee, standing between Mean Ani and Self-Destructive Ani. And once Curiosity takes the lead, I gotta say, my opinions about everyone completely change. It turns out that almost every single woman—headpiece or not— has a WILD story of her own. A story of deep pain, bravery, and triumph. A story of feeling like a failure. A story of being made fun of for her kooky style. A story of an unfortunately timed queef or an embarrassing stumble during a sacred intimacy ritual.

I clutch my heart at times. I cry with laughter at times. But mainly I realize that Jealousy and Judgment have trapped me in a cage of isolation. Prevented me from connecting with amazing people and experiencing their BIG, FUNNY, MESSY magic.

Everyone is standing in a circle around the fire for the closing ritual; we all hold hands. This time, I don't feel so weird. We are close by sharing one commitment we're going to make to claim the path of the priestess.

"Even though I'm still pretty new and don't quite get what a priestess is, I'm committed to learning, coming here and cleaning, and meeting everyone, including me, with a bit more curiosity." I beam.

A collective deep breath washes through the circle.

"And so it is!" everyone cheers.

9

Goddess Bitch

"Do we sweep up the cobwebs or do we leave them sacred?" I call to Maeve from across the dome temple. She's organizing the candle cabinet while I spruce up the floral arrangements on the temple's main altar. Tonight is the Dance of the Rose ritual. I wish I could tell you I know what that means.

"That is ... the witchiest question ever to exist—I love it, I'm obsessed. But let's, uh sweep 'em up for tonight? Make the place feel clean and organized so people can show up as messy as they want," Maeve hums, excitedly.

"On it. And can you actually break down what's going down tonight? Are we, like, busting a move in the name of the Goddess? Is it something I need to memorize?" I rush to the woodstove and start sweeping up the soot and putting away bundles of rosemary and lavender and twirling up the cobwebs.

"You'll see." Maeve raises her brow. "Twenty-two minutes. Twenty-two women. Two serpents. Lots of chocolate and roses." I watch her busily replace the tea candles in the hanging lanterns.

"Maeve? I'm not gonna lie, this is sounding a little orgy-esque."

The sound of Maeve's signature cackle is like surround sound in the temple dome.

"I had one of those once, after a Van Halen concert. But this is not that."

Maeve is a total pixie, flinging her tiny little body all over the temple in preparation. She pauses for a moment to tie up her dirty blonde hair, revealing a faint crescent moon tattoo on the nape of her neck. She scrunches her button nose (its tiny size, I've learned, is the result of a nose job she endured in hopes to make her more "castable" when she was a young actress), picks up an oversized basket of freshly chopped kindling, and bends down to place it by the woodstove, revealing a massive tattoo of a tree that sprawls across the entirety of her petite little back. She's in her fifties, but you'd never be able to tell—she can flip from being an ancient crone running a Goddess Temple, to a young hopeful hippie hanging at CBGB with legendary groupie (and sick memoirist) Pamela Des Barres.

Tonight is the first ceremony I'm helping out with. And in all honesty, I'm *shitting* myself.

When we finally are done setting up, the temple dome feels as magical as it looks. Dozens upon dozens upon dozens of lit candles flicker, their orange glow the only source of light in the dome. Ancient-sounding music plays softly. The woodstove roars. The giant, ornate altar stands proudly in front of the dome windows. It smells of smoldering lavender and rosemary.

One by one, people begin to pile in. A group of women and non-binary people enter, their faces serious as they silently make their way to an open seat. Once everyone is seated, we are provided with instructions from Maeve, who sits in the circle with us:

"Two will come up at a time. The rest of us will witness in empty presence—meaning no intention, no trying to fix, tweak, or have any agenda other than witnessing." Maeve gently lectures. I take in the group, which is definitely different from the initial one I met in this space. Bodies of all shapes and sizes are sitting, listening, and about to witness *me*. A narcissistic shudder—equal parts nerves, equal parts turned on by the pending attention—bolts down my spine. *Get empty, Ani—pay attention.*

"You never know what your movements will unlock in others. And you never know what theirs will unlock inside of you. You will receive and give exactly as you should—this is not about performance; it is not about trying; it is about slowly letting whatever wants to move through you, move through you. It's a story without words, a transmission, a download without explanation or speaking." Maeve turns to an older woman who is the only one sitting in a velvet chair to the side of the circle. "Gaila, it's time for the temple serpents."

The older woman bows her head solemnly, then reaches down for her basket, her long, thin, salt and pepper curls falling to one side.

"Snakes are not evil," Maeve's eyes pierce the room. "They are a symbol of the Goddess. Tonight, you'll have a remembering. Something deep and inexplicable. A homecoming."

"Don't question it," her eyes meet mine from across the circle. "You already know how to do this."

Staying true to myself, I'm questioning it. *First of all— is there a difference between snakes and serpents? Are they like, trained or something? Or am I about to get my shit rocked by a real snake with real fangs? Also, what if God doesn't move through me and I miss the transmission? What if my download is glitchy? What if—*

My thoughts are cut off when the two younger priestesses sitting at Gaila's feet offer to carry the basket up and walk it wordlessly toward Maeve. Gaila, easily in her 70s, follows them. Maeve locks eyes with her and bows. The eerie, ancient-sounding music gets louder. I can't look away, my whole body buzzing but grounded. I flash on parties where the bros would hold the legs of the person doing the keg stand; how times have changed.

Wordlessly, the two younger women move in front of the main altar and stand before us all. They close their eyes, and stand facing us. Then they begin to move, slow, steady, graceful, and powerful. The air is dense, the energy of anticipation spirals and cocoons all of us as they swirl their hips, slowly, peeling off their tops, letting them drop to the floor, their eyes still closed. The two priestesses drape a snake on Gaila's shoulders first, then Maeve. And they begin to move with the snakes as they weave around them, under their breasts, up their backs, down their arms. There is no fear, just pure presence.

I only flinch when I feel a warm teardrop fall on my inner thigh, but I never break my gaze. Every movement Gaila makes is so intentional, yet also without thought. I've never seen an older person move like this, her own inertia moving her slowly, spiraling with a snake, small billows of smoke moving with them. The tiny flames of the candles cast light on her expressionless face, which emanates a raw emotion, casting a spell on me. The snake slowly slithers as she spirals, spirals, bends, and spirals.

Twenty-two minutes later and I know life isn't ever going to be the same again. My heart, which has become so hardened towards beauty, is cracked open—it's as if I have been wearing a veil that has been lifted and I am seeing clearly for the first time. I watch as each pair goes up and dances as if they are being moved by magic. I am completely enthralled; each body is as unique as the human moving it. I've never experienced this kind of beauty. I've never seen bodies evoke this kind of awe and energy.

Then it's my turn to go up. I walk up like I'm about to enter the gates of the underworld itself. I slide my spaghetti straps down and slink my arms through, letting my top fall to the ground—the only thing on my body is a long black skirt I borrowed from Maeve. I close down my eyes so I don't have to think about, never mind *see*, anyone's reaction to my body. I breathe into it, placing my hands over my lower belly, and feel the smallest bolt of electricity from my hand to my belly button.

Wake up.

I whisper internally to my body.

Wake up. It's time to wake up.

The music sounds like the Armenian songs of prayer I grew up with. My hips start swirling ever so slightly like I added oil to a rusty machine. The cogs start budging. I jerk forward before slowly starting to swirl and suddenly I feel the cool skin of the snake's belly being placed on my shoulders. It immediately slinks down my chest, slowly wrapping around my bare waist, then slithering up my back. I feel its tongue graze my neck as it makes its way down my chest, steadily dictating the way my body moves. I carefully move to my hands and knees, rolling my hips, the snake snaking its way around my whole torso.

Then a surge of energy bolts my spine straight. I gasp, grabbing at my lower belly. I gulp another sudden breath of air, my head turned upward, eyes closed, chest open, and slowly heave it out. I am vapor, drinking in gulps of awe-stricken air.

I am cataclysmic. I don't have control. My legs are earthquakes and the aftershocks move through my pelvis and up, up, up, up my spine. The snake spirals around my left arm and moves up my neck.

I am making love to the awe that I'm letting in. What feels like black tar stuck inside of me begins to melt with the warmth of my body as I circle my hips, on my knees, liquefying any fear into fluid motion as I start to move deeper, bigger.

I'm on all fours, swirling, unfurling. My body is molten magic. My blood is magma. My core is the crust of the Earth. Etheric energy emits from my hands. I move to my knees again, bending my head and chest backward, slowly moving my hands down my chest, then over every square inch of skin. My cells buzz like bees. The snake rests in between my breasts, slinked over my shoulders.

I curl down. The snake coils around my arm again. I hear myself let out a wail. I wind my hips deeper, planting my forehead on the ground. My hair falls out of my bun and tickles my shoulders, and I am spiraling my entire body. The snake uncoils from my arm and slides down my back.

A smirk stretches across my face. I am crazed, connected, conjuring. I hear myself laugh, my face still buried on the ground. The sound reverberates from my bones so loudly that the calcified, hardened pieces of my heart break off and fall into the black hole in my gut.

My eyes are open.

AFTER THAT NIGHT, NOTHING IS the same. But not in the I'm-healed-from-body-shame way that I initially thought—that faded pretty quickly after, when I caught a glimpse of myself in the mirror later and realized my boobs look like Mr. Krabs' eyes.

But still, I have a hope that I've never had. Like there is a different path than the inevitable doom I always thought was coming.

Nothing has ever clicked like priestessing does. Priestessing makes everything sacred. Cleaning is a sacred cleansing ritual. Choosing an outfit evokes energy. I twirl around fire at night and live my life in service, especially outside of the temple. If a baby is crying in a market and a parent is overwhelmed, I offer to help. If a public bathroom is filthy, I feverishly clean it so I can leave it more beautiful than when I arrived. If there's an elder in the community that needs household support, I go. The focus of my life is now *practical priestessing*.

With Maeve, I am being initiateded into to hold the major thresholds of life, in service to people through the gates of change.

Menstruation, marriage, birth, divorce, menopause, seasons, cycles, sovereignty, elemental magic, sex, and death. All literally and metaphorically.

I embrace death. After the Persephone archetype with Diana—and realizing that my "darkness" was not in fact my "shadow" and something to fix or get rid of, but rather an inability to bypass the very blatant reality that every single thing will die, shift, and change—I start training to be a hospice volunteer to be with people as they pass. I get involved with death cafes, where a bunch of people gather over cupcakes and tea to talk about the one thing our culture refuses to face: the end of life.

And day in and day out, I work to heal my shit.

But as I descend deeper into my death studies, I realize how much grief I have about being alive.

I feel like I'm missing out on so much shit. I have wasted so much of my life in fear, or in trying to be something I'm not, just to have a glimpse at feeling connected. But at the end of the day, I was desperately trying to make myself "good" enough—and I'm starting to get that itch again. I've always felt like I'm on the outside looking in at life. I scroll through Instagram and see people who are doing big things in the world, going out with their friends, laughing, and I'm still here trying to heal enough to enjoy the small things.

I slide my snake cuff to my upper left arm (a symbol of the priestess) to let the world know I have something to offer. I walk between worlds, one bare foot in each, all while knowing I don't really have a leg to stand on.

I am a ghost in this town. I walk into a patchouli-scented room and I am sensed but not seen. I'm transparent, but terrified of people seeing through me. I hover around when chaos is conjured and then disappear, and every time someone tries to extend a hand to me it moves right through me.

I watch people laughing at jokes I still can't laugh at because laughing is hard for me. I'm a dense, heavy energy that darkens the room when people are basking in each other's light. With every mention of connection and community in these spaces, I feel like I'm on my tiptoes looking through a window at a reality I can't reach.

I'm just passing through.

IT'S NIGHTTIME. IT'S RAINING. Patrick Swayze is swaying his tail next to me while I stare into my dead eyes at my white wooden vanity in the never-been-visited-by-others Fun Girl Salon. It is littered with dried-out old makeup that I haven't touched in forever.

"Same," I whisper to Patrick.

"Jesus fucking Christ! I want fucking friends!" I snap, into my reflection.

"Well, look at ya. When was the last time you brushed your hair? Wore glitter? No offense, but who would think you were down for a good time?" my reflection tells me, matter-of-factly. I can't even be mad. The bitch is right. I slap on some concealer to hide my dark circles. I layer on thick squeezes of foundation in an attempt to enliven this corpse. I paint my lips bright red. I line charcoal around my lifeless eyes to make them smolder until they are on fire. I glow. I squeeze into the skin-tight slutty black dress I haven't worn in forever. I slip on motorcycle boots and feel like I am standing on solid ground for the first time in months.

My hair is ironed sleek and with every flattened curl, I feel like I can see straight for the first time in forever. Then my hips swivel me into Rivershead, the local townie bar. A gust of cigarette smoke greets me and embraces me like an old college friend.

"Whiskey neat, please." I lean over the bar, giving the bartender a seductive gaze through the cigarette haze.

He slides a thick glass down the dark wood bar. I wrap my hand around it and bring it to my lips.

I slowly sip it, catching his gaze again. A sudden vision of him throwing me against the wall flies through my brain. I spin around on the barstool and scope out the room.

"KOALAS HAVE CHLAMYDIA," a voice rasps loudly from a table across from me. A group of guys are sitting at a long table and all I can see through my thick liquid-lined lids is the scene from the Last Supper.

All of them are so ... *Oregonian*. White, with long stringy hair, at least one article of clothing with fractal designs printed on it, and horrifying Nosferatu teeth. But a girl's gotta work with what she's got.

I squint to see which one is the closest to okay and am shocked to discover one of them is cute. He has a tight brown mop of curls, big brown eyes, pillowy lips, and actually looks freshly showered? I shoot him my signature lizard gaze from across the bar. His cheeks turn pink. He smiles sheepishly.

"Did you know koalas have chlamydia?" The raspy voice, suddenly next to me, has infiltrated my home base in a sneak attack while I was distracted by the sheepish cute boy.

"Uh, no." I take a prim sip from my glass and try to lock eyes with the cute boy again.

"Yeah, they do." Everything about this guy reminds me of an oily little kid on the bus that would say "hi" really quickly and deadpan, and then run away thinking it's the height of humor. This guy fucking loves Spongebob still. This guy definitely jerks off in a sock and then tosses it on the ground. This guy definitely—

He's still staring at me, awaiting a response.

"Cool, dude. Are you from here?" I force myself to ask.

"Born and raised in little Ashlandiaaaaa! You're not from here, I can tell. Girls like you are never from around here." My pussy retracts like a turtle in its shell.

"Very nice. I just moved here from New Yor—"

"OHHHHHHHHH, no WAY! I've ALWAYS wanted to go there, you gotta meet everyone. Yo, yo, yo, she's from New York," he announces to the Last Supper crew.

Three girls who look like they got their outfits from an LL Bean and 2005 Wet Seal collaboration have suddenly appeared. They are rolling their eyes and ignoring me.

"I'm Derrik," STD Koala boy announces.

"I'm Ani."

"That's hot. You're, like, *exotic*."

"That's tacky to say."

"Oh, she's feisty. You're so New York—putting me right in my place." Derrick licks his lips. I try not to vomit.

Two more whiskey neats, one fifty-minute soliloquy about traveling and music festivals later, and I've lost any semblance of couth that I ever had.

"Jesus Christ, dude. Read the room! Take a fucking breath! I can't tell you how uninteresting this is to me, my God." I pat his arm and nod my head for assurance. "Listen, you're very sweet, I see you. You'll be a lot more successful at this if you leave room for the other person to get a word in—a little advice from my heart to yours. But—" I pause "—I do want to know who your curly-haired friend over there is, though." I bat my lashes.

"Fair, fair. That is *SO* New York, you're hilarious. That's Oliver. He's quiet, but the best guy."

"Introduce us?" I give him my best doe-eyed plea.

"Really?" he says, surprised at my choice. "I mean, okay."

Derrick is right about one thing: Oliver is indeed a man of few words. But he smells like tea tree oil, fresh ginger, and the earth of a newly turned garden, and listens with wide-eyed curiosity to every word I say. When he does talk, it's so fast and mumbled I can barely make it out, but it's charming. He's excited. My heart begins to melt for Oliver, who I learn is a gardener and a chef who grew up with a hippie-feminist permaculture-obsessed mother in an off-grid homestead with no electricity and an outhouse. I tell him about growing up where my family's motto was "keep your mouth shut and your shoes shined" and how my outdoor time was made up of strip malls. Oliver is of the woods—and not in the Pacific Northwest ax-wielding-flannel way; but in a Hanes pack of five white shirts that he takes really good care of, and wears with a scarf that his mom gave him, that is actually a purple and electric blue pashmina, kind of way. He is a total earth spirit and it's actually so beautiful. It's so ... real.

Oliver is like whiskey. He feels safe. And warm. And just the right amount of sweet. The next thing I know our lips are pressed together at the bar. Then Oliver is in my bed. I melt into him more. His lips are soft and gentle. My body is melting in his warmth; his gentleness evokes sweeter, slower movements. The same innocent jitters of a first slow dance in middle school bubble up in my stomach.

And it is on this random Thursday night, in a little hippie town, with this curly-headed man, that I, Ani Ferlise, have my first orgasm while having sex.

And I am fucking *hooked*.

"ANI, SWEETIE, I CAN'T KEEP having sex like this," Oliver says after I practically backflip in a dismount off of him with my arms raised in triumph, completely blissed out. It is exactly three weeks and 127 orgasms later.

"What do you *mean*?" I snuggle up to him in concern.

"Well, you know, when guys ejaculate, they deplete their shen."

I blink.

"You know, like, their chi?"

I blink again.

"It's, like, their life force."

Blink. Blink. Blink.

"Ani, I'm so tired."

"So, what are you saying? You want to stop?"

"I just need to replenish my shen. Let's just do it less."

By nightfall, I am in the classic strung-out-on-caffeine (but from tea, not coffee, cause, ya know, it's better for you or whatever) position: on the floor, legs in a pile underneath me, hunched forward in the dark, frantically researching how to have sex and not deplete your life force.

I sift through hundreds of ads for penis enhancement supplements, probably get several viruses on my computer, and am exposed to countless disturbing cartoons of giant sweaty throbbing dicks in the process, only to end up where the only good answers come from: Reddit.

I TOOK THESE DROPS TO RESERVE MY CHI DURING SEX AND NOW I FEEL AMAZING.

I click on the link and speed over to the website.

I am ready to get a flight to LA to pick up these drops in person when I realize they offer overnight shipping.

$175 later, I am dripping the special energy shen drops under his tongue.

"For your chi!" I chirp.

10
True Love, Bitch

Oliver. Ashland. The Temple. I have finally created a home for myself that feels like a *safe space*. But I don't want to be safe anymore. I want to feel alive.

I want to live my purpose. I want to do more. I am craving change.

So I am flying the coop and moving five hours away to Portland.

I pack Patrick Swayze into his little carrier and look at the near-empty living room with its bleach-stained, scraped wood floors (oops) in my little Ashland home. The house still feels like magic, even with the dust bunnies and echoey halls. I walk into the kitchen and graze my hand against the cabinet where I kept my herbs, then walk to the bedroom that held my first positive sexual experience, then into the Fun Girl Salon that ended up being the most happening nightclub in town, even if it was off to a lonely start. A bittersweet hit of nostalgia punches me in the gut.

Small town living where people walk their sheep on leashes like dogs, ask what Starseed family you're from rather than what you do for work, and need energy drops so they can have sex, has got real tired, real fast. These aren't my people. Again. And I don't want to be cut off from what's really *happening* in the world. *Portland* will be my new beginning—where I will find passion, purpose, and be able to bring all this priestess work I've learned into the *real* world.

I am with Charlie, Lucas, and Sophia Rose, my fellow Messy Bitch, Joan of Arcs of the Dark, who I met on the dancefloor at the only nightclub in Ashland. That's the thing about us Messy Bitches: we get the gift of night vision and can see each other in the dark. It was through them that I realized the life I've been living wasn't completely right. We've connected over some epic life shit, too: Breakups. Makeups. Rebirths. Small town dramas. Real-life traumas. And lots of cold brew iced coffees during sacred long drives where we monologue about life while watching the world fly by in a speedy blur.

And that's exactly what we're doing right now. Driving the 285 miles to Portland.

"I can't believe you're doing it, dude. You're really moving to Portland. Who are you going to hang out with?" Sophia asks breathily while exhaling a long drag off an American Spirit from the backseat, her curls whipping in the wind from the window.

"I just feel this for you, this is so right. I feel it. I don't know why. But I do," Charlie says, whipping out her phone from her Carhartt pants to take one of her signature iPhone pictures of my hand on the steering wheel.

"I'm hungry, can we get food? I want chips," Frankie, my Sagittarian siren whines pleasantly, extending her miles-long arm up to get a better view of the extra-long, red, glue-on nails she just bought at CVS.

I lean forward in anticipation—as if this will get me there faster somehow. And finally, we pull up to my new life in northwest Portland. There she is: the smallest gray house with a bright yellow door on a teeny dead-end street. In comes that familiar eerie, exhilarating, tingly, magical nudge inside of me that makes me hold my breath on the inhale (kind of like that moment before having an explosive orgasm, which I can do now if I haven't made that clear yet).

In the backseat, Patrick Swayze is as wide-eyed as I am. I march us to my golden door, turn the key, and fling it open so hard that it slams against the wall, chipping the plaster.

I have fucking arrived.

***

"Girls!" I announce proudly, "Let's do some magic, yeah?"

It is the night before Halloween and the Moving Hunks (exactly what it sounds like) have now brought all of my furniture in. We've been in my new home for exactly five hours, and we're surrounded by piles of boxes and half-eaten to-go containers of Thai food, getting ready for our first big night on the town. Everyone gathers gleefully as I pour shots of whiskey.

Lucas and Charlie are dressed as Lindsay and Tobias Bluth from *Arrested Development*, Sophia is a flapper girl, and I am dressed in my handmade, very sexy Guy Fieri costume: a flame bowler shirt tied up with fishnets; booty shorts that I bedazzled with the word "Flavortown" on my ass cheeks; signature sunglasses on the back of my head; hair in obscene pigtails.

"Okay close your eyes, take a deep breath, and then raise your glass." I call out in my cool new living room, which is lit up by a neon sign I unpacked that says "Psychic Reader." The four of us gather in the center of the living room under the blue and red light, Lucas almost eating shit when she trips over a box—yet she manages to not spill even a drop of her whiskey. We raise our glasses. "May this weekend bring everything we want and need, beyond what we could imagine. May we be completely aligned with the most epic, beautiful magic. And so it is." We clink glasses as we open our eyes.

"And so it is!" they echo.

"Oh, and we're all pretty constipated, so let's add some movement in that department. And so it is," I add.

"And so it fucking is," Lucas bangs her glass against mine so hard it cracks.

We end up at a trashy bar in Chinatown. Frantic energy roars inside of me. And it isn't my IBS flaring up this time. It's like I am looking for something I lost. My eyes frantically scan the bar, which is bubbling to the brim with characters: a man with a shark hat talks to someone dressed as Johnny Bravo who is surrounded by a group of women dressed as emojis who are being checked out by a smattering of Zombie guys. The atmosphere is primal: a modern-day mating dance as women dressed as sexy cats offer their hindquarters and grind with men salivating like a pack of wolves to Cardi B.

Soon enough, my Flavortown hindquarters are engaged in a casual discussion about human suffering and the concept of God with a man dressed as a hotdog. I'm sipping my drink restlessly. I listen to the hotdog. I respond to the hotdog. I scan the crowd. I sip my drink. I listen some more. I bring up the concept of intergenerational trauma and how it impacts our perception of life to the hotdog. I scan the crowd again. And then suddenly, like I'm wearing a pair of spy goggles from a futuristic '90s movie, my eyes zero in on a dude in an electric pink onesie.

"Excuse me, I need a second." I cut off the hotdog and creep over to the bar to get a closer look. There he is—raven black hair, stubble on his face, a ring on every finger—and my *God*. The man must be about 6'3". The name "MAMA" is stitched onto his onesie, which is zipped down to expose a healthy puff of chest hair, lean abs, and several layers of necklaces.

He doesn't notice me. He's lost in the art of pouring cobalt-colored drinks into flimsy plastic cups.

"I'm taking a cig break!" he yells mid-drink pour. He has a cartoonishly deep voice like Tony Robbins. I know nothing about this man. But I feel his energy and suddenly I'm Pepe le Pew following the green scent in a *Looney Tunes* cartoon. I watch him swag over to the corner of the outdoor tent and light up a cigarette that he pulls from his light blue American Spirit pack. Now is my chance. I swoop in front of him.

And holy-shit. He's not 6'3". He's at least six-fucking-six. I'm-five-fucking-one. I feel like a fart in the wind next to him! But *still*. For whatever reason, I *know* he's mine. Like the great Joan of Arc once said in her divinely guided state: "I am not afraid, I am born to do this." I walk over to him with the tenacity of leading a revolution in France.

"Hey—" I purr. He looks over my head. I'm about to bitchily add "down here," but he meets my eyes before the retort leaves my lips. I give him my best "Lizard Gaze." You know the look, right? The one where you suck the soul out of his body with your eyes, like a lizard's tongue catching a fly.

"I just wanted to introduce myself. I'm one of the great loves of your life."

He takes a long inhale of his cigarette and squints, not breaking eye contact.

"My name is Ani." Dear sweet Jesus, what am I *doing*?

I twirl at my Guy Fieri pigtails and my strip lashes suddenly feel like they are blinding me. Nonsense damage control words are about to explode out of me like vomit, but I swallow them down like a pro and scoot in closer to him, firmly clutching his gaze like a coveted prize I won from a carnival game.

He doesn't say anything but a heat radiates between us. It's so hot I'm not able to stop myself from erupting with: "I am going to absolutely ruin your life in the best way." *Welp, didn't see that coming.*

He grabs a shiny red cherry out of the drink he's been sipping on the DL, hiding it in the pocket of his onesie. He throws the cherry up so high that I lose sight of it. Then he lifts his head and catches it in his mouth.

He looks back down at me and winks. Wordlessly, he walks back to the bar.

***

I am back inside, staring blankly at the DJ, swaying my "Flavortown" bedazzled buttcheeks slightly—in what one might call a dissociative style of dance—to Usher's "Yeah" while actually being completely immersed in my monsoon of thoughts as to what the fuck just happened. I feel a TAP TAP TAP on my shoulder. I swing my head around to see a girl wearing a sexy nurse's outfit. She is holding the world's worst sugary nightmare hangover drink.

"From him," she says vacantly, nodding to the bar.

ALMOST THREE MONTHS GO BY and I don't see or hear from the mysterious man in the pink onesie. I do my best to forget about him. After all, I have plenty to distract myself with. Like Instagram. In fact, I'm in the middle of mindlessly scrolling when I get a new follow alert. It's from a man named "Rune." I click on it and it's *him*. In comes a comment on my latest thirst-trap selfie (I'm in an organic cotton botanical dyed bra and undies set adorned with moons): "Hope all is well, you wonderful witch" it reads, and I fly into his DMs faster than the speed of light.

"I want to know you. I want to hear your story. You down?" I type furiously, before hitting send and throwing my phone against the wall at the sheer audacity of myself. Who is this impulsive and uncalculated bitch? I don't know her. It's like my craving for him has my overthinking ass in a chokehold.

I flop on my bed belly first and scream into the pillow. Then I run to the mirror and immediately strike a Tyra Banks-inspired smize and pose.

Remember yourself, Bitch. You're hot, you're cool, you're magical, you're powerful, you got a portal to the otherworld between your legs, and you can have orgasms from not just vibrators and electric toothbrushes used as a vibrator now. You are—

DING.

"Come meet me at this bar Elvis Room. I'm here. I want to know you. Badly," he immediately replies. Butterflies start moshing in my gut; my veins are electric guitar strings.

I use the jolt of adrenaline to kick all the clothes on my floor and into the closet—just in case he comes over later. I put on tight black skinny jeans that are just stretchy enough so I don't feel like two pounds of sausage in one casing and sit in my vanity chair, turning to the side, and staring at myself to see how my flowy top slinks down my shoulder just right, revealing a black satin strappy bralette. I lock eyes with myself, give myself a proper lizard gaze, and my pussy smirks through my jeans. I'm ready.

The Elvis room is an Elvis-themed bar (what a shocker!). Within thirty minutes, I walk in and am greeted by the smell of sticky sweet syrup, rum, and the seventy pounds of lavender essential oil I doused myself with before I left. There is Elvis paraphernalia everywhere, which gives me mild anxiety while I look for him.

"We're downstairs to the right," he texts.

We? Who is *"we?"* For some reason walking down the stairs is the single most harrowing, demoralizing thing I can think of. I really can't tell you why, but I can't imagine anything more cringe than walking down the stairs toward a group of people already sitting down. Why am I doing this to myself? WHY? I look down at my phone and see his hot ass fucking face on Instagram. Possessed, I walk down the stairs à la the big reveal before prom in every '90s movie.

I notice him when I'm halfway down the stairs. His eyes catch mine while he's mid-sentence. He immediately stops talking and holds my gaze.

"Fuck," I see him declare to his friends.

I sit back and coolly lean against the booth as he tells animated tales of Portland nightlife. A natural storyteller, like he's on a stage. And I'm thrilled to be his audience.

I lean forward and our knees kiss beneath the table. A shock runs through me. He pauses his story for a moment and his face gets stone serious. For a second. And then there's that smug (sexy) smile. Everything fades away. No one else in the bar exists. Nothing else in the bar exists. Not even the emotionally-jarring Elvis paraphernalia.

As I tell him about my work, he brings his face closer to mine. I inch my legs closer to his until our limbs are tangled vines. I tell him a story about temple dancing with snakes. His hands fall against my knees. My hands linger against his face. We argue, tempestuously, about the concept of "morality." I interrupt him mid-sentence because I can't hear what he's saying anymore. My brain is on vacation and my body is steering the ship. I'm out of control and I'm loving every second of it.

"Rune, you are so falling in love with me," I drop my hands from his face into his lap.

His eyes burn into my lips. Our lips almost touch. "Not here," I whisper. My face is on fire.

I've never seen a man that big move so fast in my life. Within seconds, he is standing on his mile-long legs. He recklessly tosses a wad of cash on the bar and grabs my hand. We charge into the night like wild animals.

We get to his house and the second the front door is closed, he turns me around and presses me against it. He pauses and hovers over my lips, waiting for the okay. I nod, excitedly. He picks me up and throws me on the couch. We kiss and it's fireworks. Dozens of sparklers. Explosions. *Bombs* of desire. Our bodies rocket into the bed, where we tongue like we're going to the electric chair. He tears off my already torn-up jeans.

He steadies me with one hand, angling me closer to him. Every touch, sound, lick, is cosmic chaos. He goes down on me, and even the stars blush in awe. I'm about to ascend to a 5D reality. I cum in two minutes. He is fully clothed and quiet. He travels up my body and grabs my chin, looking at my eyes like they are supernovas. "I love you, Ani Ferlise. You were right," he breathes. I think I'm going to cum again. (I mean he said *I was right*). Then he slides off one of his necklaces—a glass pendant with swirls of blue and red. He tucks it into my hand. "Here. For when you want to be reminded about what I just did to you." I *am* going to cum again.

Two weeks later, we're on a flight to the East Coast so he can meet my entire family. Time flies when you're having fun, but time moves like a space rocket blasting through the cosmos when you're in love.

I told you. I **knew** he was mine.

"ANI, DON'T DO IT. He's a total heartbreaker. He's never committed to anyone ever and girls just fall at his feet. He blows through everyone. Don't do it," my new friend Anna begs me over the phone. "He's a dick."

My spit thickens in my mouth like it does before you vomit. Rune is now fully living in my little house with me. She tells me he left another woman, Sabrina, for me. He wasn't single on that magical, Elvis-laden night we first kissed while we were flooded with hormones and hope until we were a tidal wave of orgasmic bliss. I shove down the vomit.

Anna doesn't get it. Clearly. I hang up the phone and try to ignore the little gust of movement from my gut. It feels like the tiniest red flag gently waving in the wind.

And then Valentine's Day hits like a fist.

He is washing the dishes from breakfast. "Check out this SNL skit," he chuckles, handing me his phone. A YouTube video flashes through the static screen. It is disrupted by a text notification. From *Sabrina*. I don't believe in snooping—I'm an evolved ass bitch—but you know those times when your fingers have a mind of their own? It's them, not *me*, who open the text.

"You know I always got you whenever you want it," it reads. I look at the kissing emoji and become a demon. *What the ever-living FUCK does she mean*? I'm pupils-dilated-dry-mouth-unblinking kind of possessed. I click the notification and my eyes topple onto their text thread. And there it is. A video. Of *her*.

First, it's her hair I notice. Her perfectly blown out, ends-curled, satin-finish hair. Her face. Her perfect symmetrical face. And then it's the body. Her naked. Body. And she's touching herself. Just. For—

him.

His response: "I almost crashed my car fifteen times watching that video."

I sit there, my thumb shaking and hovering over the screen. Rage ripples through me like the ocean before a tsunami. The waves violently crash on shore and swallow a small village. And suddenly everything is still. I am the hair-raising calm before the storm that makes the animals flee on instinct. I smile and arch my eyebrows like a psychopath.

I will fire the first shot.

He is peacefully drying the dishes when I stroll toward him. I shove his phone into his face.

His eyes are full of animal fear. "Ani, I've been so good to you. I've never been this good to anyone."

I now know why they name hurricanes after people. My vision turns blinding white. My pupils turn black. A Medusa-like coldness washes over me. And then an incinerating fire blasts from my pupils.

"Hmm," I grin big, like a serial-killing sociopath. "I wish I was surprised that we're here. Everyone warned me about you. I mean—even your friends," I giggle. "YOUR people." The sociopathic grin grows. "No one had a lick of faith in you dude. You proved everyone right, huh?" I bat my lashes. "You know why you can't have anything, Rune? Cause you're *nothing*. You are actually a fucking nothing. Honestly, I am embarrassed our names are even associated 'cause you're such a loser." My words gain momentum. "Every single person you know and love asked me why I'm with you because of how untrustworthy and weak you are. It was cringe for you, dude. You're a joke." He won't even look at me.

"Ani," he says, eyes-to-the-floor, throwing gasoline over my wildfire. "I've been so good to you." His voice is soft. He's still wearing yellow rubber gloves from the dishes. He looks so pathetic and so young I *almost* feel bad.

"Get your stuff and FUCKING GET OUT of my house."

"Ani, *what*?! I didn't cheat on you! I didn't know what to say to her!" His voice gets high. Squeaky, like a hysterical teen girl. Then he tears into his closet and starts to load a duffle bag, still unable to look at me.

More fuel. More fire. "Have fun finding a place to go," I purr. I clock him checking out. I channel Dorothy Parker and sharpen my tongue, "You are such a lonely, sad, pathetic person." I twist my words into his heart. "You wanna know the best part? I know how to love. I will just experience this exact thing with someone else. But you will be stuck in this pathetic spiral, alone, forever."

"But I was *good* to you. I didn't actually do anything with her. I really did so good this time. I was good to you," he repeats, still in his stupid yellow kitchen gloves.

After he's gone, I run out to my black Volkswagen and speed five hours back to Ashland to see my Fairy Godmother, Brigid.

As I drive, the song "Wedding Bell Blues" by the Fifth Dimension plays on repeat. I am so engrossed in playing Sabrina's masturbation video over and over in my head that I don't realize I've been listening to the same song for ninety minutes.

That motherfucker, he used me! He played me for a fool! I rage from within, as my speakers coo "Bill, I love you so, I always will."

Why. Why? Why did she have to—

"... ahhhh but am I ever going to see my wedding dayyy ... "

Have *that* body?

Five hours later, I pull up to the electric iron gates at Brigid's. It occurs to me that I barely remember the drive.

I burst through her doors, and her house still smells like a magical spice cake. As I sniff the air, she appears and I collapse into her arms.

"I feel so hurt," I gasp. The shoulder of her wool sweater is already soaking wet from my sobs. She pulls me close. I cry harder. "He is disgusting. He is nothing. Truly, nothing. Fucking absolute nothing." Sloppy tears dribble from my eyelids.

"Darling," she whispers. "It's time for some cake. Come sit down."

She guides me to the kitchen and sits me down with some spice cake. It sits in my lap untouched.

"He is a huge sack of shit, he is NOTHING," I sneer again, starting yet another long-winded soliloquy diagnosing him with every personality disorder in the DSM.

"Sweetheart, who are you really talking about here?" Her hand is warm on my cold shoulder.

And all the walls of illusion crash down around me. I am laying in a pile of broken bricks as my foundation crumbles. Me. I am talking about me.

I am in stunned silence as she settles me into a big leather chair in front of a fire that roars in a stone hearth. I watch herbs dance majestically in the embers. She sits down on the couch across from me.

"Darling, eat your cake, it helps with this kind of thing." I do as she says and slide my fork through a thick layer of vanilla frosting. I lick it. Shit. That *does* help.

"Stop chopping the guillotine," she says. "On yourself."

I take another small bite of spice cake.

"And on others." The fire glows against her face. "The way you talk to yourself is the way you will talk to others. I *know* it's how you've been talked to. I *know* it's hard. But sweetheart, just because it's what you've known, and just because it protects your precious heart, doesn't mean it's not violent."

Her words cut through my delusion. Through my pain. Through my limited perspective. They set me safely into the brutal arms of the truth.

"Look with fresh eyes here, honey. A boundary has been crossed. How do you want to show up for this? If this is love, ask questions."

I spend the next two days with Brigid, digesting cake and wisdom. I really can't speak. I walk around her house in a daze of memories, spaced out and staring at the walls in silence.

I've used my words to cut a partner down when I felt threatened. I mean, I was a total ass to Johnny, specifically. I would verbally flip over boulders if he said one thing that "proved" he didn't "fully" love me.

I've always seen myself as sensitive and caring, but maybe that's just it—the thing no "empath" wants to admit. We're not just these innocent little lambs needing shelter from the big bad world. We can feel EVERYTHING. Like, say, what another person's core weakness is. And then we can use that weakness as a weapon against them. I am capable of being the most manipulative bitch around. And this quality of mine reminds me of someone from my past. Someone who would unleash his rage at the drop of a hat for reasons I could never quite figure out. Someone who ended up leaving scars on my body. My heart. My psyche.

Huh, who knew?

My own medicine is Ipecac. I'm going to puke. And I deserve it. I need to call Rune. I sprint down the long hall of Brigid's home into the room I am staying in and pick up my phone. My hands are shaking. I pace in front of the bed and click his number.

He answers in one ring.

"Hi." Fear coats his breath.

"Rune. I—" I struggle to get the words out. "—I am so sorry. I should have never talked to you that way. You are not nothing. I felt so threatened and I lost it. I don't—" sharp inhale—"I don't have an excuse"—sharp inhale—"because there is no reason you should ever be talked to that way"—sharp inhale—"I am going to make this right —sharp inhale. "If you let me"—full-body exhale—"come up with a game plan so this never happens again." SOB. SOB. SOB.

"Where are you, Ani?"

"Ashland."

"Is it okay if I come to see you?"

CHOKE. "Yes." *SOB.*

Five hours later, he's at Brigid's door. "I'm sorry. And I'm going to show you that I am, not just say it," I wobble into his arms.

He steadies my furious trembling by gripping me tightly. "I'm sorry. I didn't know how to handle that because I didn't want her to feel bad, and I did her wrong by just up and leaving. I handled it all wrong," he says. His arms feel strong around me. "She was good to me, and I wasn't good to her. I didn't want to hurt her feelings. It should have never impacted us. I am so, so sorry," his cigar-smoke voice and warm breath on my neck.

We decide right then to do a ritual that night to consecrate our relationship in the way we want—not quite marriage, but promising each other real, connected, compassionate partnership. No more angry Ani, judgmental Ani, jealous Ani—they have no place here. Brigid has an actual sword in her house (as any good witch would!) and I'm going to use it as a prop. First, I go outside with him and build a small fire. I stand in front of him, watching the flames flicker against his somber, serious face. I feel that oh-so-familiar cringe as I trot to grab the sword from inside.

Stop being a dick to him, Ani! This is your love!

Then I run back inside and grab the sword, which is mounted up high on the wall. The weight of it makes me stumble, and it almost crashes on top of me but I jump out of the way and get a hold of the handle so it doesn't cut me or come crashing down. "Real funny," I murmur aloud to God. Who'd think the Creator of All There Is would be so on the nose. Then I walk back outside, sword in hand, and every step feels like it's echoing through my body. I feel like I'm walking the plank.

"With you, Rune, I lay down my sword." I cringe at how awkward this feels. I keep going.

"My commitment is to see a therapist to look at my defenses to make sure they don't become *offenses* to you. I am putting my weapon down from this moment on."

I kneel to lay the sword by his feet while trying to swallow my pride and the expletives that are dying to come out. *Get over yourself, Ani.*

"And with THIS," I speak loudly to drown out the sounds of the hellscape battlefield that's raging in my chest.

"My intention is to create a safe enough space that you can come to me with anything, and I can hold it. And so it is." I stand and kiss him, my lips locked in the chokehold of contradiction, tongue-tied while tying tongues.

He reaches into his pocket and pulls out two rings with matching purple stones. One more oval in shape (his); the other a perfect circle (mine). "This marks my commitment to you. To always tell the truth, to always treat life like an adventure with you, to protect you and your heart. You are mine, Ani. And I am all yours." He says this with a smile as he slides the ring onto my finger.

11
Feminine Bitch

"The anus is a portal to GOD!" my teacher's voice bellows through my computer speakers, waking me from a sleepy haze. I slink from my desk onto the floor, covered in what are supposed to be lavish sheepskins but are actually yards of scratchy, questionable "material" from the glamorous "Joann Fabrics." It's 4:45 a.m. I am up early 'cause I'm next-level priestessing by embodying the *Divine Feminine* and training to be a spiritual sex and love coach.

I am in what I call the "magic room" of my new house with Rune. The magic room is a space all of my own with altars, flowy drapes, candles, and sheepskins (aka the hairy, itchy, dirt-cheap fabric that I may or may not be allergic to). Bouquets of dried flowers hang from the ceiling.

It is here that I start my mornings with my rock-solid, four-hour routine. I meticulously light my candles. There are about twenty of them, and they each have a different significance. I whip out my "rewiring the mind for success" journal prompts and write the same things over and over again, channeling all of my energy into changing my brain so I can stop sabotaging myself, heal up, and lean into my pleasure and my power. Again.

Once my brain has been reset, I sit in front of two mirrors and start a breathwork practice. Deep, slow, inhale in the mouth; long, extended exhale without a pause after. Then I begin my daily self-pleasure practice. No porn, no thoughts or fantasizing; I'm just supposed to breathe, feed my body pleasure and then, when I orgasm, send out a prayer for what I need.

The pseudo-sheepskin and fallen dried-out flower petals itch my thighs as I lay there spread eagle, staring blankly at a whitewashed picture of Mary Magdalene on my mirror altar as I furiously masturbate—*I mean* self-pleasure—in a hazy, glazed over state.

That's right. Ya girl got her shit together. I have a magic room. I'm a good partner. I'm building a business. I'm softening and healing. I'm facing my shadows. I'm learning. I'm blessed. I'm grateful. I'm amplifying my pleasure.

I also (still) fucking hate my fucking life.

I "cum" and it feels like my pussy sneezed.

IT'S BEEN A YEAR SINCE the sword ritual, and Rune and I have completely stopped going out. I am in constant training sessions and courses, studying to start a coaching business (and to understand my own shit). Rune now works at an upscale bar, is a scholar on "non-violent communication," attends group therapy, and volunteers at the Suicide Prevention Hotline.

He's doing everything right. I love him. I'm proud of him. Gone is the drinking and the drama and the naked text messages from girls with frizz-free hair and perfect fucking tits (*shit*—I mean, beautiful breasts. All breasts are beautiful and there's no such thing as perfection. *Whatever*). So why is it that during every wedding we attend together, I find myself broken into hives, hiding in a bathroom stall, dry heaving? Why is it that the thought of standing at the altar with him makes me want to rip my skin off? Why does the idea of having sex with him seem as boring as taking out the recycling on garbage night?

Why am I still so restless? I finally have everything I "called in" years ago when I was up all night at my crystal-covered desk in Ashland, frantically scribbling out everything I was certain I needed in order to stop feeling like the biggest loser alive.

I have an amazing boyfriend who would do anything for me and loves me more than I've ever been loved. I live in a beautiful house that is three minutes from downtown Portland but tucked away deep in the woods, hidden among the treetops. I have a day job as a copywriter that allows me to work remotely, and I am in training to be a sex priestess which—let's face it—has *always* screamed my name (your biggest wounds are your biggest medicine—right?). I also have a whole toolbox worth of supplies to help me stay strong, when my old friend self-hatred pounds against my bedroom door at 2 a.m. For fuck's sake, I have a *Magic Room*. I have literally nothing to complain about. And yet, sometimes, when I find my eyes in the mirror, I still see two hollowed-out sockets staring back at me.

My nightly gratitude list is as follows: my home (that doesn't really feel like home), my job (that I actually can't stand); and Rune (who I haven't wanted to fuck in months); and my body (which I spiral about daily because I am doing all this work and still can't seem to "love" any single part of it down to my grubby little hands); and my life (which I feel like I'm watching fly by in a distant haze).

I walk up to my bathroom after another long morning routine session and flick on the lights. The bathroom of our new house is straight out of the seventies: metallic pink and gold wallpaper with a bright pink tub. The decor alone would ordinarily have lit me up, but this all feels barely real, never mind something to be enjoyed. I move slowly over to the sink and catch my soulless eyes. I can't look away. A sudden snore coming from the bedroom makes me jump. I break my own gaze and feel hot rage shoot through me, only to be snuffed out by a downpour of sadness.

Something needs to change. *I* need to change.

So I do what I do best—I look for yet *another* mentorship.

Cue Raella, a gorgeous red-headed Jessica Rabbit-esque sex bomb that I wanna be just like when I grow up. *Ahem*, I *mean*, a coach who teaches about the Divine Feminine, but who also looks like she is actually happy. And like, shows herself crying on social media and calls it beautiful instead of wrong (and she also looks gorgeous when she cries, which is like, insane. I look like a swollen, post-mortem version of myself). Her vibrant energy seems to infuse everything she does. She looks like she's actually having fun with her life.

I scroll through her Instagram and watch a video of her dancing through an airport, and it actually isn't cringe or even that weird. She pulls it off. WHY? *HOW*? I need to know this woman's secrets and I need to know them fast. I scroll some more. And there, in big, blinding, swoopy golden cursive, is the holy motherfucking grail: "Eroticize Your Energy:

An In-Person Retreat to Embody the Divine Feminine and Melt Into Love and Life."

I send her a message that I want in. Then I curl out of my gremlin-who-hasn't-seen-the-sun-in-a-decade-position and click-close my laptop. I throw on my red, monochromatic, organic cotton priestess getup, fluff up my wild, natural-colored curls, and slip out the door for a date with Rune—which will be us going out to eat, and "processing" through something.

THREE WEEKS, SEVERAL THOUSAND attempts to feel anything, and one quick flight later, and I'm en route to my first meeting with Raella at a pagan temple in California. I'm anxiously awaiting the key I've been searching for as I walk into the dimly lit space. It's gorgeous and jam-packed with candles and roses and smells like copal and also ... someone is *totally* wearing Bulgari Rose Essentielle perfume! I can't remember the last time I smelled nice perfume and not just essential oils at one of these gatherings.

I scan the dozens of women there, all in their twenties and thirties. There are three slightly older women that look like they also have a house in the Hamptons, two kids in the Ivy League, and definitely refer to shirts as "blouses." I sit across from them in the giant, candle-lit circle, and can't help but stare as they nervously adjust themselves and avoid looking at anyone. A sudden, highly intrusive thought of one of them playing the well-to-do woman in a porno who is miserable in her marriage and who goes to a gay bar and fucks an androgynous lesbian in the stall, flies through my brain.

Get it together, Ani. I sit cross-legged and continue scanning the circle. The women in the room are like the diet version of the hard stuff I experienced at the Goddess temple in Ashland. Like everyone here totally shaves their bodies and would *never* post pictures of their faces covered in menstrual blood on social media (true story). The pretty haircuts and lack of unnecessary loud-breathing or melodramatic stretching (and most pressingly, the clean fingernails) make me believe that everyone here definitely works a corporate job or is an "entrepreneur." OMG! My heart flutters like a butterfly. There's someone here with lip fillers! I haven't seen lip fillers in real life in so long! I feel the same kind of nostalgia as I would driving past an abandoned Blockbuster.

Nobody is talking to each other, just gazing at the flames and "dropping in" (aka getting comfy and settled.) There's a sitar version of what I think is the song from *The Nutcracker* playing. Or maybe it's *Swan Lake*.

Then BAM! A gust of energy hits everyone like a lightning bolt, interrupting my unnecessary sorting of symphony ballet songs and lip-filler longing. No one has to turn their head to know Raella has entered the temple. She saunters through the room like a fairy and glides over to a seat upfront while everyone nervously fidgets into position.

Damn. Raella *is* stunning. She has a small frame with hair as vibrant and as flowing as the long skirt floating around her small limbs. She is soft and gentle and opens her eyes wide like a baby deer when she speaks, but especially when she listens.

"Good evening, beloveds. I am so glad you're here and choosing to devote your beings to the sacred work of embodying the Feminine. In a culture that prioritizes the Masculine, and teaches people to shut down any sensitivity, this work is necessary, revolutionary, and sacred," Raella gently coos, still managing to project across the room.

Then she begins her lecture on what the Divine Feminine *is*. And fifteen minutes into her poetic lecture, I realize that despite the fact that I have a Magic Room and am enrolled in nine online fucking classes to learn about this shit, I know NOTHING. I don't know how to feel radiant and what it means to "lean into pleasure." In fact, every time I even hear the word "pleasure," I am creeped out and can only associate it with emaciated men who have really curly hair and still drink breast milk at age fifty for "health reasons" and call it "Mother's Milk." GAG. I clearly need to be here.

"The Masculine is to be strong and steady so that the Feminine can flow, because the ticket to happiness for the Feminine is to be in her wildness, but contained and protected by the Masculine," Raella continues, interrupting my extremely haunting spiral. I sit up straighter and focus.

"He should be able to hold whatever face of the Goddess you are bringing that day—sad, sexual, soft, chaotic. A balanced Divine Mascu-line is someone who will keep you on task while you flow through all your expressions. And for anyone with sexual trauma, a man grounded in his masculine can hold space for all of your experiences. The reason you ha-ven't been able to melt into orgasmic bliss isn't that you are broken, but because you haven't been with someone who can truly hold you," she con-tinues, her dewy face catching the golden hour light as if she'd planned it.

Well fuck, I don't have anyone fucking holding my Divine Feminine, I think.

My hand shoots up without me telling it to.

"Yes? Is there a question?" Raella squints to see me.

"Yeah, I have one. Well, maybe not. Well ... if it's not taking away from your talk?" I rub my thighs and feel an ingrown hair I can't wait to get later.

"Let's hear it."

"Okay." I gulp. "So what if, like, you love someone but they definitely can't hold you like that?"

Raella swooshes her (chic as fuck) long red skirt to the side and leans forward even more. "And what makes you think he can't?"

"Because he does things that show otherwise. Like this one time, I asked him to help with the dishes. I go to dry them and notice there's still shit all over it. Like *dude*." Words tumble out of my mouth and gain speed as they go downhill. "Sorry, I mean, food. There's food all over the dishes still. And I tell him about it, I say 'hey, there's still shi—I mean food on the dishes—'" I am so revved up that my East Coast accent comes out. I sound like Tony Soprano. "And then, he stands there, and ... he starts like *cryin*." My hands are like snakes coming up from a basket as I start waving them around, talking with them. "And I ask him what is happening, why is he getting all upset, and he starts sayin' how he can't do anythin' right. But like ... there was shit on the dishes still ... so ... like, he didn't do it right. Now what?"

I force my hands back down and start picking at the ingrown bump, unable to look up at anyone.

"Ahh. *Yes*. Great question and great example. You have to come back to your softness and let him take the lead. Let *him* find the food on the dishes.

He felt emasculated, and if you want someone to truly show up for you, you have to give him a chance to do so without you jumping in to fix it. Let yourself receive. Then he can stand in his masculine and hold any face of the Goddess you bring."

Yeah, by then I'll have received fucking e.coli from shit-covered dishes. I stew as she starts to talk about the sacred Magdalene, lover of Jesus and face of true Divine Feminine love, as I frantically try to pop the ingrown—tight-lipped and shut down.

There follow several sessions of dancing out different emotions, breathwork experiences where we heal our trauma together, and a sister-hood masturbation circle to send out sex magic and prayers for the burn-ing Amazon rainforest (I hear one of the Hamptons ladies cum and it's nothing like the porno I imagined.) After two days, I am ready to go home.

AS I DRIVE MY BLACK Volkswagen back to Portland, weaving in and out of lanes, I become fixated on what now feels like my obvious next step: getting Rune to do the work, too. We have to be in this together. I am doing my end, but he needs to catch up so he can hold me, and I can be softer to him because my needs are being met. *That's* why nothing has been work-ing; I might need to chill but *he* needs to man up. That way, I can fully "give myself" to him and he can feel empowered and aligned by stepping up into *his* Masculine. And then we can have sex again! Simple.

As I drive, my mind's eye flashes on Raella's soft undulating hair and long skirts. Her polished nails. I decide that before I do anything else, I must dress the part. I look down at my tattered, thrifted, fast-fashion skirt and stare at my chewed-down nails on the steering wheel. I meet my eyes in the mirror framed by my dried-out greasy hair. There's *nothing* Divine or Femi-nine about me. I don't want to have sex with me; why would Rune?

It's time for a change. A physical change. And so I make a commit-ment: for forty days and forty nights, I will only wear long, flowing skirts with no holes in them, and I will wear my hair curly and natural instead of my signature half-up, half-down pin-straight style with the fried ends. (I know I'm dramatic with the forty days and forty nights, but hey—I've always had a flair for biblical theatrics.)

The first thing I do is book a nail appointment. Then I touch the distressed ends of my hair and call the salon for a chop, so it will look healthy and *flowy* instead of barely moving after I take it down from a bun that's more like a knotted bird's nest. I stare at the exposed flesh of my legs, covered in razor burns, and buy a new razor and shaving cream. As soon as I get home, I get on my laptop and Poshmark for the next several hours, buying up long skirts and matching tops, so I can fully embody "the look." Less Ashland priestess, more chic LA Divine Feminine Goddess.

Lastly, I buy a pair of simple suede boots with a modest two-inch heel. Feeling a deep sense of pride in myself for being so proactive, it is time to finally give away my studded motorcycle boots, leather leggings, and band t-shirts. I grab my entire collection of vibrators while I'm at it, having learned that they prevent you from really *feeling* and disconnect you from your pussy magic, and I throw them away with the remaining parts of the old me.

Several days later, I am draped in a whole new look. After a hair appointment, I take a deep breath as I pull up to our house. I check myself out one more time in the rearview mirror: my hair is silky, blown out, shorter but softer, bouncier, and healthier; nails painted to perfection and beautifully shaped; skirt fitted tightly on my waist and billowing to my feet; feet encased in sensible suede boots. I open the front door and approach Rune, who is sitting on the couch watching TV. I suck in my stomach, strut toward him, and gently crawl into his lap.

"Baby! You look amazing! Good for you, honestly. You're hot!" He gasses me up with his Tony-Robbins-rasp, smiling and looking at me from head to toe before bringing me closer to his chest. I nuzzle in.

"Mmmm ... Baby, thank you." I gaze dramatically up into his eyes from underneath my false lashes, trying to entice him like a gamine Audrey Hepburn.

"Babe." He furrows his brows. "Did you take one of my Adderall? Why are you looking at me like that?" Clearly, my doe-eye is looking more coke-eye. I tone it down. Relax my lids, to ya know, "soften."

"I have to talk to you about something," I say, scooching myself up to get down to business, accidentally putting my weight on his balls, causing him to jerk and wince. "Sorry, sorry." I attempt the soft doe-eye again, adding in a flip of my soft silky hair for good measure. He looks at me quizzically, holding his nutsack.

I continue primly, "I need you to be more masculine, like Divine Masculine, like in-your-power masculine. I need you to make more decisions and take charge more. I need you to be able to hold whatever face of the Goddess I bring to you." I'm trying to sound earnest but I'm serving toddler-thinking-they-look-adult-after-covering-themselves-in-makeup. I can see a smirk starting to stretch across his snide little face and I have to shove down my annoyance by taking a deep breath. "I'm serious. I need you to do this so that I can truly heal, *okay*? I know our sex life has sucked. This is how we are going to get better. I'm traumatized and trying to heal and I need you to help as my partner and lover by embracing your inner masculine." I look at his face to see if he's getting it. The smirk has quickly been replaced with a blank, confused stare.

I push forward. " ... and that basically looks like YOU making the decisions and letting me work through my sexual trauma *with* you, so I can just express whatever face the Goddess is asking me to." I take a breath. "And you can hold that."

"Okay, I hear you, but why do you keep saying 'whatever face of the Goddess'?" he teases. I don't really know either, but I'm pissed and ready to snap. *He isn't taking this seriously enough GOD DAMN IT.*

FINE. I don't actually know what I'm talking about or what it would actually look like for him to "hold whatever face of the Goddess" I bring. Does he just listen to me stiff spined and intense eyed as I rage through intense recounts of my traumas?

But maybe all those times I was a complete and utter cunt to him were actually totally cool. Maybe a real man would completely understand and not take it personally and then fuck the shit out of me properly after I cunt-out. Who the fuck knows, but I can't let on that I barely know what I'm talking about and hope to God he just thinks of *something*.

"Rune—can you just be more in your fucking *masculine*?" I snap, "For fuck's sake, like, set the scene for sex, and choose what we're doing at night. I'll make it worth your while by being in complete devotion to you.

What do you say?" I plead, trying to widen my eyes like Raella.

"Of course, babe. I love you. I'm proud of you for facing this, and I got you." He holds me closer and I believe him.

I let out the first sigh of relief I can remember taking since I started doing all this exhausting goddamn work.

BY DAY EIGHTEEN OF MY forty-day and forty-night feminine embodiment deep dive, I am about to lose my fucking mind. I haven't had sex since I got back from Raella's workshop, because Rune doesn't seem to know how to set the scene. He is also not making *any* decisions, let alone all of them. In fact, not once since our talk on the sofa has he stepped into his "masculine."

If I am going to be my most empowered, feminine, pleasure-filled, radiant self, then *he* has to be able to meet me there, right? I feel a deep resentment boil in my chest. I got us a couple's massage complete with CBD kombucha and a soak in some fucking mineral water or whatever you call it—and he still can't arrange a dinner or, at the very least, fuck me good? *Monster.* Tacky at the very least. That's it.

I pull out my laptop and assume my signature, hunkered-down-on-the-ground, hunched-over research position. I find a couple's Tantra workshop on Portland Eventbrite happening Saturday night.

And quicker than one of my pussy-sneeze morning orgasms, we are walking into the sun-drenched open space room in southeast Portland. We are met with a room of guys with low ponytails, paperboy caps, and small hoop earrings (and who definitely only have sex to Sting's "Desert Rose"), and women who look like they would want to fuck guys with low ponies, paperboy caps, and small hoop earrings who only fuck to Sting's "Desert Rose." AKA—short, spiky-haired, long denim skirt, art teachers from the '90s dressed in Whimsigoth attire. If you're picturing Jamie Lee Curtis in *Freaky Friday* post-makeover, you are correct.

A woman who you can tell looks better without any makeup on begins to guide everyone through sacred intimacy practices with their respective partners: timed unison breathwork and sitting criss-cross-applesauce on each other (which I find out is called "Yab Yum"), and connecting with each other's root, heart, and third eye.

I try to drop in with Rune, but every time I close my eyes and put my forehead on his, I picture a sea of low pony-tailed men in this position, but naked to the sounds of Sting when they get home. I know, I fucking *KNOW* that for some reason their necks get really red when they're having sex. Rune's breath smells like the Doritos he ate in the car before we came (Cool Ranch—*ew*). I feel like I'm crushing his leg and he won't tell me because he knows I've been self-conscious lately so he's silently suffering. I exhale a sound to let go of the tension as directed per the no-makeup lady. It is the sound of someone who hates this, who hates herself, and who hates the fact that she's dating someone who chooses Cool Ranch Doritos over the red ones, and eats them before a fucking intimacy workshop without thinking about it.

After the workshop, we go to dinner at some Mediterranean place. We sit down and order immediately, which feels bleak for some reason.

"Let's talk about what that brought up for us," I say, before embarking on a fifteen-minute monologue as I process the feelings the whole experience brought up for me. The waiter brings the appetizers and Rune starts frantically eating olives and hummus from the mezze platter, licking the excess hummus off of his fingers while glancing around the restaurant and adding the occasional "mhmm."

Even though I want to snap like a Soprano at the disrespect that is occurring at this table, I swallow it down. I don't tell him he has hummus on his lips and that he sounds like a guy breathily grunting and cumming in a bukakke porno when he eats.

Instead, I take a deep breath, smile, and hand him a napkin, then shut my mouth like the fucking compassionate Divine Feminine bitch that I am.

OKAY, IT'S DAY TWENY-FIVE now and instead of having mind-blowing orgasms with my Divine Masculine partner, I am spending even more time alone in my Magic Room. Trying to connect with my body and heal my sexual trauma, doing these deep breaths into my womb. I'm not going to lie: the breathing into the womb thing is actually really nice. It's like slowly blowing into a bonfire and feeling the warmth grow and flames glow. Okay, I could get used to this.

Then I retch out of nowhere.

For fuck's sake.

I long for my beloved collection of vibrators that I threw away in my rebirth ritual to try to "re-sensitize my pussy," and don't want to admit that I miss them more than I miss sex with Rune.

And every day, I dutifully soften/widen my eyeballs and put on an ankle-grazing skirt (that I constantly trip over) and do my rituals with my long pretty painted nails (that make texting feel super weird with that tapping sound that gives me a strange sensory episode). I also can't actually masturbate without feeling like I'm ripping apart my clit. I then zip up my new boots (they clack too loud and I get weirdly embarrassed when I'm the only one making that much noise), and try and conjure up my sexual trauma so that I can "face it, release it, and heal it."

Fuck yeah, dude!

By day thirty I find myself looking in my bathroom mirror again. My lips are tight and my eyes are full of fire. I try to soften. It's not working. Without my signature eyelashes—without any sparkles or makeup—I am rocking only the dark circles that make me look like Yzma from *The Emperor's New Groove*. My hair is both greasy and dry at the same time, the deep conditioning treatment having long worn off. It's so curly, it looks like I have the Liberty Bell on top of my head. I'm wearing another long, solid color, flowing skirt with a matching solid color top. "I don't look ... good," I whisper to myself. "You don't feel good, either," my pussy, who now for some reason has the voice of a chain-smoking seventy-year-old, chimes in. I hop on the pink plaster counter and cross my legs to shut her up and make some model poses in the mirror, trying to catch a glimpse of hope for myself.

I am a motherfucking chode of a foreign entity in a bizarro Ani suit moving like I just inhabited a body for the first time.

I take out my phone to distract myself, hunched over in the orange light of my bathroom counter. By now, I am stalking every single Divine

Feminine mentor I can find on Instagram, and every other post in my feed is of a soft, radiant, billowing, sexually liberated, and "conscious relationship having" Goddess girl who loves to say the word pussy and call me babe and share that she also—PLOT TWIST—listens to gangster rap. Just another *face of the Goddess*, I guess.

The kind that writes captions that spew shit like: *RAVISH ME. I am surrendered enough to let life and my man ravish me and fuck me open to God. That's what you're missing, babe. Let your ESSENCE do the talking. Stop doing—you are subconsciously blocking yourself and taking control by doing, doing, doing. Just BE—magnetic. Soft. Receptive. Then the powerful man you've been waiting for to fuck you into divinity will come. Devote yourself to the path. To yourself. To your man. To GOD.*

I slam my phone down on the counter. The screen cracks but I'm too "surrendered" to care. I leave the bathroom only feeling ravished by thick, dense, sticky molasses-level hopelessness. But I will face and "release" that in the morning.

"RUNE?" I CALL INTO MY dimly lit house on a chilly day, as I reach down to unzip my suede booties. It is day 32.

"Up here! Come up!"

My muscles tighten with every step I take up the wooden stairs. Halfway up, I am so tense, it's like my blood cells are playing my thigh muscles like the violin in an Alfred Hitchcock. With every slow step, it gets louder.

I cautiously open the bedroom door. I wince. The room is covered in lit candles. Rune is ass naked on the bed with my sequined pineapple pillow covering his dick, laying there like a Michelangelo statue. Something overwhelming comes over me. Something that I cannot control in the slightest. It comes from the depths of my soul. I burst out laughing.

"What! I'm setting the scene like you asked!" he shrieks, trying to be heard over my (definitely not gentle and feminine) 10-year-old-boy cackle.

"I... I'm... sorry," I manage to squeak out between breaths of hysteria, "I don't know why I'm laugh—" I look at the candles reflecting off the sparkly pineapple covering his flaccid dick and I burst out laughing like a lunatic yet again.

Then starts to laugh too. Hard. It's the first time we've laughed togeth-er in ages. All the weeks spent trying to be *gentle* go out the window, as I laugh so hard I let out a giant, schoolboy snort. We still don't have sex, but I snuggle up close to him and relish in the connection—it's the closest I have felt to both being human and connecting with one in months.

But by day fifty I am still nowhere near where I want to be. I don't feel traumatized, but I also don't feel soft. I don't feel angry, but I also don't feel sensitive. I feel dead. I am not having sex, nor am I interested in having sex.

Maybe I'm not trying hard enough. Or maybe this isn't the right path for me. Regardless, *fuck this*.

12

Blow Up Your Life, Bitch.

If I splash ocean water on my cheeks and pretend that they are tears, would it count as feeling something?

The white foamy water creeps up and kisses my feet before it retracts. It's early March, and I'm on Venice Beach in California for a Divine Feminine business training that's taking place this week—we're gonna learn how to run a business and let our sales be sacred and our marketing be magnetic. We will call ourselves "soulpreneurs" who deeply embody our FEMININE POWER.

I smoosh my toes in the sand and curl my lips. I don't want to go, but I also do. Priestessing in 2020 looks like having a business, and I have been busting my ass trying to build this thing. A sudden wave crashes hard and water rushes around me and cocoons me. I can actually hear my hair frizzing. I stomp away like a kid in mud.

Okay, Ani, be in your feminine. Magnetism. Transform the rage into power. And walk.

I put my shoulders back and swivel my hips down Venice Boardwalk with confidence.

Strut, strut, strut, glide, glide, glide.

I make my way through the sea of moody Jim Morrison impersonators, eager musicians playing into echoey microphones, and aggressive boys with a lot to prove whizzing by on skateboards. The catcalls are as loud as the waves and there's an electricity in the air, which is peppered with bursts of random, roaring belly laughter, and snippets of deadpan conversations detailing the latest hot gossip with enough dispassionate vocal fry to burn the healthiest of vocal cords.

I stare at the real world and realize how badly I've been missing it. Then I stop dead in my tracks, because a man is making a ratty bear puppet dance while "House of the Rising Sun" blares.

"Same," I whisper aloud to no one.

I gaze at this high art and I actually start to tune in to myself. *Fine*—I miss like, normal people—like this puppet guy! But it's like every time I find myself craving normalcy, a line-up of flowy-haired priestesses from Instagram floods around me, snapping their fingers like the Sharks and the Jets in *West Side Story*, reminding me to be mindful and heal and surrender and lean into my fucking "pleasure."

A man who looks like a young Elton John but like, swollen, cuts in front of the dissociative puppet dance. He's wearing a light-up cowboy hat, cowboy boots, a purple suit, and big orange tortoise-shell sunglasses and I just *KNOW* he's so hot and sweaty and uncomfortable right now.

"You're a shiny, pretty lil' thing, aren't you?" He's trying to do an Elvis voice, but he sounds like the kid from *The Brady Bunch* doing his "pork chops and applesauce!" bit.

And even though Swollen Elton John is cringe as all hell, I'd be lying if I said it didn't feel a little nice to be hit on. I smile a Cheshire cat smile, my (very natural looking) fake lashes like exclamation points over my dead-inside eyes.

"Thank you." I peer into his eyes and nod my head. But he looks suddenly disinterested and starts walking away.

"No, really. Thanks," I call out earnestly.

I watch my connection to the "real world" gallop away down the boardwalk, his blinking light-up cowboy hat getting smaller and smaller.

I WAKE UP THE NEXT MORNING and reach for my phone. The first confirmed COVID death in LA has officially been announced. I look out the window of my friend Charlie's place. The boardwalk that was so full of life just the day before is foggy and completely empty. I check Instagram to see what's happening, and it is filled with startling infographics.

I sit on the sofa with Charlie, a bag of uneaten potato chips between us as we watch the news in dense silence. We exchange one glance and make a feeble attempt at eating chips, but food feels foreign in our mouths. The somber newscaster tells us that life as we know it will never be the same again. I gear up to make a joke but no words come out.

We are officially going into lockdown.

My stomach drops. I'm 962 miles from Portland and Rune. There's no way I can get on a plane, they are all either booked or canceled, plus I'm terrified. Instead, I frantically rent a car and drive the fifteen hours and thirty-seven minutes back home. The only stop I make is at a small town in Northern California to get groceries. It's eerie, like a zombie apocalypse movie. Smiling people stroll leisurely through the store and chat with each other, unaware that a flock of flesh-hungry living dead is coming for them. I study their faces intently. All the stores in Portland are allegedly empty.

My head throbs. I pray to the Goddess over, and over, and over again as I drive, drive, drive.

Please make this be fear-mongering and not really bad.

Please keep everybody safe.

Please don't make life blow up.

Please, no disasters.

Please.

ON THE MORNING OF MARCH 13th I finally wake up in my own bed, and it feels like an elephant is standing on my chest. Inhaling feels like sucking through a tight straw. Chills cover my entire body. My muscles ache like I've run a marathon. I can't stop coughing.

Two days later I'm in the middle of hacking up a lung when an email comes in:

"Ani and Rune, The landlord wishes to move back into her house at the end of your lease in May. Renewal is unfortunately no longer an option. Best of luck."

Cheers to finding a new home in the middle of a global pandemic while sick with what is potentially the virus responsible for this deadly shit show!

Five days later I'm still too sweaty and feverish to have processed the concept that I need to leave my home in less than six weeks.

DING.

"Hey Ani, can I call you at 11 a.m for a moment? Won't take long."

A fire alarm blares in my bones. Nothing says good morning like a sudden text from your day-job, real world boss asking to meet. I suck in my stomach and hold my breath until air rushes out of me like a deflating balloon. My brain tries to convince me that my instincts are just primed for fear, but I know what's coming.

"Ani, you know I don't want to do this, but my hands are tied right now. This is a lot more serious than we initially thought and we don't know how long it will last. We are having to make major layoffs, and unfortunately, that includes you. Best of luck though, I know you're going to do amazing things!"

March 24th, 2020

It's time to go back to the drawing board, but I'm a broken pencil.

Rune and I are sitting on my baby blue velvet couch in the home we're about to lose, biting our nails, nervously scanning the Zillow app as we search for a new place to live.

"How about this one?" Rune asks, showing me a house in one of the nicest neighborhoods in Portland on his phone. It has a white fence and a child's swing set in the backyard.

"Or this one? This one is so nice," he adds, flipping to another home in the suburbs. It has a fucking *playroom* with a plastic pink castle and scattered broken toys surrounding it.

"Same," I whisper, staring at a barely visible stuffed fluffy green monster with one eye that's being crushed by the toy chest.

I have been keeping calm for most of this whole COVID experience. I have been entrenched in my faith. Dutifully doing my practices. Grounding. Showing up for my community by hosting free rituals even though

I feel sick all of the time. But now, looking at these gorgeous homes with the man who is going to be my forever, my chest tightens. My airflow constricts again. Living in a house with a swing set makes me feel like I'm going to swing right off the edge. I don't know why. The butterflies in my stomach feel like a swarm of maggots devouring a rotting corpse. My body hurls itself off the couch. I pace in a circle.

"Baby, what's wrong? What's happening?" Rune asks, standing up and putting his hands on my shoulders. His hands feel like sandbags weighing me down when I'm already drowning and I almost lunge for him. His eyes are cartoonishly big: round and stretched open wide. I wrangle out of his grip like a fish out of water and continue to pace. Faster this time.

Circling on the rug. Circling, biting my nails, not sure where to look, circling, spiraling, circling, spiral—

"I can't do this!" I shriek, "I can't live in one of those fucking houses!"

I claw off my shirt and throw it to the floor. I slink out of my flowing skirt and then I'm a pile of flesh and bone on the floor. I am Ani, deflated. Cracked on the floor like an egg with a broken yolk. I press my forehead into the pink Urban Outfitters rug. I feel as dramatic and as deranged as I look, as little gasps escape my body like steam from a Manhattan street. I've officially lost my shit.

I can't even look at Rune, who is standing over me in silence. I want to scream that I can't do this—that I'm addicted to negativity and I'm never going to heal—but I close my mouth tight to hide the track marks on my tongue.

I can't handle his reaction to the disaster I've become. I'm supposed to be the grounded one. The one who has "done the work" and can handle whatever life throws at her. I finally lift my head and look at him with one eye sealed shut. Because, you know—keeping one eye closed will shield me from the fact that I am now ass naked in a weird rendition of "child's pose" having a nervous breakdown over a very nice life that most people would kill for.

I'm so bent out of shape I'm starting to look like a corny statue installation at a liberal arts college.

THINK.

I just gotta get out of here. But I can't go to Brigid, I can't go to the Temple, I canNOT go to another apprenticeship. My heartbeat slows down. I exhale and open the closed eye with a sudden bolt of insight. "Babe, what if we just, like, left?" I ask with conviction. "I don't want to be here anymore. I can't do Portland anymore. What if we quarantine in Airbnbs for a while?" The words are tumbling out of my mouth faster than I can process them. "Put everything in storage, and get the fuck out of here?"

Rune is quiet for several seconds. Then he shrugs his shoulders as he nods his head. This broken rock is about to become a motherfucking rolling stone. And with that, we have a shiny, brand new plan. I spend the night picking out the few coveted items I'm going to bring with me: a box filled with crystals and cards, a refurbished Vitamix I bought during a bout of PMS insomnia, and some flowy priestess dresses. I say goodbye to everything else for now.

ON THE MORNING OF MAY 1st, my little Volkswagen Tiguan is packed to the brim with five plastic bins and my abnormally fluffy and squat dog that I named Anoush—"sweet" in Armenian. She's my new official emotional support dog. Patrick the cat is gone, passed away a month ago, and took a piece of my heart with him. We are all off to quarantine for a month in Yosemite, California.

I'm going to use this time to ground. To nourish myself and connect with the earth. To pray for everyone and everything amongst the tall trees and fluffy earth. I will smell juniper as I pray in the hot tub and I will make sweet love to Rune under the stars because the pressure will be off. I can be in complete service to my brand new clients. I can use the Vitamix to make sauces from plants I forage out there.

We get there and it's pitch black. I haven't had service for a half-hour. I can't even see our dream cabin in the woods until we go inside and flip on the lights. It has the same bile colored carpet as my college room, but I focus on the wholesome framed pictures of bears catching fish in a creek.

At 3 a.m., I'm jolted awake. Our bed is *vibrating*. A dark, mass-produced print of a bear with a salmon in its mouth drops from the wall to the ground and the frame smashes into tiny pieces.

The earth is literally shaking. Cue in an angel or God herself cheesily narrating: "It is this moment when Ani realizes that she can't escape her inner turmoil, despite moving her location."

Same, I think to myself. *Fucking same.*

Two days later, Rune and I are walking Anoush in the pitch black. Our flashlights shine against the vacant street where our Airbnb lives, light-years away from a proper town. I keep looking over my shoulder into the pitch black. I have the same feeling I get when walking home from a bar alone, late after closing.

The next morning, an older dude who looks like he's in the cast of *Napoleon Dynamite* frantically bangs on the door. "I just checked the security cameras 'cause we got an alert," he drawls. "We saw you two walkin' with your dawg, and there was the biggest mountain lion we ever seen right behind yah. Be careful around these parts!" he warns, widening his eyes to drive the point home.

I let Rune do the talking and stare at our new neighbor's mustache hairs and think about Burt Reynolds for a second, but then about how these metaphors God is throwing my way are getting a bit redundant—we get it. I'm avoiding shit. Now leave me alone to bask in my bullshit in the hot tub outside.

***

We've been at the Airbnb for a little over two weeks by the time May 18th comes around. It is my 28th birthday and I'm celebrating by raising money for The National Domestic Violence Hotline by posting some stories on Instagram. I suddenly notice that someone has serial "liked" sixteen of my posts in just a few minutes. I am overcome with that creepy, lion-stalking feeling again. I click on the account. It has zero pictures. Zero followers. It follows one person and one person only: *me*. The name on the account is Michael Lunger.

After almost seven years with zero contact, he is back. He is *watching* me again. My mouth is so dry, there's no spit to swallow. My fingers tremble like last week's earthquake as I click to block him. I steady myself on the pale green wall and my vision blurs. Then I drop to the floor and land on all fours and release a loud retching sound.

Suddenly, my hair is jet black, pin-straight, and lengthened with extensions again. I look at my shaking hands and they are covered in fingerless gloves, chipped knockoff O.P.I. Lincoln Park After Dark nail polish on my bitten-down nails. I look down at my body, which is covered in piercings and cigarette ash and glitter. And I'm back. Back in college. Back in terror. Back to wanting, *needing*, to know everything about where he is now so I can keep my enemy close; watch him like a hawk. I'm the girl whose closest friends are her panic attacks and spiral thoughts. Whose fear rumbles through her body violently, shaking her like a tiny sailboat in a rambunctious storm, the waves throwing her around until there is nothing left to do but puke into the water.

I lean against the creepy, vomit green walls in the Airbnb bedroom and try to feel the ground beneath me. I press my hands hard against my eyes until I start seeing patterns against my lids. I cannot be that girl again. I am *not* going to be that girl again. I've done far too much healing to even recognize her inside of me anymore. I need to tell Rune what *really* happened in Michael's room that night. I've never told Rune the full truth in an attempt to not "victimize" myself or "trauma bond" with him—but I can't pretend this didn't happen anymore: being physically held down, tossed around like a rag doll, told I was nothing, threatened, stalked, hunted. Everything I've tried desperately to padlock from my memory is suddenly breaking down my door.

I am trying my best not to hyperventilate as I stumble into the living room, where he's sitting at his makeshift desk in front of the wood stove that he has balanced a ring light on for his Zoom calls.

"Rune," I choke.

He closes his laptop, looking concerned.

The words spill out of my mouth manically. I sound like I just railed ten lines of blow as I tell him everything. Shame slithers around my body tighter than the snakes I used to dance with. I can't look Rune in the eyes, but when I glance over, I notice he's avoiding my gaze at all costs. When I'm finished talking, I plop down on the couch as my heart drops to my stomach, and I bury my face in my hands, rubbing my eyes harder, harder, harder.

Rune is silent. Deafeningly silent. His eyes are everywhere but on me. Finally, he walks toward me and kisses me on the head. The kind of head kiss you give to a little girl who has just scraped her knee. He turns his back to me and toward the stove where dinner is sitting in a pot. "Want some pasta?" he asks.

I walk upstairs, my body is lead and I feel dead. As soon as I get back to the ugly green room, I lay down on the bed, squeeze my eyes shut, and try to will myself to sleep. But all night, a voice screams in my head: *GET OUT OF HERE.* In the morning, I run downstairs and see Rune at his work desk. He is already back at it, making cold calls and selling people his real estate services.

I *cannot* be this isolated anymore. I *cannot* be locked in this wildlife-decor-infested cabin, far, far away from civilization. I can't sit still in this loneliness, nervously waiting for Michael to find me. Again. I need to run away. Again.

"Babe, what if we go stay near your family and quarantine? I don't think I can be so far away from humanity anymore." I am literally pleading with him.

He turns his head to look at me for the first time since I spoke up, which in hindsight was probably a stupid mistake because I'm already constantly turning him off with my incessant negativity. "Sounds great, I'll let them know." He returns his face to the screen.

ONE LONG DRIVE HALFWAY ACROSS THE country, we arrive at our newest digs for the month.

June is spent watching the heavy shadow of our society grow so big, people from all over the world can see it.

People in the spiritual world—people that I trusted—take to social media to say, with full confidence, that "Hillary Clinton *eats babies.*" That "Bill Gates is microchipping us." Or that: "*All lives matter.*"

I see my favorite celebrities exposed for brutal acts of sexual assault.

I see thought leaders accused of raping hundreds of people who trusted them with the most vulnerable parts of their healing. I see transphobia and racism in people leading wellness circles and running "spiritual" Instagram accounts.

It's a weird, un-namable thing: to be both unsurprised and absolutely shocked at the same time. Like one part of me is stabbed in the back while the other one is yelling at her, saying "I told you so!" and pushing the knife in deeper.

***

The Airbnb looks like a creepy dollhouse. Dark brown wood. Tan-stained walls. Tight little squares for windows. Sinister crawlspaces. I make the upstairs attic a pocket-sized space of my own. Whenever I am home, I am there. I even start sleeping up there.

I tuck myself into the white, ruffly, twin bed, far away from Rune, just to have a break and recharge and pray. I slip into a dream.

"She's coming for you. Oh boy, is *she* coming for you," an otherworldly man with a long face laughs, shaking his head. In the dream, I'm in the living room of an old farmhouse. It looks like it's from the early 1900s with just a hearth and a candlestick.

"Who?" I ask like a little cosmic brat. I mean, seriously? There isn't enough happening in the *real* world to have to deal with this strange drama in the *dream* world?

"Bathsheba, she's coming for YOU!" He laughs harder, and a portal opens up in the living room, through which a rageful, wild-eyed woman swiftly emerges. She grabs the candlestick and uppercuts the man from under his chin so hard that his head comes clean off his body.

To which I mutter, "fuck all this, I'm out" and book it for the stairs. But the rageful woman rematerializes directly in front of me, wild eyes ablaze, two massive circles of fire. Her hair is alive with the electricity that's coursing through it. She looks like she is from an old painting. Strong shoulders. Rounded features.

She is so close to my face that her nose brushes against mine. Her fiery energy burns my skin. Then she says something to me and I jolt awake. I blink my eyes, which are thick with sleep. I try to make sense of where I am. What did the woman with flames in her eyes say? I can't remember. I scan the room. I'm back in the creepy dollhouse Airbnb. Phew. It was all just a weird dream. *But who the fuck is Bathsheba?*

I leap out of bed and fling open my laptop and type the name "Bathsheba" into Google. And there she is.

Bathsheba, I discover, is a young girl who was kidnapped and raped because the King thought she was "hot." So hot that he wanted her all to himself. He killed off her husband by sending him to the frontlines of war and took her as his own. She is known as a whore in the Bible for "sleeping" with him.

And through the screen of my laptop, I come across another Bathsheba. This Bathsheba is a woman from Rhode Island—the place of my birth—from the 1800s, who was accused of witchcraft and exiled after the loss of her child. The movie *The Conjuring* depicts her as a demon. People still defile her grave in Rhode Island to this day.

In the dark, my eyes dart from tab to tab as I read on, absorbing the stories and information, trying to piece together why *this* name, *this* figure, came to greet me in what is quite possibly, the most visceral dream of my life. Here's what I deduce from the confines of my little attic: There are three core archetypes that women are accused of being when they are not "pretty" or "perfect" or "pleasing."

The witch.

The bitch.

The whore.

And as the social media wars escalate and expose what needs to be seen by the masses—the ones who speak up are accused of being *witches, bitches, and whores*. It is making more sense to me that Bathsheba showed up in all her wild-eyed, angry glory. She represents all the parts of us that are capable of channeling our power into change. The Witch is someone who knows their power and capabilities. The Bitch honors their boundaries and refuses to people-please. The Whore owns and honors their body and desires.

But where have the Witches, the Bitches, and the Whores been in all of this "divine feminine" training I've been doing? I think of what Diana has taught me, Maeve, and even Brigid! Amidst all the flowy skirts and softening of eyes, somehow I've managed to overlook these very important, very sacred pieces. Pieces that have nothing to do with gender or gender roles, and everything to do with advocating for yourself and others. Pieces that allow us to move the needle in a way that maybe isn't the most palatable—but is the most powerful.

It is the Witches, Bitches, and Whores who eat chaos for breakfast to feed the person they are becoming and the world they are trying to create. Fire erupts inside of me and incinerates all the delusions I have been harboring about my own life.

I'd come to believe that the restlessness inside of me was connected to my traumatic past and the dark turn in current world events. But maybe I've been despondent and dispassionate about my life because this—when all is said and done —is not the life I want to live. Maybe it's that fucking simple—and that complicated. Maybe the life I have created with Rune is beautiful. But something can be beautiful and not be right.

Maybe Rune is beautiful and—

not right.

It is sunrise when I clip Anoush to her leash and begin to walk to help me digest the slew of questions swirling through my brain. I walk for miles, holding these newfound realizations heavy in my heart. I gain more and more clarity with every step. By noon, I do what every Messy Bitch does in times of crisis: I call on my guides. Which, in this case, just happens to be one of my best friends, Jill.

"Hi, Jilly. I have to tell you something. I think I'm leaving Rune," I'm shocked at how easily the words flow from my mouth.

"Ahh, yeah. I knew this was coming."

I gulp. She *did*?

"How do you feel? What made this come up for you now?" she asks, her voice strong and gentle. (This is the beauty of having a best friend who is also a gifted psychic and astrologer.)

Jill and I talk until sundown and she tells me stories about leaving her partner of five years back in 2018. I tell her all my fears and how scary it is to leave something that is actually really ... good? By the end of the call, we have decided I will give myself three days to make a final decision about whether to stay or to leave.

When I get back home, Rune is on his laptop doing his real estate thing. I walk by him and crawl into my little attic lair and pray for guidance, clarity, a sign, something.

THE NEXT MORNING, RUNE AND I decide to walk Anoush together. It is the perfect midsummer morning, and we are both feeling like we could really use some one-on-one time. We start to crack jokes about our families and us as little kids. My heart begins to soften the hardness in my chest.

What was I thinking? This is great. Maybe it IS just your trauma, after all. And the reason you're blocking real intimacy is because you've never truly experienced it before?

"That's how I want to be when we raise our kids," Rune says proudly, finishing up his story about his parents letting him party in their basement back in high school.

"What do you mean?" I ask.

"When we have our kids, I want to be like that when they start experimenting with drinking. My parents were so cool about it. I want us to be like that with our kids, too."

Breathe out, BREATHE OUT, BITCH. This is NOT a fucking main character movie moment. This is your life, don't be a dick, say SOMETHING—

"—You *do* want to have kids with me, right—?" Rune finally asks. His pace gets slower and I can tell he doesn't know where to look.

"Well ... have you ever heard of attachment styles? Sometimes it makes it really hard if you've experienced trauma to truly be able to see a future with someone, you know?" I stutter, gracelessly. "When I think of a future with you, I start to panic—"

THUD. THUD. THUD. My heart slams against my chest like a countdown before dropping to my belly like an atomic bomb, and my words are blaring out of my mouth faster than the sonic boom.

" —But I think it's only because I've never experienced true intimacy before, you know? You can read all about it here if you want?" I start to pull out my phone, only to see his hand gently lower it. He looks me in the eye and stops walking. He stands directly in front of me. All 6'5" of him in his bright green Nike matching shorts and shirt set.

"Ani?" He asks slowly. "Do you—" his hand still over my phone, leaving me with nowhere to run. "Do you not see a future with me?"

I am a little kid playing a heated game of "Hide and Seek" and the person I am hiding from has just walked into the room.

"Well, I mean, if you could just hear me out. It's not real, it's trauma. It's called attachment trauma," I look at our shadows warping against the blaring pavement beneath me, but it's got nothing on the heat coming from his gaze. "Like, I can't right now. But it's my trauma, not me, and I can heal it!" I am begging. I look at Rune. Now he's a little kid, too. A little kid who has just found out that Santa isn't real and that grown-ups lie and nothing is what it seems to be.

Why am I saying this out loud? It's only been two days since I even started *entertaining* the idea that my three-year relationship isn't working. This could be PMS. It could just be a bad mood!

"I need some time with this. If you can't see a future with me—if you don't want to marry me and have *my kids*? Ani? Don't waste my time." His voice shakes. "I *know* what I want. And I know I want to marry you. I know it's you. You are the mother of my kids. The love of my life." He exhales. "If I'm not yours, tell me now. Please—" his voice quivers "—don't drag this out. Don't waste my time."

My gaze darts from the pavement to his shorts; I am unable to look in his eyes. "I hear you. Give me a moment and let me get my shit together. I'm really overwhelmed. Let's connect about this later tonight, okay? I love you."

We return to our creepy rented dollhouse. Before he can say anything, I run up the stairs to my little attic abode, and frantically Google "attachment styles." I send Rune all the relevant links I find floating around the internet. I'm grossed out with myself. I'm basically saying "See! This is why I don't love you!" The wellness, self-help version of "it's not *you*, it's *me*." I tip-toe down the stairs. I find him sitting silently on the couch. I walk to him and something else takes over me—I'm not sure if it's a self-sabotaging demon or a compassionate angel, but I'm choking up and my feet are stepping toward him.

"Rune—?" His eyes are red, tears are barreling down his cheeks. His stare is fixed on a small tree outside the window.

"I feel like you don't even like me. I know you love me—but you don't even like me," he whispers.

A bullet lodges itself in my heart and I let out a small cry. "I'm sorry," I say, meaning it more than I've ever meant anything. Fat, heavy droplets spill from my lids and splatter against the dark wood floor one by one, no matter how hard I blink or look up and try to stop them. "I'm so sorry," is the only thing I can manage to muster, any more words and I will crack. I try to get it together. This isn't about me. My body is convulsing, but I hide it by swaying and looking at the droplets on the thick planks of dark wood, then up at the popcorn ceiling with its water stains. Months and months of built-up truths I've refused to look at stare me, unblinking, in the eye.

"—I can't—" my voice cracks, my face burning hot.

"—be doing this—"

"—to you—" I break.

I hear a whimper come from his throat, the sound of a stifled sob. He looks out the window, but not at me.

13
Fall, Bitch

I start to peel out of the driveway. A million razor-sharp icicles pierce my chest. I'm crying so hard that I'm sore in my nail beds. Anoush is next to me. She paws at my arm and I pet her, crying even harder knowing she has no idea this might be the last time she ever sees him.

I look back once more, and he is sitting red-faced and sobbing on the edge of the driveway, unable to look up from the pavement.

I try to pick a song on Spotify to distract me as I drive away from the life we have built together. Nothing is coming.

What the fuck.

What the fuck did I just—

What the fuck did I just—

What the fuck did I just do?

As I drive down the highway, trying to search for a feeling of empowerment in my newfound sovereignty, I decide right then and there that I need to have something for the "reborn" version of me to look forward to. I spend the rest of the cross-country car ride fantasizing about my new life: I'm going to get a trailer! I'm going to live in it and travel around! Mostly because I actually have no idea where I want to end up and the thought of settling down somewhere gives me crippling anxiety!

Exactly twenty-one hours later, I snake into my mother's long, winding driveway in Rhode Island, where I will be staying temporarily. I am excited to be by the ocean, which is a just short walk from my temporary abode. There's a lot of healing to be had, and nothing heals more than the ocean. The air is so salty and muggy that my eyebrows start to frizz the second I step out of the car.

"Ready, Gunky Girl?" I turn to Anoush, who's side-eyeing me, clearly unamused, from the front seat.

"I know, it'll be fun!" I force a smile.

She looks out the window and sighs before we hop out of the car and into our new life.

I spend the rest of the summer trying to summon the classic "glow up" that is supposed to come after a soul-scorching breakup.

And ... well ... we're in a literal global pandemic. I can't see friends. I can't go out. There's no reason to get dolled up. Instead, I spend every day being in service to my clients, replying to faceless Instagram followers, and sharing things online that I'm not ready to share in the name of being "authentic."

I also develop a sick, twisted, self-defeating addiction to calling Rune. Like any addict, I can't help myself. I reach out to him every day and every night. I am desperate for a fix of him. I am shameless. He never answers my calls. Every time I am met with his generic voicemail, the reality that this is *actually* over becomes increasingly high-definition. I am not de-ranged enough to play the "victim" here—*I* ended it. He is hurt. But, at the same time, he had totally checked out of the relationship long before I ended it, so he's not really a victim either ... Right? Well, at the very least, we both deserve *closure.*

I pick up the phone and call again.

It rings.

And rings.

And rings.

"Please leave your message for ..."

FUCK. God, fuck him. If he could have just grown up and owned his shit, this wouldn't be happening.

Days go by. I keep calling. And calling. And calling. If I'm not obsessively calling Rune, I am obsessively researching ways to craft a new life, or obses-sively writing down every convoluted thought that flies through my head in a journal. Scribble after violent scribble trying to make sense of things: *Am I a narcissist? Am I a mess? What is my dream person like? When was the last time I felt— good?*

It dawns on me that I haven't felt good in years. The last time I remember feeling good was when I lived in Ashland. More scribbles. More research. More calls. More voicemails.

I look in the mirror and I see a ghost. I am the ghost. Fake Venus flytrap lashes stripped bare. Faraway eyes. No sparkle or lipstick or anything colorful or fun or pretty on my face. Hair overgrown and looking like the letter "A" 'cause the top is greasy and the bottom is dry and frayed at the ends. I have no idea what to wear anymore. I don't know where home is. I have nowhere to go that feels okay. I am not okay. In fact, fuck *good*; all I want is to return to a time when I felt *okay*. It certainly isn't going to be in Rhode Island—I feel like I've regressed being back here. As for my fantasies of nomadic living, I can't afford a trailer to travel around the country in. (And if I'm being honest, the whole concept does give me murder vibes, seeing as how I'm probably too far down my narcissistic rabbit hole bullshit to stay aware of my surroundings.)

I am scribbling away in my journal at the dinner table that has yet to have dinner on it, the only light coming from my laptop, which is playing binaural beats for self-love.

If I want to feel the way I felt in Ashland ... maybe I need to go back to Ashland?

My brain lights up at the thought. And it wouldn't exactly hurt to be in close proximity to Rune, too. He moved back to Portland after our stint in his hometown to be with his new real estate team. They're the kind of guys who DJ "on the side" and love molly and house music and posting motivational quotes on Instagram with, like, a lion or a stock-photo image of a generically good-looking guy wearing a too-tight suit in the background. His new life might not be my vibe, but I know if we could just see each other, he would remember that we aren't frigid enemies. I don't want to get back together. But I want us to be family. He is my family forever, no matter what. And with that, I'm going back to Ashland, bitch!

In a harried frenzy, I pack my Vitamix and a handful of crystals, grab Anoush, ignoring her incessant eye-rolls, and make yet *another* cross-country move, where I will stay at a seventies-themed motel until I find a new place to live.

THE SECOND I SEE THE mountains of Ashland, I force a sigh of relief. Manufactured calm. Almost as good as the real deal.

I find my brand new apartment to rent the first week I'm there.

I text him: "I want to go through our storage unit."

He answers a day and change later: "Okay. I'll get my stuff."

The confusion of being back where it all started faintly plays like a radio in the back of my head, but I turn up the volume on my excitement to drown the sound of impending chaos out.

***

"Anoushik! Play! You're a dog!" I call out to the pile of fluff that is laying on the picnic table of the dog park. She hops off the table and slowly makes her way toward me, ignoring the dogs pining for her attention, then plops down at my feet, releasing a sigh of exhaustion from her twenty-second trek.

It's Sunday, I just signed the paperwork on my new digs and I am certain I'm about to feel *so* good and so grounded again. I sit on the bed and Pinterest decor with one hand and pet Anoush with the other.

Suddenly, my screen flashes and vibrates.

Rune. Is calling. Me.

It feels like I'm freefalling in a dream.

I slide my thumb to answer the call. "Hello?" I manage, even though there is a freight train barreling through my chest.

"Hi, Ani. I hope you're settling in well." I can tell he's trying to sound "cool," but he sounds ... cold?

"Regards, Rune, glad we can circle back and touch base," I mock playfully, in a pseudo-corporate voice that mirrors his. His silence shows me that he is not getting it. Okay take two: "Well, how the hell are ya? What's going on in your world! Long time no talk."

"I'm well, I'm well." He sounds like he's about to compliment my firm handshake and ask about the ol' ball and chain before we close a deal in a beige office.

"So," he continues, "I just wanted to let you know that you are amazing. I'm so proud of you for working on your sensuality."

HUH?

"You are so powerful—"

I zero in on an acorn on the ground and the rest of his words get tuned out by the sound of the alarm reverberating in my bones throughout my whole body. *No.*

I see him lying in bed naked with a girl wearing pearls. I can't move and all I want to do is run and get off this fucking phone. I am nuclear. He's moved on.

"Rune," I cut off his pseudo-sincere soliloquy " ... did you move on already?"

I am blinded by a flash of her big white shiny teeth.

"Ani, I'm not going there with you."

Him running his hands over her long, toned legs and ripping her flowy dress off. "Does she wear pearls?" I press.

Rune pauses. "Sometimes."

It's a three-minute drive home from the park. I hold it together for two, and I'm one minute from my door before I can't hold it anymore.

"Oh my God," I whisper. I can practically hear them purring "I love you" to each other while spooning naked in their bed.

You broke up with him! He is not yours! I know she always smells good, Rune— BUT IT'S BEEN ONE FUCKING MONTH. YOU WANTED TO MARRY ME.

"Oh ... my God." I am hyperventilating so hard I can't see. I pull over, grab Anoush, and power-walk the rest of the way to my house.

I burst through the front door. I get a glimpse of my reflection on my phone screen. I'm wide-eyed, terrified, panicked. I need to do something, anything. Every time I think I reach the point of a panic attack, it somehow just intensifies more. Pure, potent panic driving my actions. I need to know who this pearly girl with the blinding white teeth and the racehorse legs is. Within seconds, I'm sweaty-palmed and scrolling through Instagram. I go to his page, and nothing new is posted. I grit my teeth; I can't find anything. I suddenly remember the sacred lesson of the Messy Bitch Sleuth. Passed down to me by generations of the Messy Bitches that came before. When you can't find what you're looking for, *always—*

Check—

Venmo!

Dopamine floods me as I click on his name and see dozens of exchanges with this sweet, shiny girl. I snort deadly lines of Venmo exchanges between them, becoming more crazed, my heart racing, pupils dilating, the stench of cold sweat bursting out of my pores. There are Venmo exchanges for groceries. Movies. Dinners. There are cute little emojis. I don't know what I am more disturbed by: him moving on so quickly or the fact that they are going *Dutch* on dates.

Sarah Baker. Of course, her name is Sarah Baker. By the time I clumsily type her name into the list of people he's "following" on Instagram I am manically high. And there she is. So un-ironically Americana with her big bellowing barrel curls and palatably on-trend outfits and ... Oh my god—*fifty thousand followers*?! Her username is literally @bakers_buns_fit. REALLY? She's a *fitness influencer*? I collapse on the bed like I'm spiraling down to the depths of hell—he's with a professional "hot girl." Alabaster teeth and all.

I try to swallow to lubricate my bone-dry mouth. My eyes quiver like nervous limbs. They are darting around the screen, taking in every ounce of information as quickly as I can. I scroll past a picture of a chalkboard that says "chase your dreams," then past a soft claw French-girl manicure with dainty little gold Mejuri rings. And then—there he is. Long arms wrapped around her fat-free yet perfectly busty frame. Their cheeks delightfully pressed together. The caption reads: "I love you yesterday, today, and tomorrow. Thank you for being everything to me and the best partner I could possibly dream of #couplesgoals"

You know in the movies when someone squeezes a glass so hard that it shatters in their fingers?

Crunch

Any delusion I have been secretly holding onto about us being a forever family that transcends romance smashes to pieces and bloodies up my hand.

None of my tools are working. Emotional regulation? Never heard of her. Breathwork? What even *is* oxygen? Ritual? I don't trust a damn thing.

Never mind *God*.

"This is just your ego, Ani. Your ego is bruised. You'll get over it," everyone says.

Maybe they're right. But does that make the hurt suck any less? Hell no.

"Ani, you're going to find someone even better!" they all continue.

I stare at the wall and wonder how the hell I got back here. Alone. On my bedroom floor. Where I have been for most of my life.

14
Winter, Bitch

I'm too old to be the sexy "hot and broken bad girl." I'm a twenty-seven-year-old hot mess who hasn't showered in days and has wasted her entire adult life in a fake relationship engaging in fake spiritual practices and failed attempts to heal something that I don't even think is fixable—me.

Every morning when I wake up, I peel open my caked-in-old-mascara eyes and am immediately greeted with visions of Rune and The Fitness Influencer waking up together. The ceiling in my new Ashland apartment serves as a projector screen showing their love story in real-time. I try to focus on the cracks in the plaster, but they constantly morph into them laying in each other's arms.

I turn over, pick up my phone, and frantically type in her Instagram handle. Again.

A new picture of them cuddling jolts me fully awake and my mouth suddenly tastes like battery acid.

"Everyone deserves a man like this one"

I am suddenly hyper-aware of the sheets tangled up around my feet. I don't even have enough energy to kick them off. They are cold from old damp sweat. I can smell my own B.O.

What the fuck is the issue here? I didn't even want him! I chose to leave! Why do I want to fly-crawl backward down a flight of stairs and projectile vomit, Exorcist style, all over them?

Anoush walks into the room and puts her snout directly in my face and does her signature "huff"—not quite a bark, not quite a whine, just a blunt declaration that she's about to piss her fur.

I fling the covers off and stand up too fast. I can't remember the last time I was able to keep food down without feeling violently ill. My hands are constantly shaking. I lean my head on the doorframe and try to stabilize myself. I see black.

You are so fucking weak. The world is in crisis and you're worried about your stupid frail ego? This is your biggest problem? Crying over someone you didn't even want? You love playing the victim, don't you? You love being miserable.

I take Anoush for a walk in my oversized pajama shirt, which has a massive picture of Chunk from *The Goonies* over it. I know I look strung out, with my hair greasy and my pace as Zombie-like as my eyes. But I look past everyone I pass, so I don't know if people even see me.

When I get back, I try to turn to reliable old masturbation to distract myself from visions of them staring lovingly into each other's eyes. But the second I touch my body I see them in the throes of love and gag. I end up laying there, my mind's eye honing in on a scene of them laughing at my frantic phone calls from the summer, her getting creeped out. "She's still so in love with you," I hear her giggle, giant teeth flashing like police lights. I imagine the way he describes our relationship to her: "Yeah, it was rough. She was just miserable. Hated everything all the time. But I think she just hated herself. Could you blame her?"

Worst of all, I keep imagining how wildly relieved he is to be rid of me.

And here's the other thing I'm starting to realize—every single boyfriend I've had has immediately moved on after me: Johnny married a Swedish model about two months after I broke up with him, and they had a JFK and Jackie O themed wedding, tweed skirt suit and all. Michael, I found out, also married some girl a few months after me, and now has TWO KIDS (terrifying). And now Rune has Sarah Baker.

It's so clear—I am the problem.

I close my eyes and count down as a way to will myself out of bed. *Three. Pause. Two. Pause. One. Pause.* And I still can't seem to move! I face the wall and stare at the layers of sloppy paint jobs, thick coats of white caked onto each other. These days, I'm either hollow or in a full-blown panic attack.

I threw away my whole good, dream life for what? Trauma? Because I thought there was something out there that was better?

This is *ridiculous*. ENOUGH! It's time to at least try and get help. I Google "local therapists." I pick therapists like I pick wine, not by provenance but by how well they're branded.

I settle on an older woman: Aria Linston. She has a sweet smile and sparkly eyes. Soft graying hair is tucked gently behind her ear. She poses with her dog, and I don't even need to read her "about me." My intuition tells me to call her, and so my fingers confidently dial.

"This is Aria!" she chimes. Her voice is sweet and crackly, like roasted marshmallows. Sold.

We set up our first appointment for the next day.

"Oh, and if you're open, I also do astrology. I would just need your birth time!" she adds.

Astro meets neuro. Perfect.

The next day, I open up Zoom, and her sparkly eyes beam at me through the screen.

"Hi!" I smile, relieved to feel a sense of comfort. A contorted form of comfort, but comfort nonetheless.

"Oh Ani, I ran your chart ... yikes. You are in the hardest transits one could go through. There's no escaping it. It's like you're getting rid of all your trauma and stuck emotion before the time you're thirty. It'll end up being good, but it's not pretty while you're in it."

I zero in on a red candle on my desk.

"...Thirty?" I squeak. "This is gonna last till I'm *thirty*?"

"At least another year, but it could go until you're thirty, yes."

THREE. FUCKING. YEARS. OF *THIS*?

"What do I do?" I beg.

"Just know that while it's hard, none of what you're going through is in vain," she says, through a furrowed brow. Daggers fly from my eyeballs.

This is NOT going to work. As soon as I hang up, I pay for the session, and I vow to never call her again.

Instead, I crawl back to the Tantric relationship coach Rune I worked with and beg her to take me on to teach me *how* to love because clearly, I have no fucking clue. (She also happens to know Rune, so maybe she can *honestly* tell me if it was him or me?) An exorbitant amount of money later and we're starting our sessions together.

Tara the Tantric Teacher has a tiny nose and a big hoop nose ring, juxtaposing her teensy frame and flowing clothes. She always has a cup of tea and she sits on a sheepskin in every Zoom meeting.

"Ani, in your next relationship, how will you know they are showing up for you?"

I suddenly want to throw up.

"So when you get ready to receive them, to really open to them, you must make sure you ..."

Her voice starts to sound like the Charlie Brown teacher as I click around my screen and Google "Airstreams for sale."

Suddenly she snaps: "Ani, are you doing something else right now? Listen to me: you need to dream of something new to move on."

I slowly turn my head to the screen and look her in the eyes. "But do you think Rune REALLY loves her?"

"I refuse to speak one more time about them. Refuse. We need to focus on YOUR future."

"But why am I so replaceable?" I croak, barely able to finish the last word without my voice breaking.

"You're not, honey. There's no replacing anyone. Maybe he just found a better fit."

"It's like I never existed like—like none of this mattered or even happened. He was my family," I break down.

"Ani," she clips. "We can't go *there*. It's time to move on. Look. Focus as best as you can. Let's talk about 'conscious relationships.' There is a man who could meet you in full presence and power, who is unafraid of your depths. There is a man who shares your values and can meet you in conscious communication."

As she talks, I envision a slew of creepy men in leather trench coats. They have little hoop earrings squeezed into thick earlobes and wear low ponytails with paperboy hats. "Spiritual men" who boast about how "conscious" they are, but use their flowery language and non-violent/ conscious communication to manipulate women into sex. I don't fucking want that, either. And I don't fucking want to talk about it anymore.

"HI, MY CLAM, HOW YA holdin' up today?" Joni has called me Clam since high school because of some inside joke I can't remember, and there's a small part of me that finds it humorous to hear it used so casually at a time like this. And then I remember *why* I'm calling.

"I can't feel this again," my voice is monotone and flat, as I dead-stare at a spot on the wall.

"I know. But you're doing it. You're moving through it. It's so hard but you're doing it! And I'm right here." Joni sounds so sure and so clear that I have no choice but to believe her. And Joni *knows* the darkness well. I've seen Joni move through deep bouts of doubt, depression, confusion, and overwhelm.

"I can't do another day. I don't get it. It's not like I want him. I just can't ... move on. *Why*?"

"I don't know why you're in this spot and I don't know why he moved on so quickly. But what I do know is this—I love you. You are one of the loves of my life. And any person would be damn lucky to be with you," Joni's voice glows in the dark, like one of those peel-and-stick stars that kids have on their bedroom walls. A tiny faint light.

"What if I came out there for a couple days?" she coos.

"Across the freaking country? I couldn't ask you to do that."

"Ewuhh—we're past that. Did you forget who you're talking to? I'm on my way," she claps back. I can hear her extra-long nails tap tap tap on her keyboard, booking a flight right then and there.

Exactly seventy-two hours later, I am driving to the Medford airport. It only has one terminal with one baggage claim carousel, and I suddenly *feel* how *tiny* this town really is.

And then there she is, in a cut-up t-shirt with her own sixties-inspired art on it, a long skirt, and enough statement jewelry to put any bohemian to shame. I hop out of my car and run towards her, forgetting to even put it in park.

"Ah Jeez!" I yell, as the car begins to tiptoe away. I hop in and slam the breaks.

"Ah Clam, what happened, yah got excited to see your pal or some-thin'?" she laughs, doing her signature Massachusetts Mother voice, watching me through the window.

I run towards her again and hold her as tightly as humanly possible, feeling a lifeline for the first time in weeks.

"Oh, my Clam, you look beautiful," she purrs, gently grazing her long nails against my back.

"You smell like home," I snot into her shoulder. I lift my head and see the giant wet mark on her and feel a strange sense of pride. My *friend* is here.

Joni and I have a tradition of joining pinkies for entire car rides, a cov-eted ritual we've been doing since high school. Instinctively, we lock them and drive off.

"What the fuck just happened?" I deadpan, looking at her with hazy eyes. We burst into a hysterical fit of laughter. The rest of the day is spent settling in. Joni helps me clean my house and set it up pretty. I don't think about Rune and his leggy new girlfriend at all. That is, until the dreaded nightfall comes calling.

Don't slip into this hell hole again. You finally have support. Use it, bitch. Don't. Slip. Down. There.

"Hey Joni, have you ever seen the music video for that 1980s song 'Into The Night' by Benny Mardones?"

"I can't say that I have?" she replies inquisitively.

"It's actually the creepiest song ever. He looks like the human equiv-alent of cigarette ash and he falls in love with a sixteen-year-old and they ride a magic carpet over the Statue of Liberty while he, like, dramatically yell-sings at her. Wanna see?"

"Pull it up."

I plug my computer into my speakers and pull up YouTube. The opening piano riff begins.

My foot starts tapping to the beat. I play the part where Benny sings about a teenage girl everyone is telling him to "leave alone."

I start to mouth the lyrics. How is this song still allowed to play? It's ultimately about a grown ass man lusting after a teenager! And I still hear it in every major grocery store chain ever.

Joni and I watch him walk up to the girl's window. Next, I am shooting up from the bed and scream *belting* in Joni's face about flying her into the night.

Joni pulls out her phone and hits record, another ritual we've been doing since we were kids. I put on an elaborate, dramatic interpretive dance to a song, and she records it while silent-shake laughing. Shit. I remember that THIS is always how I've processed the ocean of emotion in me.

I grab my twisty witch's broom I have proudly displayed in my bedroom to use as a microphone and leave the room. Then I dramatically re-enter with my witch's broom mic-stand in front of me, singing with as much gusto as Benny in the video.

Now, I'm crying. Like actual *tears* are flooding down my face. But like any iconic superstar, I channel it into my performance. I look at Joni, unblinkingly. Her eyes are welling up. (Joni can cry and laugh more easily than anyone I know, and it's contagious.)

Then I whip the mic-stand broom between my legs like a witch flying and lift one leg and hop as I belt into the air.

I drop the broom and fling my whole body down, flip back up, whip my hair behind me, and raise my hands to the ceiling.

I'm sweating and crying and grabbing Joni's cheeks and scream-singing millimeters from her face without breaking eye contact. She roars with laughter.

Two hours later, we are still playing the song. I do my entire interpretative dance to it at *least* forty times. Joni is now laying on the bed exhausted and exasperated, petting Anoush and sighing every time I press the replay button.

"Clam! Please! Not again!" she whines through a fit of joyous giggles.

"Did I hear an encore chant?" I say in my best seventies-corny-variety-show-host voice and hit play for the forty-first time.

"Okay ... one more time!"

I let this one be the most dramatic, releasing every ounce of emotion that's been stuck inside this body.

It dawns on me mid-performance that this is the first time in fucking years that I've accessed a part of myself I thought was dead. Why it has to be to what is perhaps the creepiest song ever is beyond me—but hey, release happens when we least expect it.

A peephole of hope carves itself into the underworld prison I've been trapped in.

TWO WEEKS HAVE PASSED SINCE Joni's visit. Much of my hope goes away with her, but I'm fiercely determined to white-knuckle my way through it.

I incessantly call reader after reader to get an analysis of "WTF is going on."

Tarot.

Astrology.

Psychics.

Numerology.

Human design.

I'm desperate for someone to tell me who I am and what is going to *happen* next.

I get on the phone with an astrologer I've met with every year on my birthday since I was a kid. Good ol' Jerry, a former monk turned astrologer with a voice that sounds like a meditative Santa Claus.

"Annie!" Twenty-seven years later and he still gets my name wrong—but with him and him alone, I do find it endearing. "You know I love you! When I saw your name in the schedule I just about leaped out of my office chair in excitement. How are you?"

"Jerry ... I'm ... awful. Never been worse. What is happening and when is it over?"

"Well, to be honest, when I come across this transit you're in now—other people in this transit either call me from the psych ward or a hospital bed," he says cheerily. "The good news is you're clearing out all the pain in your subconscious. All that stuck stuff in there. You're in the belly of the beast—the core wound. Annie?" He asks. "Permission to be blunt enough to make a monk blush?"

"Jerry, nothing you say could shock me at this point. Shoot."

"This isn't about him. This is about the pain you've carried your whole life. This is about a reckoning with God. This is about never letting this stuff stop you from doing what you want in this life and knowing your capacity for happiness! It's hard now—but it *will* get better. This is all part of your destiny." He pauses again. "And you're going to write a book," he adds cryptically.

Oddly enough, every reading I've gotten has told me the same thing: this is the hardest time ever, but it has nothing to do with the relationship. It all has to do with something much *deeper*. They all strangely predict that someone new will be in the picture around March. This person will allegedly change my life. In the fall, I'm going to have to choose between two people.

But I'm too stuck in my current reality to find relief in their predictions.

After I hang up with Jerry I run to my closet, pull out my tattered, well-worn motorcycle boots and slide them over dirty pink socks. The second the boots grace my feet, it's like a key is unlocking a giant chastity belt. A giant chastity belt I didn't even know I was *wearing*. Why in the ever-living fuck did I ever take these boots off? Why? I click my bad bitch boot heels together à la Dorothy in *The Wizard of Oz*, and call out to Anoush laying on the floor behind me, "there's no place like home!" She frantically wags her tail while the rest of her body remains completely inert.

I realize it's not just the boots that are bad bitches. It's me. I'm a *bad* bitch. And it's time I dressed the part and started living *badly* (like good, strong badly) again.

Next, I dig out all of my old bold, audacious, velvet, and sequined clothes. I put on eyeliner, I blow out my hair, I throw on a velvet jacket and big hoop earrings. When I go out to walk my dog, this time I feel like I'm strutting. I see a flier posted on a telephone pole in town for an outdoor concert the following night. It's a Led Zeppelin cover band with a female lead singer. Who is *also* a priestess. If this isn't a sign I don't know what is.

I sashay straight back home with my game face on, Anoush strutting behind me like the supermodel dog that she is.

FRIDAY EVENING IS FINALLY HERE and I'm getting ready, blasting "Dazed and Confused" while fastening a velvet choker around my neck, painting my lips a bold red, and creating a cat eye so sharp it could *cut* a bitch. Over it, I apply the signature glitter liner that I haven't seen in years. Every little golden sparkle on my lid feels like part of a yellow brick road back home, and I see a little piece of myself again in the mirror. I slip on my silk bralette and step into my pleather leggings (the only pair I've found that doesn't give you that cheap-plastic fish market ass-gina smell) and complete the look with my newly upgraded motorcycle boots and oversized black velvet blazer. My hair is down, the two front pieces dyed platinum blonde.

I pop a Big Red into my mouth.

I look ... good. Great, even. Hello body. Hello velvet. Hello jawline. I'm like coven hot. Like witchy hot.

I spritz myself with rose perfume that has moonstone and lapis gemstones in it, kiss my dog goodbye, and head to the concert by myself. This is a reclamation: the only company I need is myself. I arrive at a back meadow of a hot spring resort, and with every step along the dimly lit path, I feel a piece of my soul coming back. I get my temperature checked, ticket scanned, and hop in close to the stage. Then out comes the priestess singer in a full leather outfit and massive, long ponytail, belting along to the song "Living, Loving, Maid."

I dance. I frantically scan the scene—like I'm looking for something. What is it?

"Immigrant Song."

I feel the unease building in my bones, so I focus on the guitarist's hands to distract myself. I don't know how to move my body. I feel like the Tin Man without oil.

"Whole Lotta Love."

My body feels clunky and like it's not really mine. I can't really feel the music at all, nor can I shake the feeling that something is missing.

"Kashmir."

There doesn't seem to be a way to get enough breath into my chest, despite my desperate gulps for more.

Fuck.

Tears pierce my eyeballs. I choke them down and push through the crowd. I sprint out of the venue and toward my car.

It's fine ... this doesn't mean anything. You're still a bad bitch, I think while my hand shakily clicks in my seat belt.

I drive up the road in silence and take long, steady breaths that come out so shaky it sounds like I'm off roading.

And then—the motherfucking annoying ass tears come. *WHY. WHY??*

I peel into my driveway as the crying gets so intense it feels like there's a balloon sucking the air out of my chest. I burst through my door and Anoush comes trotting up to me wagging her tail frantically. I sink down to the floor with her. I can't keep it together. The mascara, eyeliner, and glitter I'd meticulously applied an hour earlier run down my cheeks and into Anoush's fur. The room is lit only by my blue and red neon psychic reader sign. I realize I still have the piece of Big Red in my mouth. I catch a glimpse of my reflection in the large, ornate living room mirror. My beautiful outfit is covered in fucked up makeup, snot, and glitter. I'm on the floor with a Martian disguised as a dog. I'm smacking my gum like my life depends on it, the pops so loud they are echoing off the walls.

And I can't help it. An involuntary smirk paints itself across my face as I sniffle the snot back into my nose and snicker. *Hey ... I've been here before.* But being in this all too familiar place doesn't feel like backtracking ... it feels like a ... homecoming. Like seeing a college friend you shared your most cherished moments with but haven't seen for years at a random work event, and you both scream and hug each other.

This girl I have tried to run desperately from. The Messy Bitch who never gives up no matter how many times she blows up her life.

Here she is.

I've missed her.

I fling myself off of the floor and grab my laptop from my bed, whip it open, and pull up Pages, because I'm still the only person in the world who uses Pages, which also makes me smirk.

I want spirituality for the ones who immediately look up their new partner's ex and compare themselves to her.

I type furiously, feeling inspiration take over my hands and my brain.

I want spirituality for those who find solace in a song when it feels like no one else could possibly understand.

I feel completely possessed, in the best way.

I want spirituality for the ones whose emotions feel so big, like a tsunami, that sometimes it's easier to not feel them.

I want spirituality for the ones who brunch. Who are insecure. Who work a nine-to-five. Who can't find a job. Who wonder how the fuck they are going to survive 2020 if another thing hits them. Who daydream about steamy lovers and then giggle to themselves after.

I want spirituality for the ones who are rawly, authentically themselves, working through all the bullshit conditioning, just trying to find their way.

Your journey is one of the most sacred—even with your mascara stained pillowcase.

I close my laptop and flop on my bed, and fall asleep with makeup running onto my silk bra.

THE FOLLWING WEEK, I TOTALLY space that I have another group meeting for a spiritual embodiment facilitator training that I'd signed up for pre-pandemic—when I was still trying to "better myself" and hadn't yet accepted that I'm basically human trash.

I hop on to the Zoom call, not even sure what we're supposed to be doing.

"Okay, my loves, time to present your final projects!" announces the program leader.

Fuck.

We were supposed to do something that shows what we have learned from all this. I have four presentations to come up with something before it is my turn.

Okay ... I'm pretty good under pressure ... but holy shit. People have written songs, made videos. *They are amazing. They present mind-blowing, well-thought-out* work they've channeled heaps of effort into.

I pull up the manifesto that shakily poured out of me the week before. With rapid-fire intensity, I furiously type out two pages of words to pair with it.

I'm up. I straighten my back, channel any ounce of fire in my body through my gaze, and lift my chin as my non-verbal "fuck it—here we go."

My voice cracks.

"I am a Messy Bitch. Like, truly, a *Messy* Bitch. Like possibly one of the messiest bitches. And I wear that title proudly," I read.

"I've thrown up that fluorescent purple 'liquor' (which, honestly, what the hell is that stuff?) in the club. And I've had the most spiritual, profound, real conversations about betrayal, loss, heartache, and what love really is in the bathroom there, too."

I glance up at the Zoom call to give everyone my Lizard Gaze to see if it will translate over the internet, but everyone is already looking pretty hooked.

"And the time I had to tuck a rogue hair extension away in my purse at a nice brunch in a hipster Brooklyn cafe that also sold lingerie (because, Brooklyn) ... If you ask me, ALL of it is what makes life worth living ... "

When I finish, I get a flood of private Zoom chats from the rest of the participants.

"FUCK. YES."

"THANK YOU."

"I've been WAITING for this!"

And then, one from the owner of an indie publishing company that reads:

"If you ever want to turn this into a book, let me know. Amazing."

I pick up my smooshy pillow that's caked in my hair grease and I proceed to press my face into it and scream in pure excitement, hop off the bed and start air spanking the air, run to Anoush and start clapping and petting her, to which she starts freaking out and wagging her tail and panting in excitement with me.

I, Ani Ferlise, am going to write a fucking book.

And for the first time in fucking years, something feels right.

OKAY, YOU KNOW HOW PEOPLE annoyingly say that happiness comes from within? Well, fuck them and fuck the whole concept. But no matter how hard I try to keep it around, the excitement of the book idea fades, just as quickly as the opportunity presented itself.

I'm still living in Rune's shadow. He creeps into everything I do. No matter how hard I try to escape it, his presence is like the sun in my eyes during a long drive: blinding, unavoidable, and following me at every turn.

I go home to Rhode Island for Thanksgiving, a holiday my family doesn't even celebrate.

I live out of a suitcase at my sister's house, a spooky, old Victorian on the water. Every night I check on "her." Ya know, @bakers_buns_fit. She posts a picture of the most basic, on-trend outfit and gets thousands of likes.

In fact, every picture is of a basic-bitch, on-trend outfit. Each one gets thousands of likes. *She seems like the kind of girl who would have a "live, laugh, love" sign in her house,* I think, smugly.

The truth is, I've been pouring my heart and soul into Instagram for three years—taking model shots, telling stories, teaching ... and I barely get any interaction. Her effortless connection with her followers stings.

What a fucking basic bitch! She's probably never suffered a day in her whole life. She probably isn't deep at all. She probably loves Ed Sheeran and hates spicy food and puts on The Notebook when she wants to feel something. I'm gonna be an AUTHOR.

I twist in my cheap fleece heated blanket on my sister's guest bed and let a bead of sweat count as a tear shed as I stare at the ceiling.

She's out there living her best life, and I'm the one who's all alone, miserable and judging her.

And here I am, the same bitch who judged all of the women at the priestess circle, all those years ago. Nothing has changed except I got even more self-righteous.

Literally, what's wrong with being a "live, laugh, love" girl? I mean, is that not the entire goal of life? To live it, to laugh, and to love? I kick the itchy heated blanket down to my ankles and starfish on the bed.

In which case, what was the point of all of this *self-work* when the outcome has been feeling even more alone, terrified, and unable to live, laugh, or love? That was the *promise.* That was what was *supposed* to happen.

And the real kick in the balls? I don't even know what her story is. She could have had the same traumas and life experiences I've had—maybe even worse—and yet somehow still be managing to enjoy her life.

But all I can do is mock girls like her. Maybe because I can't remember the last time I truly lived, laughed, or was able to love myself.

And here I am, alone during the holidays under a heated blanket I haven't washed in weeks, in yesterday's mascara, going through her photos as she shines brilliantly with her pearly whites.

Fuck it. I want to be a fucking Live Laugh Love girl. I want to brush my teeth every night and I want the life I was living with Rune to be enough for me. I pass out, my phone in my hand.

IT'S NEW YEAR'S AND I have nowhere to go. We're still in the pandemic, and all my immediate friends are with their significant others.

I decide to do a ritual because even if I'm not sure that anything even exists "out there," at least I can trick myself into thinking I'm not completely alone by being dramatic. And there is nothing more dramatic than ritual.

I have a statue of a Goddess made of clay. She is a spiral Goddess with a round belly, her hands stretched to the sky. I put the statue on the dining room table and light a candle, then get up and grab a can of IPA from the fridge and a cup. I pour out half and give it to her as an offering. Then I chug the rest, sitting with man-spread legs, slouched down in the chair in front of her like a rebellious teen in the principal's office in a family friendly 1990s TV show.

I'm not even sure what I'm doing or why, but as I begin to feel buzzed off half a beer, I start to speak out loud:

"Okay. So listen. This whole thing? Sucked. Big time. And I just don't get it. I'm mad. I'm scared. But I'm going to choose to believe that this is going to get better. I know how you work, I've heard the stories of the underworld and losing everything and ego deaths and what not. I am not sure if that's what's happening here. But if it's not, so help me God ... dess ... sorry. So anyway, if this is it, it's not really worth it. So show me that it's not? I guess? Please? Show me that this isn't all in vain."

Then it hits me: I'm by myself on New Year's, speaking out loud to a statue I got on Etsy.

I also made an offering to the *Goddess* of an IPA that was definitely made by a hipster-bro that would mansplain Bitcoin to you and not ask you a single question about yourself and gets monthly subscription boxes for his beard-care.

I am completely losing my mind.

12:01 a.m. hits, and I head up to bed, slipping under the disgusting heated blanket I still haven't washed. I pray for tears because it feels like my head is going to explode from the pressure of them collecting behind my eyeballs.

I AM GOING TO WRITE THIS fucking book because my life really does depend on it at this point. Like, literally, I need something to live for. And what does a gal who needs a reason to live write about?

Her deepest traumas!

Day after day. In detail.

After every story, I can't stop pulling up motherfucking Facebook, slamming my fingers on the keyboard like someone hacking the motherboard in a nerd movie, searching all the people I'm writing about.

I start with Michael. There he is. Posing with his wife and child. I cannot believe he literally has a fucking *family*. He ate my face and now he has a family.

I move on to my boss from camp. I swallow. The hairs on my arms raise. And wouldn't you know? The first photo I see is him and his freshly wedded wife, wearing matching "just married" sun hats on beach chairs, holding hands on their honeymoon.

And lastly, I type in Rune's name.

Oh great, not only is he with Live Laugh Love Happy Fitness Girl Baker, he also bought a MOTHER FUCKING Porsche.

I can't help but feel pure, unbridled rage.

Pure existential rage.

The anger is so alive inside of me I hear it snap in my bones.

I slam my laptop shut so hard I crack the screen. I sit in the silence of my sister's home and glance around the kitchen to try to steady myself.

Then I whip out my Goddess statue from my backpack and put it on the kitchen table in front of me, interrogation style.

"There's no fucking punishment for people who are bad, huh?" I hiss at the inanimate statue.

"And only rewards when people are good?! Michael is taking *family portraits* and his wife is commenting on what a 'great dad' he is. He fucking destroyed my fucking LIFE. FOR YEARS," I am yelling, my whole body shaking, my lips curled tight, my tongue practically forking as I continue to hiss.

"How COULD you let this happen? How COULD you let bad things happen to good people until they become fucking assholes themselves? Why?! There is no fucking fixing this. There is no fixing me, LORD KNOWS I have tried! And yet these motherfuckers just get to enjoy their fucking life?"

I'm ready to grab an imaginary overhead swinging lamp and shine it directly in this inanimate statue's eyes, bad cop-style. But instead I inch closer and glare into its cold, dead eyes.

"I spent YEARS suffering in the aftermath of that relationship. Terrified that he was going to post my nudes online and ruin my life. Constantly panicking that he was going to show up somewhere and finish what he started," I sneer and lean in even closer.

"I could have been normal. I could have loved Rune and 'lived, laughed, loved' with the best of them. I wouldn't need to desperately prove myself all the time." I jolt up from my chair like a rock in a sling shot, knocking the chair over behind me and slam my hands on the table.

"MAYBE I wouldn't need to try so hard to be sexually empowered. Maybe I would just actually *be* sexually empowered! And you rewarded him with a FUCKING FAMILY?"

"I am STILL cleaning up a huge FUCKING MESS that I didn't even FUCKING MAKE." I slap the statue so hard I clear it off the table, and it shatters it on the ground.

I drop to my knees and let out a primal, guttural scream.

And there I am. Sitting and heavy breathing in a pile of broken plaster. It's as if I am sitting in the broken brick of the bullshit foundation I've created.

And for the first time in my life, I feel rage burn away the fear inside me.

I am electrifyingly ANGRY at life. The order of things. The unfucking-fairness of it all. All these years of trying not to have a "victim complex," which only kept me stuck while they just went ahead and lived their lives.

I hobble to the cabinet and pull out a stale box of Chips Ahoy, ignoring the plaster digging into my bare feet.

I start shoving them into my mouth. Suddenly I know exactly who I need to call.

Mel is a tall powerhouse of a human with bellowing blonde hair. She always sports a fleece adorned with running horses. She is the kind of person who passionately and compassionately confronts people from her past. I have watched her do this and call people to talk about how they crossed her boundaries, with no expectation for them to make it right, or make her feel better.

I shoot her a text.

"Are you free to talk about some heavy shit?"

Within three seconds, my phone is ringing. Mel knows when her superpowers are needed.

"Yo, I'm fucking pissed," I answer. And all of it comes out.

"Ani ..." she breathes. "What if all this fear and hatred and disgust ... what if it's not yours?"

"I don't get what that means though. I truly don't. Because I'm here. I'm feeling it. And there are *very* clear reasons as to why. All of this ruined years of my life. While everyone was out having fun and doing 'normal' college shit—I would be shaking in my room, feeling every pore on my body, thinking *I* was the one who was gross and in the wrong. It's just ... Mel ... why the FUCK do I not matter to anyone? It's like I never even existed? To them, to God, to everyone. And yet all of this shit haunts me every goddamn day, no matter how hard I try to heal it," I clap back.

But she comes right back at me. "That fear? It's not yours. It's their fear of getting caught. All that secrecy? Not yours either. You actually have nothing to be ashamed of. Nothing to fear. It's *their shame, their fear*. You don't have to carry it anymore. And all that stuff about not mattering."

Maybe it's the portable heating fan blasting in my face. Maybe it's the sugar from the half box of crumbly Chips Ahoy I've devoured. Or maybe it's the warm, liquid-honey reality that's seeping into my system right from Mel's mouth, making me feel like I just took a shot of a truth serum.

This has nothing to do with Michael, or Rune, or his girlfriend. Mel is describing a wound I was carrying LONG before them.

The "I don't matter" wound. Fuck. It goes all the way back to God.

When I was a kid, I would wake up in the middle of the night terrified. Terrified of all the things I could do that would make God want to punish me for all of eternity. I never felt good enough for God. I never felt good enough for love. I've never felt good enough.

And the mess this has got me in? It's not one I made—but it is one that only I can clean up. I didn't make the mess, but it's on me to throw it in the trash. Right there, with Mel and her honey voice speaking in my ear, I decide: I will not waste another fucking second of my life holding on to garbage that isn't mine.

THE NEXT DAY, I MEET with a trauma coach named Corey. She has short hair and a nose ring and doesn't get mad when I'm late to our sessions, and she has been helping me slowly process all of this.

"Corey ... what if this is it?" I ask.

"Explain that, Ani."

"What if this is my baseline? What if no matter what happens, I'll always come back to this? What if this is who I really am, how I really am? What if *this* is what life is? Unfair and unexpected, and there's no such thing as actual safety? What if life is like the myth of Sisyphus, the guy who rolls a boulder up a hill for no reason only to have it roll all the way back down?" my words tumble out of my mouth like the rock I imagine rolling down the hill under Sisyphus's feet.

"Well, Ani... what if it is?" she pries gently.

"Umm?" I croak like a high school Valley Girl who just heard someone say her hair was frizzy.

"What if this is it? What if that's what life is, Ani? Now what?" I don't understand how her voice could sound so gentle but her words feel like the first gust of the harsh winter wind when you open the door to leave the warm cozy restaurant in New York City.

As many times as I have asked myself that question, I never paused to think of what the actual answer would be.

If I *am* Sisyphus on the mountain ... then what am I gonna do about it?

I think of when I moved into my first place in Ashland, and it was covered in animal feces, hadn't been updated since 1955, and had a cat infestation. No *really*—cats would break in through the AC and would gang fight in my house. I'm pretty sure they heard a single woman was living there alone, slid on their leather jackets, and said "come on boys, we got ourselves a spinster."

One time I even fell through the bathroom floor because of how rotted it was. But I made that house into the most beautiful home. I scrubbed it all down and blasted bleach on everything, decorated, and covered the walls in artwork. I even put a mirror ball in the part of the house that was the most dark and dreary!

I made that dilapidated house into a decked-out disco home.

And that home became a Mecca for all who needed a place to be held in any way.

It held Lucas after her boyfriend cheated on her ... again—and she was finally done, and took a bunch of molly, and just wanted to have a sleepover and watch *Gilmore Girls* and snuggle in my bed.

It held full moon dinners, where I would cook a massive meal and invite all the older women I knew to come have dinner with the gals my age, and they would share stories and we would all laugh as we received their wisdom, lessons, and blessings.

It held Bri when she stayed with me for two weeks while she changed depression meds and couldn't stop crying and puking.

It held themed parties, from dressing as memes to "wild things" to 1960s inspired, and everyone had a place to sleep after and coffee and breakfast in the morning waiting for them.

It held new friendships coming together, and me as I set boundaries for the first time in my life.

It held my tears, my clothes, my glitter, and enough twinkly lights to be the sole reason global warming is a thing.

And if I could make that house into that kinda home ... maybe I can make my *life* into its own disco-driven dream.

Maybe all Sisyphus needed was to stop, and give up hope that somehow, this time, it would be different, and he wouldn't have to repeat the whole process.

Maybe what he actually needed to do was take that energy and build a Studio 54 from the broken rocks surrounding him at the foot of the mountain.

I have spent MONTHS lamenting how I'm not supposed to be here, that I worked too damn hard for life to be this way. But actually ... what if this is it? The thought is incredibly freeing, like it's the most insanely liberating breath of fresh air I have had in months. There's no *should*— "should" has been like a shackle around my ankle anchoring me to a reality that isn't happening.

What if life just fucking sucks?!

What if the beauty of life is that life isn't beautiful at all. That everyone you love will die, and that every time you love you're just setting yourself up for pain. What if the beauty is laughing and dancing anyway!

What if life isn't beautiful—but we sure as fuck are.

What if I can't trust life, or God, or the cosmic order of things.

What if all I can trust is that—despite it all—we *will* dance again.

"Well ... I guess I could make it work," I say to Corey, but mostly to myself. "But I'm going to need a disco ball."

15

Spring, Bitch

Nothing makes my pussy more dry than gym culture. The sticky smell of sweaty balls and foam floors, the hormone-induced stares and glares, and the constant reminder that I should have some kinda "goal" with my body. "Ten lunges with the kettlebell, go that way and come back," Ilaria, my trainer, commands, not only with her voice but with her gaze, which is gleaming through the most dramatic strip lashes you've ever seen. Especially at 7 a.m. when my Dunkin' hasn't even kicked in yet.

I can't remember the last time I was in a gym. The gym is where self-hatred wears a mask of "strength, determination, ambition, and never giving up" (those words are literally imposed on stock photos of people working out from 1999 on every wall in this place).

But what is most disturbing as I look around this Diamond Fitness are the grunts and faces everyone makes that induce intrusive thoughts of them either cumming or shitting. No matter how hard I try, there is no *not* seeing it. The sixty-something man wearing a toupee? Shitting and cumming. The meathead who looks like every bully in a 1980s coming-of-age movie? Shitting and cumming. The guy who may or may not be my gynecologist but I can't tell 'cause he's not wearing a white coat? Shitting and cumming.

But the same psychic who told me about the book claims the only way this emotional turmoil will leave me is if I *move* my physical body. So I dutifully signed up for personal training with the lovely, bold, iconic Ilaria. Ilaria wears outfits that match her sneakers and is always in full glam: hair and makeup and lashes for days. Today she's wearing her long, wildly curly hair in a slicked back pony, has on a violet matching set, and is rocking the perfect electric blue liquid eyeliner.

"Ani ... you're confused," she chuckles as she curls her three-inch acrylic nails around the ten-pound kettlebell. "You squat, move it to the right, and step," she instructs, handing me the kettlebell.

"Right, sorry, monkey mind—got distracted," I giggle, hiding the fact that I just imagined everyone within a fifteen-foot radius either on the toilet or starring in a 1970s porno.

"What, is that your *boyfriend* over there?" she teases through a lit-up smirk. Her eyelashes look like they add exclamation points to everything she says.

"What! Who? *That* guy?" I look over at toupee man, who right at that moment decides to hock a loogie on the floor, and we both cackle.

"That's your crush!" she teases, as she laughs even harder.

Something about our cruel mocking of this man warms my heart. Working out with Ilaria and laughing at her jokes has become the highlight of my day. As much as I hate gym culture, I actually can't wait to see her in the mornings. I jump out of bed at 6:30 a.m., throw on my workout clothes, pick up at the Dunkin' drive-thru, and burst through the doors to see her gorgeously made-up self. And as we go through our series of half-assed lunges and conversations about flirtation, I feel the smallest reprieve from the darkness I've been in.

"You know Ani, I don't even look at men's faces anymore here. I don't bother. I can tell who they are by their calves," she blurts out while I'm mid-lunge. Her refreshing bluntness causes me to actually fall to the floor, laughing.

"WHAT? Ilaria ... why their calves? Are calves hot to you?"

"Oh, Ani, *My God* —I love them," she purrs. "You know, we gotta get you a man. Who do you like? Seriously."

I feel my stomach churn, and suddenly the mixture of Dunkin' and working out on an empty stomach isn't sitting so well.

"I don't know. I'm kinda going through it right now." I feel tears starting to prick my eyes, and I swallow them as best as I can. I walk away from her so she doesn't see me tear up. I'm making a half-assed attempt at putting away the kettlebell when I realize she's standing directly in front of me.

"You know, hard times happen, but it will be over soon. One day this isn't going to hurt any more. You show up, you get through it. I can see your pain, I understand. And it will be over," she speaks in a hushed tone to me, as tears fall out of my eyes like a leaky ceiling on the rubber-matted floor.

"Some days it just feels like it's never going to end," I whisper, fighting with everything I've got to not burst into uncontrollable sobs.

"Ani, you know something—*I* had hard times. I couldn't leave my bed. And now I'm here, and I found purpose. I feel sexy. I didn't have any of this before. I come here, I know everyone, I have friends, I am the happiest I've ever been. I never thought I could have this. Just keep going, okay?"

Usually, when people tell me it's going to get better, or that "this too shall pass," I want to do a backflip and punch them in the face, Quentin Tarantino style. It always feels like a subtle *fuck you*. Because sometimes, everything is not okay! And sometimes the depression is just not going to pass any time soon, so just let me stew in my misery!

But something about the twinkle in Ilaria's eyes makes me believe her. "Hey, Ilaria? Do you think I should get my lashes done again?" I ask, wiping the tears from my cheeks and cracking a genuine smile.

I've never seen anyone's eyes light up so fast. "With those eyes? You'll be able to get anyone you want. DO IT."

TWO DAYS LATER, I WALK into the electric pink and blue lash studio I used to frequent, where I see all my old friends: the women of "Love Your Look." Rose, Briana, and Brooklyn have supported me in everything I've done back home in Rhode Island—from moon ceremonies to the launch party for a tea line I created. I'd lay in one of their chairs as they meticulously adhered the most dramatic, 14D curl lashes to each one of my own, and we'd unpack every facet of our lives. Brooklyn, trying to reckon with what she wanted in her love life, versus what society wanted for her. Briana's journey falling in love and then into new motherhood. Rose's experiences holding circles for women at her church and taking care of all the people in her world.

The second I walk through those doors, I feel comfort. Brooklyn walks through to the waiting area and I just about jump on top of her, I am so excited.

"ANI! It's been YEARS, how have you been?" she gleams, opening the door for me to follow her. I am trying my absolute best not to do the absolute most as I fight the urge to start crying again—which appears to have become my new way of greeting people.

But these tears aren't like the ones I've been shedding since the crumbling of my relationship. The ones that felt like they were trying to release the 800 pounds of pain caked on my heart. They are tears of relief, like when you get lost in the mall as a kid and then finally see a familiar face.

Brooklyn and I chat incessantly as I follow her through into the bright pink lash room, lay on her chair, and close my eyes. And I swear to the Goddess that with every eyelash she glues on, a tiny piece of my soul comes back home into my body.

There are few connections deeper than the ones with the people who do your hair, nails, or eyelashes. What might start off as nervous small talk becomes a sacred bond, developed over each hour and fifteen-minute appointment. It's a rite of passage, and as I feel the heaviness of my lashes increase, and the stingy smell of the glue burning my throat in the best way, I feel like Brooklyn is rowing me out of the Styx.

I always know the appointment is over when the fan comes out, which they say is to dry the glue but I think is actually to soothe the smoldering sensation the glue causes on the ol' eyeballs.

"Alright Ani, you are lashed up and back in the game!" She hands me a bright pink mirror as I sit up. I blink a couple of times, feeling the weight of the lashes and pull the mirror towards my face.

And if they say eyes are the window to the soul, well, my soul has the most beautiful, luscious curtains in the free world. Maybe it's the lashes, maybe it is the conversation and connection; either way, I recognize the girl staring back at me for the first time in a long, long time.

"Brooklyn!" I gasp. "I fucking LOVE it."

I speed home and burst through my sister's doors. (Yes, I'm still there. Yes, it's been four months. No, nobody is thrilled about it.) You know that quote that's like, if you want to make God laugh, create a plan? Well, if you wanna make depression laugh, same. So, limbo it is.

My sister, Alex, is in the kitchen, busily making a sandwich.

"LOOK!" I shout, batting my freshly fluffed lashes that are acting as exclamation points. She jumps. Her eyes open wide in shocked horror.

"Dear God, Ani—don't you think that's a little much?" she asks.

I beam with pride. If Alex thinks it's too much, that means it's *hot*. Now I *know* I'm **really** on my way back.

But when night falls, the high from my lashes withers away. Once again I'm full of creeping dread, a restless itch, a vacant numbness. I flop on my heated blanket (still not washed) and flip open my laptop.

Don't do it, Ani.

I go on my browser and type in Instagram.

But, you're hot! You should just see what she looks like and see if she measures up!

I type "Sarah Baker" into the search.

Ani you fucking idiot don't you motherfucking da-

I click on her handle.

"STOP!" The word leaps out of my mouth and reverberates off the walls of my room. "I'm not doing this again." I pick up my phone and do the only thing I can think of to make myself feel okay. I download Tinder and get to work setting up a new profile.

I start picking through a series of well-rounded selfies from when I hadn't yet identified as a succubus and still felt like a real live human. One where I'm smiling in a field in a yellow and white jumpsuit; one where I'm with friends dressed sexy with one eyebrow coyly raised; one where I have my hood up and I am powerfully gazing at the camera; and of course, one with me and my pup Anoush, looking eerily like twins.

Then I write my perfect bio: "A real down to Mars girl." (The reference is sure to separate the cool guys from the squares.)

And right before I release my profile into the great expanse of the Tinderverse, I do what I was taught to do with crystals. I place my phone in my left hand, put my right hand on top, close my eyes, and set my intention.

"May I connect with exactly who I need to ... and so it is."

Send.

Within moments, the first person pops up. Adam, 32. Picture with a dead fish.

Next.

James, 29. "What are we getting ... pizza, or tacos?"

Next.

Brett, 31. Corinthians—

Next.

Lucas, 34. "I'm not looking for anything serious, just out of a serious partnership. Loyalty is everything. My ex en—

Next.

Ethan, 28. "Are you a pizza girl, or a taco girl?"

WTF is up with pizza and tacos? Am I missing something? How did Rune land a model within weeks of our breaking up, and I'm left with "loyalty is everything" Lucas as my best option?

One more swipe.

And wait, here's a promising one. Tall. All of his pictures are in a sepia tone. Says he's a movie buff and a writer. But his dog is cropped out of all his photos.

I send him a "like" with a message.

"Hey, this 'like' is actually for the dog that you cropped out of every photo because I want them to know they're valued."

I throw my phone across my bed in excitement and satisfaction. Charming. Cute. Funny. Conversational. I *nailed* it.

Moments later, my phone pings.

IT'S HIM. I feel the same kind of rush I experience when I see a waiter walking up to my table holding a massive plate of spaghetti.

"Oh, it's because she died and I can't get myself to look at any pictures yet."

Cue the waiter walking right by my table without even tossing me a glance.

I nod my head in silence, and with that, I delete Tinder and call Charlie for some reprieve. We haven't really connected since the shit hit the fan, and I *know* that if anyone could laugh at my Tinder tragedy, it's her.

"Is this my Ani Punani?" Charlie giddily chides, calling me by my pet name.

"Charlie, I literally just flirted with this guy's dead dog." I am the embodiment of the word "flaccid."

"Well, hello. Yeah. That's uh ... that's gonna need some context." We both burst out cackling. I send her a screenshot of what just went down, and I hear her cackle even louder. I keep trying to get a word in but every time I try and finish a sentence, my words go up seven octaves and turn into roaring laughter gibberish. At some point, we aren't even laughing at the Tinder tragedy anymore, it's like something has come over us.

After a solid few minutes, we take a final deep breath to settle the hysteria.

I release what's left of my giggles. "God, I missed you," I sigh, still trying not to completely lose it again.

"My Punani, I missed you so much. How are you?"

"Charlie ... I'm pretty awful. Did it have to be a motherfucking Instagram model?"

"And did you see the Porsche? Like, come on, try harder."

"Yeah, I know, but dude ... couldn't I just be fucking happy? Why couldn't that whole thing, Rune, Portland, life ... just be right for me? I had it all. Why was I so miserable? You know I rarely feel attracted to people. I always find a problem. An issue. I feel like the biggest, most ungrateful, awful brat of a human who can't just be happy." The words leave my mouth heavily and I can't look away from the wall.

"Hey ..." her voice sounds unsure. "Okay listen, can I just say something that may or may not be the wrong thing?" The mix of intrigue and anxiety breaks my foggy wall gaze and I actually tilt my head to the side in shock.

"I mean, yeah, duh, just say it," I say. I do my best to sound cool and collected, but inside anxiety pangs rage in me, and it suddenly feels like my belly is housing the Rolling Stones at Altamont.

"Ani... I don't know ... I really just think—" her voice trails off.

The anxious rage wins. "Alright with the suspense! I'm shitting bricks over here just say it, Charlie!"

"I think maybe you like women more than you think and I think maybe it's time to explore that!"

Okay.

Um.

Okay?

Wait.

I *mean.*

So Charlie is a proper lesbian in the lesbian world. And she is also one of my best friends, and has been able to see me in ways most people can't. The basis of our friendship has always been the brutal honest truths we're probably not going to hear from anyone else. But—she's clearly just projecting. It's not that there's anything WRONG with being a lesbian, I'm just not one.

Why am I having a hard time breathing?

"Listen, I mean, I'm just like everyone else. I made out with my friends in college every weekend. And sure, I only really watch lesbian porn. And *yes*, I made my girl Barbies make out when I was little and didn't want anything to do with Ken. But honestly, those are just normal things everybody does. That doesn't mean I'm gay. That would be disrespectful to people who are *actually* gay."

"Ani," Charlie pauses, gently. "My love." Gentle pause. "That's not what everyone does." Gentle pause. "That's what *you* did." Sharp pause. "And I think you're more gay than you realize."

"So, not everybody writes erotic poetry for their girlfriends for birthday gifts?"

"Nope."

I stare at the scratched wood floor beneath me, my hand gripping tighter around the phone

"Ani. Who is the background of your phone right now?"

I look at my lock screen and am greeted by a picture of Joan Jett in a white tank and leather pants, looking sexy. Did I say sexy? I meant to say sweaty.

"Yeah, okay. And who is your top Spotify artist?"

I nod silently to the Goddess that is Cher.

"That's what I thought. But seriously—all jokes aside, you've said why you *shouldn't* explore this, but you never said you didn't want to. You got *one* life, Ani. If you want to, you can explore. If not, then screw it—you don't have to. But just know you have the option."

I thank her for her reflection and rush her off the phone. Then I sit cross-legged, silent and stunned, on the scratched up floor. The yellow light radiating from the vintage space age lamp makes me feel like I'm in a low-budget soap opera. Why does what Charlie said feel so fucking scary? I suddenly feel the same way I do every September, when you can just feel things shifting. It's disorienting but you can't place why.

Fuck it. Maybe I'm bi. And if I'm going to "experiment," maybe I can finally get good and kinky for a while? Become a unicorn and join a couple? Maybe my life can be filled with threesomes and sexual experiences that I can't even imagine.

Or maybe I'm just a nightmare of a human trying to grasp onto anything that I can change about my situation.

MY THOUGHTS TURN DARK AGAIN. Each night becomes a battle between me and that motherfucking voice.

You're a failure. Look at you, in your sister's home. You're probably a narcissist. A toxic narcissist. Did you take the online narcissist test?

My skin crawls as I lay in bed and writhe because my skin feels like a too-tight, itchy-wool turtleneck. I kick off the covers and rip off my pajamas. I get on all fours and stretch. I jump and kick and smack at my skin and feel the familiar bubbling hot magma of rage building up. The kind of rage when you spent hours meticulously stringing up twinkly lights, only to plug them in and they don't goddamn work. The kind of rage where you're in a rush and someone cuts in front of you on the sidewalk and walks at 0.1 MPH because they're on the phone. The kind of rage where you try on every item of clothing in your closet, change your hair, and redo your makeup for hours, but still feel like shit.

The kind of rage that breaks you.

I pick up my pillow and smush it up and try and try and *try* to rip it open. After forty-five seconds of pure exertion, my lips tightly curled, hot angry tears streaming down now, arms shaking, I throw it to the side and flop down, defeated.

Is this rock bottom yet?

I reach for my laptop and type in "Dolly Parton Interview." Dolly has always been a source of comfort and inspiration to me, and if I can't feel the presence of God—*maybe* I can feel Dolly.

First thing that pops up:

"Dolly Parton Contemplated Suicide"

Dolly Parton. Loving, happy, charming, sweet Dolly Parton, once found herself writing a suicide note because she didn't think her being here was *worth it*. And then her DOG jumped on her bed, and that was the only thing that stopped her.

I look down at my fluffy chow Anoush who is side eyeing me after my graphic display of rage, visibly judging me, and read on.

If Dolly Parton, the bringer of total goodness, has experienced the dark night of the soul, then *none* of us is immune.

My fingers fly across my keyboard, as I search every single person I am inspired by—Cher, Stevie Nicks, Oprah.

And I come across story after story of people facing the depth of the pain it takes to be alive. It turns out all these people, who have stewarded so much beauty, and who are so radiant and powerful, have been in this place, too.

What if being here, feeling the rage and humiliation—witnessing the annihilation of all I know and all I am — barely having the will to keep going — what if this actually *will* pass? There's so much literature on tortured artists, and how creative people are destined to walk through life as a tortured soul—but what if we are *all* artists? And what if the tortured soul part wasn't a static state, but rather the birth of creation?

I glance over at the mirror and see my mascara-stained cheeks and sweaty naked body crouched over my laptop. I look less like an artist, and more like whatever it is that greets you at the seventh circle of hell. I bury my head in a pillow to force my eyes closed.

Maybe ART is my only hope?

I walk over to the mirror and move my cheeks from side to side, trying to get a glimpse of "the artist." If the old me is completely dead, who is the new me? I rush back to the computer and type in "western rhinestone cowgirl style."

And with that, I buy a pair of white cowboy boots that have skeletons taking a selfie on them, because nothing says "I'm barely hanging on but trying my best" like skeletons taking a selfie. And nothing says *Dolly* like white cowgirl boots.

I take the brown, scratchy pseudo-fleece electric blanket off the bed, march down the too-steep Victorian stairs, and throw it in the wash.

One cap of Tide + Downy, one pair of boots, and one clean blanket later, and the too-tight wool sweater feeling is gone. Maybe I can walk out the other side of this shitstorm in Dolly's shoes.

"REMEMBER WHEN WE WENT TO that show in your Bassnectar phase, and we were sitting on the grass processing how amazing the drop was, and that girl didn't see you sitting there and literally walked directly into your face—like her entire pussy practically went into your mouth and you literally weren't even phased and continued talking as if you didn't just go to third base with someone by accident?" Vita laughs so primally over the phone that my dog comes in from the other room to make sure everything is okay.

I spray my coffee out of my mouth and all over my sister's circular dining table.

Vita, My Sweet Vita. We've danced through so much darkness together in our lives, through dingy nightclubs in New York City, to even darker festivals filled with light shows and huge pupils, to the darkest times of all, coming out of abusive relationships in college.

We bonded over music. Poetry. And, of course, most importantly we bonded over our total Messy Bitch-ness. We cried, we shook in fear, and we validated each other. And no matter what, we always ended up choke-laughing through the trauma.

One night, we were at an 1980s arcade bar, surrounded by green neon lights, new wave graphic posters, and a Rubik's Cube dancefloor. Vita's signature long, black extensions perfectly framed an insane amount of cleavage squished together by a tight black bandeau that read "slut," paired with leather leggings she said were too sexy to give up even though the plastic leather smelled like the worst kind of fish.

We were taking shots of Johnny Walker and chasing it with espresso, a lethal combination set up to unearth every ounce of anxiety laying dormant inside of you. In an attempt to distract ourselves from the conjuring doom of the panic attacks that were sure to bubble out of us any minute, we headed to the dancefloor.

Within minutes, we were manically stepping side to side across from each other to the dance hits of the '80s, while yelling in each other's faces over the music. Duran Duran's "Girls on Film" was blasting, and our bodies were on autopilot, and there was no one else around, and there was nothing else to do but have this conversation.

"Ani, I swear to God, I don't even think it was consensual."

GIRLS ON FILM.

Vita did a turn and snapped, while maintaining eye contact to gauge my reaction. We were doing some version of the Hustle now, Vita's eyes welling up, my brows furrowed, both of us desperately trying to choke back the tears.

"Vita, I have no words, I'm so sorry. This is a big one to digest."

GIRLS ON FILM.

I grabbed her hand and twisted her around as we both started synchronized shimmying while locking eyes and trying not to cry, completely detached from our bodies.

And that is how we began our journey of healing. Vita and I somehow manage to laugh in the face of any evil that comes our way. And although we would have our FaceTime dates after I moved to Oregon every so often, we haven't seen each other in the flesh *in years*.

Now that I'm on the East Coast, setting up shop in the dark, it's time for an in-person meetup.

But first, I have a stop to make.

I make my way down I-95 in a rental car that's shaped like a sugar cube with Anoush by my side. I'm playing my "Even Cowgirls Get the Blues" playlist and wearing my new white cowboy boots, trying to embrace this southernly sad version of myself. I see the exit for my college and I quickly peel off and make my way down.

I pass the Chipotle I haven't seen in close to a decade—the one where I spilled diet Coke into Vita's Chanel. I feel a twinge of that bittersweet nostalgia, like reading notes in the back of your yearbook.

One stoplight later, there's the entrance to my campus. I feel like I've inhaled on a joint too quickly and the hot smoke is burning the back of my throat.

And beyond that entrance, down to the right, three streets down: Clarence Street. The street where the fucking frat house lives.

My speed grows with my building rage as I fly past the gas station where I would buy my Four Lokos. Past Bling, the underage nightclub where I made out with my RA and then got thrown up on by someone dressed like Superman.

I peel down Clarence to the cream colored nightmare of a house with the big brown chipped paint door.

I throw the car in park.

Electricity radiates off of my body like a severed electrical wire in a lightning storm. Spark. Spark. I feel like I could eviscerate a person with a simple glance. Spark. Spark. And I'm not going to lie: it feels damn amazing. I cast my eyes toward my hands. They are not shaking. I am not afraid.

I look at Anoush, who is blissfully unaware of where we are, and why, and the dangerous flames inside of me transform into a radiant warmth.

This is my life now. I'm not in that fucking house. I'm in a sugar-cube-shaped car with my fluffy dog and I've lived in motherfucking *Oregon* and studied with a *witch* and danced with LIVE snakes and was eventually able to actually *enjoy* sex.

That warmth melts the frozen tears that have been stuck inside of me into a soft liquid.

I tell the old me, the one who was trapped inside of that hell house, that one day life is going to be so wild and so weird. I tell her that her life will be far from perfect but she will still howl with laughter. I hold her and assure her that her body isn't gross. I tell her that one day she will find herself sitting in a circle of women of all ages, self-pleasuring as prayer, and that in the moment it isn't going to be as weird as she thinks (but she will still laugh at the weirdness of it all after).

I watch her come out of that house. And I watch her close that big brown chipped door, and get into the sugar cube car and sit on my lap. I hold her close. I hold her with power. I strike a proverbial match and burn off any last ties she has to that place. She sinks into my bones. She's home. I'm home.

If no one else, I got me now. ... I got me now, fuckers.

The heat blasts from the air vents and dries out my tears. Anoush has one arm leaning on the center console and her paw is right next to mine. I grab it.

"Ready Thelma?"

I turn down the heat and turn up the music. "Believe" by Cher blasts out, and it's as if God themself is giving me a message, and I can hear it.

AN HOUR LATER, I PULL into the long, dirt road leading to Vita's door in Wine Country, Long Island. I grab Anoush and roll my cheetah print suitcase up the steps of her beautiful little gray home, which is surrounded by big, bare trees.

I hear the yap of small dogs going crazy, and the door flings open. There, in all of her big, bold, Leo magic, draped in a satin sapphire-colored nightie and long black extensions, stands my Vita.

I drop my bag and topple into her. We instinctively begin jumping up and down and chanting, "WHAHAPPENED WHAHAPPENED" in thick, Long Island mother accents.

Vita's girlfriend is there, along with someone I don't know, who is pouring herself a glass of white wine in the kitchen. I recognize her from Vita's Instagram. She has long curly hair, a tall, slender body, and the fiercest jawline I've ever seen. She's wearing black jeans and a black leather jacket, and those New York cool girl pointy booties (if you know, you know).

I physically push Vita out of the way, and march right up to her.

"Hi, nice to meet you, I'm Ani."

"Hi—Savannah." She leans in and hugs me and my face is pressed into her leather jacket, and she smells like fancy perfume and clean laundry. I clam up immediately: *what the fuck is this?*

It was just two weeks ago that Charlie planted that gay little seed in my head, and now I'm feeling shit just *hugging* this random girl? What is happening?

And then we all head out to dinner at a Michelin starred restaurant that Vita and her girlfriend frequent so often it's like going to the neighborhood diner for them.

I sit next to Savannah, across from Vita and her girlfriend. Savannah and I share stories. We laugh. I feel her leg press against mine beneath the table. And then there's a bolt of lightning that awakens my pussy from the dead. I clench my Frankenpussy tight to keep her from maniacally laughing.

Yeah okay Ani, calm your clam. Who's to say she'd ever be into you anyway?

My cruel inner demon is left stunned and blushing as Savannah drapes her arm around my shoulder and brings me closer to her.

"That's right. Scootch in closer," my pussy whispers in her deep, smoker's voice. I imagine her with long coral nails, lighting a skinny cigarette.

"Gotta run to the ladies room. Vita? Wanna come?" I shoot Vita a look so loaded that I am practically blinking Morse code.

Vita, just buzzed enough to not pick up on the heaviness of my gaze, but wanting to pee nonetheless, joins me towards the bathroom, dry martini in hand.

"VITA—" I lock the door like a frantic thirteen-year-old who just found out the hottest, most coveted gossip in school and is ready to *dish*, as Vita immediately strips completely ass naked and unceremoniously plops her spray-tanned ass against the porcelain toilet.

"I know, Sweets. I gotta tell ya—she only wears that leather jacket when she wants to fuck a girl. You're it." Her words slide dramatically out like the last of her martini sliding into her perfectly painted red lips.

I spiral. *What if I don't like it? Even worse, what if I'm bad at it? Jesus. I feel like I just figured out straight sex like ... now I gotta go back to square one?*

"Vita ... I don't know how! What do I do? How does one actually like ... lick a vagina ... if that's what's happening here?" I snap half excitedly and half nervously. "Show me! Do it in the air!"

A glazed-over glimmer bathes a warm light over Vita's black eyes. She smiles maniacally like Tonya Harding at the end of her routine. Without missing a beat, she makes intricate patterns in the air with her tongue.

A few hours later, I am ass naked, making intricate patterns on Savannah with *my* tongue.

I have my fourth explosive orgasm of the night.

Turns out, I am not making this gay thing up.

Definitely. Fucking. Not.

16
Summer, Bitch

"Friend ... you licked a vagina." Sage's voice always sounds like the men in *The Sopranos*, even though she grew up horseback riding in Newport, Rhode Island and knows what a regatta is.

"Yes, yes I did." I mirror her tone as if we're about to start dishing the hot gossip on the Gabagool.

"And you liked it?" she asks.

"Well—remember that scene in *Forrest Gump* when he touches Jenny's boob and immediately cums all over her roommate's bathrobe? It was like that."

"Damn. Good for you." I picture Tony Soprano nodding on the other end of the phone.

"And Friend ... we watched *Cats*. Like the creepy CGI musical. And I cried when Jennifer Hudson sang. I truly don't know what is happening to me."

"So, now what?"

"I'm not sure."

It is a sacred ritual: driving in my car with the window cracked, iced coffee in hand, chatting on speaker phone with a friend and digesting life. This time, I'm heading back to my sister's house after a potentially life altering week with Savannah. It dawns on me that she and I established a morning routine before even going on a date. Damn ... maybe I am a good ol' fashioned U-Haul lesbian. It feels like a piece to a puzzle that I didn't even know existed has been placed, but I'm not sure what to do next.

Like, I'm not sure who I am, where I'm going, what I'm going to do, what's going to happen next, if I *am* gay, or if I'm bi, or some combination of both—or if that even really matters. I'm not sure if I'm spiritually open or horribly traumatized, endlessly hopeful, or mentally ill, or if all those kinda mean the same thing. I'm not sure if Rune ever loved me, if anyone ever has loved me, and if this is how everyone feels. I'm not sure if I've ever truly been a decent person or loved anyone the way I want to be loved. I'm not sure if I'm excited or slap happy, if I'm drunk on delusion or illuminated by insight. I'm not sure if I'm ever going to be the same or if I even want to. I'm not sure if I'm ready or if I'm reacting. I'm not sure. It's like ... I am everything and nothing.

I pass farm after farm, green exit sign after green exit sign, absorbing the music that is blasting from my stereo into my being like vitamin D from the sun. Today it's the Cocteau Twins. "Heaven or Las Vegas," specifically. Over and over again. I remember when I first heard this song—it was during my solo cross country road trip after leaving Rune, when I still felt excited and hopeful about the breakup. It came on a random playlist as I was driving through Utah, and when this song played I prayed for my life to become as wild and unfamiliar as the landscape was to me.

Speeding down I-95, my smile grows with every passing exit sign; if I don't know who I am or where I'm going, that means I can be whoever I want.

I have been a gal who smelled like frankincense essential oil, with chewed-up nails and undiagnosed ADHD, thinking about what T-Pain is while trying to do a Tantric Meditation.

I have been a gal who has moved cross country multiple times, and who, when tasked with packing only the essentials from her entire life, brought a box filled with items for her altar, a refurbished Vitamix, and my blankie.

I have been a gal who was terrified of looking stupid or embarrassing myself during sex, and who also sat in a sex magic circle in a house that smelled of lentils and lavender, using my orgasm as prayer for the world.

I have been a gal who was bullied and teased, and who would look in the mirror at my protruding belly and budding boobs, and drop to my knees to pray to God that one day I'd be beautiful enough for people to actually want to hang out with me.

I have been a gal who smoked cigarettes but never inhaled. Who studied with a witch and foraged food from the woods. Who was raped. Who was straight.

I have been a gal who built her life on a foundation of sand, and who bulldozed that life because I could feel it collapsing beneath me into a muddy mess whenever the slightest wave would come. The past few months, I have hated the me that tried so hard to make it work in Portland, and I have hated the me that left it all behind.

But as the etheric synth wave styles of the Cocteau Twins carry me forward ... I realize:

all these versions of me ... they haven't been that bad.

The wind from the window is softly whipping at my hair and I feel cosmically alone, in the unknown, and it doesn't feel scary. It feels ... like potential. Because, for the first time, I can feel the beauty of it all.

Isn't this what makes life so fucking kinky? That the more painfully, devastatingly beautiful it is, the more pleasure there is at its core?

Is this what freedom is ... or did I just have a week of really great sex?

I'm not sure!

Who the fuck knows!

But here I am!

Life feels like a big, cosmic kind of FUCK IT.

I also want another iced coffee at 4 p.m. because ... fuck it! I don't care if I'm up all night. I'm the motherfucking Queen of the Holy Dark, and I still run on Dunkin'.

The orange and pink letters are beckoning me into the drive-thru line, and I think back to when I was a religion major, learning about the Goddess Inanna. Me and her have a thing or two in common. She was the Ancient Sumerian Queen of the Heavens, and she loved to adorn herself in beautiful, ornate jewels ... and then she decided to leave everything she knew behind, and take an innocent little trip to the underworld to go to a funeral. A trip that completely humbled her and stripped her of all her earthly magic, and then everything was taken from her.

First her crown.

Then her necklace.

Then her breastplate.

Then her golden, gemstone-infused hip girdle.

Then her anklets and bracelets.

And then her Queen's robes.

And then ... she died, and was left hanging from a meat hook with her eyes gouged out.

Which is a pretty extreme comparison to make, but there have been times back there where I've kinda felt like I've been hung out to dry, too.

But guess what.

Inanna rose again. With the help of her loyal friend, of course, because not even the Queen of Heaven can come back from the dead without her besties to help her through.

And she became the Goddess of all that is.

Now, I'm not vain enough to think I'm an actual Goddess, and I'm not even sure that I would be a very good Queen as of right now– it would be a very "let them eat cake" moment I'm sure. But what I can say is that I'm crawling through those gates. And in this moment, with my ears ringing from the blown out drive-thru speaker, I know that there is no other place in the world for me to be, and nothing else I should be doing other than this.

"GODDESS, PLEASE GIVE ME A SIGN through this next song. When I click shuffle, whatever song plays is going to be a message from you to me. I'm listening. And so it is."

I'm sitting alone at my new kitchen table, with only the light from my spell candle and my laptop. I'm in a new apartment, which is actually my mom's boyfriend's depression pad. He got it when they broke up for a month but he never stayed in it, and it feels fitting that I'm gracing this space.

It's my birthday in an hour. I'm ringing in my 28th year covered in snot and self-disgust. For every moment of crystal clear clarity and celebration, the come down is twice as bad.

I press shuffle on Spotify.

Ani DiFranco's "Not A Pretty Girl" comes on.

"Ha!" my pussy mocks, raspily. I cross my legs hard.

I feel about as stable as the table in the YouTube viral sensation "Scarlet Takes a Tumble" as I feverishly scribble in my spiral bound notebook, trying to make sense of things.

According to this same journal, I have gotten everything I asked for. In the Summer of 2020, when everything was crumbling around me, I wrote out everything I was calling in. And I have it.

I have been dating Savannah, and it's been going great. I feel like a whole new bitch, I feel more free, more expressed than I ever have been. I have amazing friends who are creative and lively and magic. I am writing my book; I have a purpose. I have been traveling and having fun. And yet ... here I am, at 12:05 a.m. on my birthday, STILL fucking crying and feeling like I am nothing. I'm supposed to be happy now! I'm supposed to feel fulfilled! How the fuck am I back here again? I start plucking at my eyelashes, which are crunchy and matted together, caked with salty tears.

You're just a miserable fucking person. Soon Savannah and all your new friends will see who you really are and you'll start becoming a succubus in their lives, too. This is why you're alone on your birthday. No matter what you have, or what you do, you're never going to enjoy it.

"ALRIGHT, ENOUGH!" I slam my hands on the rented mid-century modern table and yell out loud to myself or God or something in between. Anoush looks over at me for a moment before going back to sleep.

"Okay, you know what? I need help." God, Goddess, whoever, please let me get the fuck over this and let it go. Please help me release this pain. Please help me to make peace with everything. Please, God, for the love of God, I need your help. Guide me. I can't keep fucking doing—AHH!!!"

I scream, interrupted by something tickling my leg. I start swatting at what must be a giant spider, but realize it is blood. I got my period. Two weeks early.

I totally ruined this probably really expensive rented mid-century modern chair, but I do know that this means something. I curl into a ball, and hold my body. My thoughts swerve in a different direction.

Thank you for everything. Thank you for this life. I want to like being here. I don't need to be happy all the time, but please, not this low again. Please. I release it with this blood. I release it all to you. I'm open to your healing and support in this release. I love you. Thank you.

I close my journal and stand up, wiping my face with the sleeve of my Fleetwood Mac sweatshirt. I realize how fucking exhausted I am, as my soul catches up with my body and I'm walking towards my bed.

I get under the covers and Anoush jumps on my feet and curls up, exhaling loudly. I match my breathing with hers until we are both asleep.

***

I wake at the ass crack of dawn, and barrel down the stairs to the coffee pot. Then I put on "The Bald and the Beautiful" podcast to give me a burst of humor on an otherwise weird start to my birthday, and to block out the invasive thought that my tits look like Kermit the Frog's eyes as I scoop them into a too-tight sport's bra.

When I walk into the musty gym twenty minutes later, Ilaria is waiting for me, doing a birthday dance by the row machine in her electric blue workout set.

"Thank youuuuu!" I beam, feeling genuine excitement about the day for the first time.

"What are you getting for your birthday?" she pries with her signature sly grin. Well shit, I forgot about that part. But as soon as she asks, the delicious demon of desire is summoned. It takes over my whole body.

My pupils dilate. "You said you do hair sometimes, right?" My mouth slowly mirrors her sly grin. "I'm sick of this blond. I want to go black. And I want extensions. I'm ready."

"YES. Come to my house at four. We'll go to Sally's and I'll do it for you."

Cut to me sitting in Ilaria's living room six hours later, watching her two French bulldogs hump each other while she feeds me sangria and coats my hair in black dye. It feels like a poetic beginning to my new year.

The last time I had my hair black, it was my senior year of high school. My sister had always called me Sister Golden Hair after that song by America, as an homage to my former golden(ish) locks. After I dyed it, it came out a weird purple-ish color, and my nickname was quickly replaced by Sister Eggplant Head.

But my eggplant head was a total act of autonomy, as coming-of-age and not-knowing-what-to-do-with-my-teenage trauma as that sounds. But it's a cliché for a reason. Not only is dying one's hard dark a metaphor for innocence lost, it's also one fucking small ass way to feel like you have a say over what happens to your body. Back then, having darker hair made me feel older and sexier, and less like a stupid kid who got tricked into jerking off a loser of a dude in a lonely field at fucking Christian camp.

I stopped dying it when I tried to lighten up by being all granola. Now, as the black dye penetrates my hair follicles, I feel like Inanna coming back into her powers back as she slides off the meathook.

Ilaria fastens in the extensions and runs the iron through my hair before the big reveal. And just like that, I am Cher. If there was ever a symbol of rebirth and power, it's her.

***

Two weeks later, Savannah, now my best friend (another gay thing is being friends with your exes), calls me frantically.

"Pack your bags, we're going to Fire Island."

VAGULY OFF-PUTTING, HYPER-REALISTIC cheetah bag?

Packed.

Pubes?

Trimmed.

Bright pink tooth gems that I suddenly think are the coolest thing to ever happen to style even though I placed them on like the braces that I had for six months in 8th grade?

Applied.

Next thing I know, I'm dragging my hyper-realistic cheetah weekend bag onto a ferry in Long Island, New York. My black pleather shorts are baking in the sun and sweat is gathering in my white skeleton cowboy boots. My long black extensions are sticking to my back, and my natural hair is beginning to curl. But I don't care. I'm heading to an island filled with gays where there are no cars, and it's the first actual vacation I've ever taken where I'm not also working or trying to have an epic spiritual transformation.

I get to the top of the ferry. The sun reflecting off the water looks like the glitter in my extra thick lashes, which are blowing so hard in the wind that I think they are going to take flight. I've researched everything about this place, where gays could freely be themselves in the summer, without fear of persecution. There are so many butterflies in my stomach that they are starting to unionize.

I stumble off the ferry with my off-putting cheetah bag in tow in one hand "AWH HI! SHE'S RIGHT HEAHH!" a raspy voice echoes from the dock and greets me. Krys is walking towards me in a head to toe black outfit and shakes her head to adjust her bangs. Before I can even open my mouth she grabs my bag with one hand, and uses the other one to give me a hug.

"Hi, welcome, nice to meet ya. Tina Burner is about to go on so we gotta go, just gimme your stuff and we'll drop it off—you hungry?" Krys doesn't wait for a pause and leads the way.

Cue the daytime gay club.

The air inside is dense and humid. Ivy is there in a yellow coquette style dress, completely unbothered that the zipper broke on the side. She somehow makes it look fashionable. Vita is wearing a face full of gems, big blue and green sparkles spread all over her chest and cleavage, and space buns. Savannah is wearing a gold sequin blazer, her curls fabulously spilling over to one side. Krys is in all black of course, with pointy booties layered with chains that mirror why people get intimidated by her.

My nerves are still popping off. Like, soaring. Like ... overwhelming. I haven't been in a sweaty nightclub in YEARS.

But sometimes nerves are excitement without breath and a disco ball, so inhale deeply into my belly and go in like a moth to a flame.

We enter the same way I picture Adam and Eve witnessing the Garden of Eden for the first time, gliding through the arched doorway, the beat of the song that's playing mirroring my pounding heart, flashing lights dancing over us.

I soar over to the bar. They have a drink with elderflowers. I remember what Diana told me about the magical properties of elderflower—it was a gift from the Goddess to protect and bless people who respected her power. I immediately order the drink from a shirtless bartender in assless chaps. He slides the elixir over to me. I turn my back to everyone in an attempt not to be weird and to still get invited places, and whisper into the cup,

"Thank you, thank you, thank you." Then I pour a little of the drink out the window as an offering.

The sticky, humid air wraps around me as I fish for my ID and it feels like a hug from an old familiar friend. Then "I Feel Love" by Donna Summer starts blaring from the speakers, and I turn and take in the scene. My eyes gape open in awe, and I'm sure everyone around me thinks I'm coked out due to not blinking for what feels like two minutes.

There's a small stage in the back of the club, where another man in assless chaps and a cowboy hat is doing a backflip. There's a group of bachelorettes in multi-colored wigs, drunk off tequila and excitement. And then there's me, wide-eyed in a corner, reacting as if I'm witnessing Jesus resurrected and coming out of the tomb.

In front of me, as buttcheeks clap and my friends clink their glasses, and two strangers hit on each other at the bar, I am struck by the resilience of humanity.

And I start to move.

Like a slutty supernova, I burst onto the dancefloor with a force that could only be described as both gravitational and cosmic, feeling myself UP and twirling around.

I swirl my hips and start to sing, letting this song be like a prayer of absolute gratitude for being alive.

There are no thoughts. I'm simply in my body, being a human, and dancing in the divinity that is being alive. Sweaty bodies in surrender, swirling with the song, moving with the magic, and hope holding us all the while.

We were all led to this cosmic moment, the disco ball being our North Star.

Months of isolation. Heartbreak. Loss. Panic. People throughout the world, facing this unknown together. People turned on each other. Stole toilet paper and accused people of eating babies. There were Zoom funerals and a crumbling of life as we knew it. Nothing was okay. And it still might not be.

But here we are, dancing despite it. Or because of it. In honor of it. And that is fucking spiritual.

The music fades to Michael Jackson's "PYT."

And then a beautiful man in the most pristine pleated pants and pressed shirt extends his hand to me, and we lock eyes and and smize at each other.

I grab his hand in a wordless response. And without so much of a half-beat missed, we are FLYING through the dance floor. The lights are bouncing off of my sequined bra-top as he spins me and dips me, and I feel like the most radiant disco ball in town.

Remember when the world popped off because Joan Osborne made that song "What If God Was One of Us" in the '90s? And everyone thought that was like... so disrespectful.

Well, I'm going to officially take my stance.

God is totally in this nightclub.

And I'm not sure if it is this man who let me know that everything will be okay without saying a word, or the DJ who is playing the perfect music, or the hot, heavy air that holds us, or the moment itself.

But I've never had hope in humanity like this.

And I've never felt divinity like I do on this dancefloor.

THE NEXT MORNING, I AM strutting down the boardwalk in a vintage romper with a halter top that's covered in little hearts and cowboy boots. I am high on newfound confidence and the "$9 nitro cold brew that I'm pretty sure called me tacky for being a medium iced hazelnut Dunkin' kinda gal.

I am greeted by my North Star: a giant disco ball at an outdoor dance bar named Aces. Up the boardwalk is a store called Dazzling Dreams, and if I've learned one thing in this life, it's that when you see something as deliciously tacky as a store called Dazzling Dreams, you don't question it, you just go in.

I scan the place, which is crammed with ornate costume jewelry that looks like something my Armenian grandmother would have worn but which is really made for drag queens, and tons of penis paraphernalia.

It is being presided over by two older men with killer senses of style and stoic faces, who I would be scared to eat a sandwich in front of for reasons I haven't yet unpacked with my therapist.

"Hi!" I chirp to them.

They stare. I smile.

And quicker than two lesbians renting a U-Haul (can I make these jokes yet?) I see my holy grail. I spot what can only be an epic gift from the highest source there is, and everything clicks. I walk up to it the way people in cartoons walk up to the most sacred of ancient artifacts.

I whip my head back at the two men.

"Can I try this on?" My smile is so big I can't even pretend to be cool for them.

"That was actually made for you. I think you actually need to," one of the storekeepers says, through the plumpest male lips I've ever seen.

I carefully move some statues of BDSM mermaids to the side, and pick it up from its shelf.

I place it on top of my head.

I walk to the mirror in front of the store.

And there I am. Resplendent in a two-foot, shiny black pleather, BDSM-chain adorned witch's hat.

Just then, Savannah comes gallivanting in.

"Is this too much?" I ask earnestly.

She bursts into laughter. "Only you would ask me if wearing a BDSM leather witch hat in the middle of the summer with virtually no other clothes on is too much. On anyone else, it would be."

"Agreed," the stoic storekeeper says, peering at me over a pair of pushed-down red frames.

***

Okay, you know that old trope that's like, "I saw her and it was like time stopped"? This is usually only uttered by people who love Michael Bublé and who make the same I'm-a-really-good-person smile in every photo ever taken. And well, I kind of get it now.

There I am minding my own damn business, when a girl with big brown eyes and sockets as deep as *The Wall* album by Pink Floyd shoots me a lizard gaze that puts mine to shame. I lock eyes with her and refuse to break it because my narcissistic ass can't even let love at first sight not be a competition. She will not beat me at my own game. And also, if we're being real, I *can't* look away.

I feel my soul leaving my body and am only jolted back when I hear the beginning chords to Melissa Etheridge's "Come to My Window" and realize my pussy is strumming it with my hot pink g-string.

What the fuck was that? *Who* the fuck was that? I rush off down the boardwalk with my cheeks hotter than the sun beating down on my (perfectly) tanned back.

And maybe it's the nitro cold brew, but who am I kidding—those ten seconds of intense eye contact have me bubbling to the brim with electric FEELINGS. Not quite nerves, not quite turn-on, but some sort of hybrid of the two that I'm pretty sure is going to make me ascend out of my body because it's creating so much sensation. But damn, if this feeling happens once in a blue moon, then I'm buying a paintbrush and blue paint, getting on my broom, and taking off to the sky.

I channel that energy into power-clacking down another slippery wood boardwalk street, my cowboy boots feeling more like a pair of those 1990s roller skate sneakers, and I peek my head over the bush on the corner to see if she's there.

FUCK. I jump back at the site of her black tank top with the extra-long armpit holes; it's a thing for some reason, but somehow she's rocking it. The back of her hat reads, "In dog years, I'm gay." Somehow, she's rocking that too. Her blond-ish hair definitely smells like Pantene, and her toned back is glistening with sweat that I want to lick clean.

She's chatting with someone I can tell knows how to fold a fitted sheet really well. I nervously adjust my witch's hat in an attempt not to ascend right then and there, but honestly, fuck it. I walk towards her like I'm the High Priestess walking toward her altar.

You got this, bitch. You got nothin' to lose.

You are an underworld Goddess, you're practically reborn. And you have Cher hair! GO!

I try to give my best catwalk down the boardwalk toward her, but I quickly realize I'm walking like I have a two-pound yoni egg between my legs. I straighten my back. Tits out. I glide.

And then ...

I glide right by her.

For fuck's sake.

I clack into a bar.

Listen, maybe I'm drunk on love, or life, or the whiskey neat I just ordered to keep my hands busy so I didn't maul her right then and there, but I'm pretty sure whatever kinky Goddess/God is up there wants us to love, right? I would say we'll cross that bridge when we get to it but I'm pretty sure I already burned it down anyway, back when I was passionately body rolling to "Pony" by Ginuwine in a patent leather BDSM sex witch hat minutes prior.

When she walks into the bar a few minutes later (okay, thank you God/Goddess!) I make eye contact with her again. Okay, take two.

"Hi. You are like, really powerful," I blurt, spilling the beans right into the giant pot that I'm stirring and losing all hope of being coy.

"Yeah?" she smirks.

"Yeah, like, I bet your mom is really cool to have raised you." *What*?

"Well, I'm sure she'd love to hear that," she smiles.

"Can't wait to tell her one day," I beam, sliding off my barstool and galloping away in my witch's hat.

UGH! I am barreling down the boardwalk again, flushed and on fire like I'm burning at the stake. I blew it. That was weird. I'm probably never going to be that coy cool girl again.

"Where ya going?" she asks, catching up with me (thank you again God/Goddess!!)

"To the beach, I need to connect with the ocean. I'm Ani, by the way. Wanna come?"

"I'm Jordan." She beams as she walks by my side.

"Do you know the ocean is like the amniotic fluid of the great mother?" I ask.

"Welp, that is something else. What do you do with that information?"

"You become reborn! Let's do it!"

And like a magnet to steel, I slink my arm through hers, pulling her in close. And it isn't a "who the hell is this?" feeling. It feels like an "oh, there you are!" kind of moment. Like we have been arm in arm a million times before and we're just catching up.

We go to the beach as the sun is setting. I gush about rebirth rituals and she tells me about how she bumped into a group of manatees in Florida once and they were as big as cars, even the babies! I can't tell if it is me, or my heart, that is skipping.

***

We spend the rest of the night gallivanting between the beach and the bar. A few hours later, we're back at Aces. The lights are glaring off the disco ball at the bar overlooking the water and Beyoncé is blaring through the speakers. I realize I completely lost track of all of my friends, and I light up when I spot them dancing, laughing, and singing.

Ivy saunters up to us.

"Oh, I'm so glad you met! Ani, this is Jordan, we dated for years forever ago."

I feel like I'm going to barf up the twelve mozzarella sticks I ate when I got off the ferry right then and there.

"Ani, can you come to the bathroom with me?" Ivy coos.

We trot toward the bathroom. I am clenching my cheeks with nerves.

"Okay, I have to say it, tell me if I'm overstepping—you and Jordan are soulmates. I see it." Her eyes glow golden as they stretch into a smize that would put Tyra Banks to shame.

"IVY!"

"I'm serious, I don't even need to give you my blessing but you have it. It's weird. I see it. I feel it. It's palpable."

We both take a sneaky peek down the bathroom hallway to catch a glimpse of her.

Jordan is at the bar, and despite our attempt at being inconspicuous, a gal in a giant BDSM witch hat and a gal covered in face gems with huge fake electric blue flowers pinned to her hair are not exactly subtle. She waves and smiles, and we dive back into our hallway-hole like we just saw our shadow.

I clack back toward Jordan taking in everything Ivy said.

"I feel like we knew each other in a past life or something, I don't know," I say to Jordan's big brown eyes as we wait for our whiskey neats at the bar.

"Well," she pauses, holding my gaze. "Do you think we were lovers?"

"Arrright, can we not make this corny?" I cackle.

"What! I don't know about this stuff but I know I want to kiss you."

My whole body tenses. I don't want to be the person I was in the past. I don't want to have some weird power game, and what if that's what I just did? She's looking at me expectantly, waiting for a response.

"What if I just successfully manipulated you?" the words bubble out of me like an overflowing cauldron.

"What?"

"What if I just reflected to you what you like about yourself and you are just enjoying the attention I'm giving you?"

"... What?" She is clearly confused. I'm clearly confused.

"Well, nature calls. Be right back!" And by nature, I mean more mozzarella sticks. I grab Vita and we run to the pizza shop next door.

We get a slice and an order of sticks heated up and grab the crushed red pepper.

"Well, what do I do?" I ask her.

"You should fuck Jordan, that would be so hot."

"Vita, for fuck's sake!"

"Well," she takes a bite and the mozzarella stretches out as she pulls it away from her mouth. "What do you actually want?"

"I want to like, make out with her and listen to her stories and walk arm in arm like we're on the Bob Dylan *Freewheelin'* album cover!" I smash the pizza into my mouth and choke on the hot, melty mozzarella along with my cheesy-ass truth.

We head back to the bar, sated on pizza and laughing at some obscure Spongebob reference. Everyone we love is here, and I ground myself in trust, and root into my North Star. Before long, I'm giving astrology readings to a line of people that has formed at the bar.

Then: "I WANT TO BE A MOM!" I hear Ivy yell, which awakens the priestess in me.

"Let's do a fertility ritual!!" I shriek back.

By now, the ocean is as black as the cosmos and the undercurrent of whiskey and connection has us swirling with the tide. On the horizon, the moon is reflecting truth and big full beams. The ocean at night usually terrifies me and gives me Titanic vibes, but right now I'm getting high off of the mystery.

Here I am, waist deep in potential, arm in arm with a new romance and her ex lover, who is also one of my new best friends. Jordan is in the middle, holding both of us in place as the waves push against our bodies.

"Can you two at least zip up your purses? Ivy, your passport is floating away! Ani, is your phone in your bag?" Jordan bends back and snatches our runaway items from the traveling current as I grab my phone from my black leather satchel and stick it under my romper's halter strap.

"I'M READY!" Ivy shrieks at the moon.

"DID YOU HEAR THAT GOD? SHE IS READY IF YOU ARE!"

"Yes, she's ready, God—Ani, please, your purse ... your vaccine card is getting soaked."

"GOD, GODDESS, YOU KNOW WHERE WE STAND!"

Dry lighting streaks across the sky like little minnows jumping in a lake. Or sperm!

"Okay, let's get back to shore now," Jordan leads us out, but I break from her arm. "One sec," I announce, and let her and Ivy head off.

I stand in the water alone, watching Jordan help Ivy with her floor length, sopping wet dress. I hear the laughter coming from the shore, the pulse of the distant music, the waves crashing, my heart beating. I close my eyes and feel the water around me. My heart beating. My heart beating.

I'm okay.

A Hymn for the Hedonistic Heretics

Starry eyed mystic sirens singing, sinning sweet nothings,
nodding to the cosmic chaotic clowns
and dreamy dancers, making love to life itself.

Finding God in a tube of toothpaste and ruby red rouge lipstick
Or good dick or pussy licks or good bods and back claws—
a round of applause for the epic performance
or the transcendent, decadent dance.

Here's to the retrograded renegades,
The unsung heroines,
The ones who get their accolades
When they pull down their dress and then the shade
The ones who were beat down, betrayed,
The homemade grenades
The ones who like to get laid and get paid,
The pervasive persuasive abrasive mystical mermaids—
The wind sings your praise
When it permeates your perfume through the air.

I want to show you the North Star that bellows out of your being
Every time you speak of your freedom
And of your disgrace
And other people's distaste—
As you are infusing your story with life,
While you're smoking death
And mating with decay
And trying to be okay
As hope floods your breath
And you dip your wick in your yearning, the burning ...
You would have been one of the first to go if this was The Crucible.
But you take pride in that.

Young Liliths, witches, bitches, whores
The ones who experience life and just want more,
The ones who came for it all—
I bow to you.
The holy grails of this living heaven or hell—
I bow to you.

Acknowledgements

I have a lot of people to thank. Like...a lot. And I'm trying to write this without sounding like it's an Oscar acceptance speech so please bear with me.

Everyone who has touched my heart or cracked it open - named in this book and beyond - deserves to have infinite belly laughs, amazing dinners, and mind blowing amazing sex for the rest of their lives for being so amazing to me, during these times and also during the process of writing this book, one of them even helping to coax these stories out of me. I can't actually write their names because, you know, they are in the book - but I've told you who you are and I love you more than words can express. Thank you. Thank you. Thank you.

And thank you to my beautiful family, my incredible partner, and every teacher who has had a hand in sharing their wisdom with me - either at the bar or in an apprenticeship and everything in between.

Thank you to my Anoushik, who has been like honey on my heart. And to every musician that has created the tunes to carry me home.

Thank you to Tanes - just literally - thank you. I love you beyond words.

Thank you to the one Miss Ruby Warrington, who heard a book in my passionate ramblings and believed in this every step of the way.

And finally, to all of my messy bitches - I love you. Thank you.

Ani Ferlise is a writer and perpetual student of life. She lives in Brooklyn with her beloved dog Anoush and works as an editor and copywriter. She can't write an author bio to save her life, which seems like a basic task for a writer, but she promises that this book is really great and you should just take her word for it.

CPSIA information can be obtained
at www.ICGtesting.com
Printed in the USA
BVHW040853130223
658403BV00002B/106